The Alliance Revolution

The Alliance Revolution

The New Shape of Business Rivalry

Benjamin Gomes-Casseres

HARVARD UNIVERSITY PRESS

Cambridge, Massachusetts
London, England
1996

Library of Congress Cataloging-in-Publication Data

Gomes-Casseres, Benjamin.
The alliance revolution : the new shape of business rivalry /
Benjamin Gomes-Casseres.
p. cm.
Includes bibliographical references (p.   ) and index.
ISBN 0-674-01647-5 (alk. paper)
1. Strategic alliances (Business). 2. Competition.
3. Interorganizational relations. I. Title.
HD69.S8G66 1996
338.8—dc20   95-44555

For Susan and Rachel

Acknowledgments

Over the years, many teachers, colleagues, and students have helped develop the ideas in this book. Louis Wells has challenged, coached, and encouraged me since I first came to Harvard as a doctoral student in 1982; he read several versions of the manuscript and suggested important revisions. David Yoffie too has been an ally, friend, and co-author on various projects. Joseph Badaracco, Adam Brandenberger, Kim Clark, David Collis, John Dunning, Charles Gomes Casseres, Jean-François Hennart, Rosabeth Moss Kanter, Steven Kobrin, Bruce Kogut, Tomás Kohn, Thomas McCraw, Edith Penrose, Julio Rotemberg, Raymond Vernon, Richard Vietor, and Michael Yoshino commented on parts or full versions of the manuscript or on a companion paper. In addition, I have benefited from the comments of participants in seminars at Harvard Business School, Brandeis University, Boston University, and Dartmouth.

I also had help in collecting the evidence for this book. The research was conducted between 1989 and 1995 while I taught at the Harvard Business School. James Bamford was an invaluable aide in the critical final stages of research and the early stages of writing. Chris Allen tracked down any library information I needed at a moment's notice. Dimos Arhodidis, Maryellen Costello, Roger Hultgren, Neil Jones, Paul Mang, and Krista McQuade collected and manipulated data or drafted case studies. Richard Luecke and Marilyn Nicosan helped with early editing. The work of these individuals and all my trips to Japan, Europe, and across the United States were funded by the Harvard Business School's Division of Research. My directors of research, Jay

Jaikumar, Warren McFarlan, Steve Wheelwright, and Michael Yoshino, went the extra mile to get me the resources I needed. At Harvard University Press, Michael Aronson has been encouraging from the start; Elizabeth Gretz edited the final manuscript.

The data themselves come from a variety of sources. Interviews with top managers at major high-technology firms were an essential source of information and insight; these managers are listed in Appendix A. The case data have been reviewed by the companies for accuracy, but the interpretation of the evidence is mine, as are any remaining errors. Dataquest, Chi Research, The Gartner Group, the International Data Corporation, Itsunami, and the Maastricht Economic Research Institute on Innovation and Technology provided statistical data.

To all these allies, *Masha Danki!*—which is how I express a heartfelt thanks in Papiamentu. My family in Curaçao will understand what I mean; geographic distance did not keep them from following my progress and cheering me on. Two other supporters deserve more credit than I can express in any language. My wife, Susan Wexler, truly made this work possible through her confidence and love, her common sense, and her humor—she created the perfect alliance at home. Our daughter, Rachel, provided welcome interruptions to my writing and managed to stay clear of the reset button on my computer. The dedication only begins to express my gratitude.

Lexington, Mass.
October 1995

Contents

Figures and Tables

Figures

Tables

The Alliance Revolution

Competition despite Cooperation

Cooperation among firms has grown rapidly since the early 1980s, as alliances have proliferated in one industry after another. At the same time, however, the competition in these industries has in many ways become even fiercer than before. The persistence of competition despite extensive interfirm collaboration flies in the face of traditional economic thinking. Why is it occurring? This book shows that alliances do not so much suppress business rivalry as transform it, giving it a new shape that is often even more virulent than the old.

The interplay between alliances and rivalry is still a puzzle for business economists. For centuries, economists have thought that collaboration between firms inevitably leads to a suppression of competition. Adam Smith observed: "People of the same trade seldom meet together, even for merriment and diversion, but the conversation ends in a conspiracy against the public, or in some contrivance to raise prices."[1] This view has been expanded and deepened over time, so that today the dominant approach in economics equates interfirm collaboration with collusion to increase market power.[2]

But prices, instead of rising, have fallen in many of the industries in which alliances are spreading. There is no uproar from the public—or even from antitrust authorities—about collusive conspiracies and cartels. In most businesses where collaboration is intense, there now seem to be more, not fewer, competitors. The race for new products is quickening, contrary to what one would expect if cartels were suppressing technological rivalry. As a result, widespread collaboration has not eased the job of business managers—they now need to attend to the rising tide of alliances as well as to the intensifying rivalry. They, too, face the puzzle of the coexistence of these two seemingly opposing processes.

The evidence to be considered here suggests an answer to this puzzle. Modern-day collaboration has created new types of competitors, restructured industries, and generated new forms of rivalry. In the process, alliances have frequently intensified competition.

At a basic level of economic exchange, collaboration between two parties does indeed suppress competition between them, as the traditional view suggests. But in the modern world of large firms, global businesses, and advanced technologies, the relationship between these two processes is much more complex. The type of business rivalry emerging in this environment grows out of the very dynamics of collaboration. Simply put, business rivalry now often takes place between sets of allied firms, rather than between single firms. This book explains the rise and mechanics of this new "collective competition."[3]

Although collective competition is a relatively new phenomenon, we can use many existing concepts to examine how it works. Economic theories of the firm and of industrial organization, in particular, are useful in understanding why firms create alliances, how allied firms behave, and how industries peppered with alliances evolve.

Adam Smith himself provided a key insight to collective competition—the idea of the division of labor. He argued that factories in which workers specialized in one or a few tasks could be more productive than those in which each worker performed every task.[4] This idea is also at the core of many alliances; frequently, each partner in an alliance specializes in what it does best, thus making the collective more competitive than the members would be by themselves. Collective competition, in other words, revolves partly around how allied firms in rival groups organize themselves to exploit the benefits of Smith's division of labor.

The New Shape of Business Rivalry

The essence of the new rivalry thus lies in the way collaboration and competition interact. These two processes do not automatically conflict—much depends on how the multifaceted relationships between the parties are configured. I will identify when collaboration dulls competition, and when it sharpens it; when competition destroys collaboration, and when it facilitates it.

Of all the ways in which collaboration and competition can interact, this book focuses on one that is central to the emerging organization of industry in high-technology fields. Alliances among high-technology firms are forging new units of economic power—groups of firms I call "constellations."[5] These constellations compete against other such groups and against traditional single firms. From this perspective, collaboration and competition often take place at different levels, with alliances at one level shaping the groups that compete against outsiders at another, higher level.

In such a world, the way firms manage the collaboration inside their constellation affects the competitive behavior and performance of the group as a whole. As a result, the performance of each firm comes to depend not only on its own capabilities and strategies but also on those of its allies and on its relationships to these allies.

CONSTELLATIONS AS COMPETITORS

Economists and business strategists have generally viewed alliances from a much narrower perspective. For a long time they saw these arrangements as anomalies, worthy only of a footnote.[6] Even when the importance of alliances was recognized, they were thought to be too amorphous for rigorous analysis.[7] This attitude among theorists is changing, as so often happens, because the world is changing. "More companies are waking up to the fact that alliances are critical to the future," Corning Glass chairman James R. Houghton has said. "Nobody can do it all alone anymore."[8] Indeed, the 1980s and 1990s have seen an explosion in the use of alliances in high-technology fields (see Figure 1).

The rise of interfirm collaboration has led to new empirical and analytical research on alliances.[9] Current scholarship stresses that alliances blur the boundaries of firms, making it hard to discern where one firm ends and where another—or the market—begins. Alliances do this because they are organizational structures that combine features of both firms and markets. Like firms, alliances are ways to govern incomplete contracts between economic actors; like markets, alliances represent decision-making mechanisms in which no one firm has complete authority, and negotiation is the norm.

But to focus on the "boundary-marker" role of alliances is to mistake the trees for the forest. The common definition of a clear boundary is

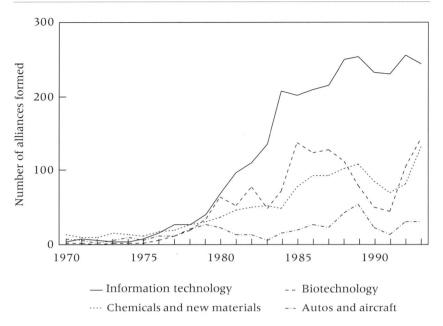

Figure 1 Alliances in selected high-technology fields, 1970–1993.
(Source: Based on data collected at the Maastricht Economic Research Institute on Innovation and Technology [MERIT]; see John Hagedoorn, "Understanding the Rationale of Strategic Technology Partnering: Interorganizational Modes of Cooperation and
Sectoral Differences," *Strategic Management Journal* 14 [July 1993]: 371–385.)

one that separates territories; a blurry boundary, it follows, is one that
joins these territories to some degree. The tighter the collaboration
between two firms—that is, the blurrier the boundary between
them—the more the firms will in effect be joined and the more they
will wield economic power *as a unit.* Unless the alliance changes into a
full merger, this unification of power is never complete. But the actions
of these firms will still be coordinated to some extent.

The following metaphor may be useful. Firms, we have traditionally
been told, are "islands of conscious power in this ocean of unconscious
cooperation,"[10] which is the open market. Alliances blur the boundaries of these islands. But they do much more. By *linking* firms to each
other, alliances create new concentrations of "conscious power" in the
market. The area between these linked islands, to continue the metaphor, is never as firm as dry land; but neither is it an open expanse of
ocean. The archipelago of islands is, in effect, a new unit of power.

Much more than firm boundaries is at stake here—the very unit of economic behavior is becoming larger than the firm. When two or more firms are linked through alliances, their economic behavior becomes a function of interests at both firm and group levels, and competitive advantage is derived from conditions at both levels. Economic power, in this view, is no longer concentrated solely in firms. Instead it coalesces in groups and is distributed among the members of these groups.

Single firms and constellations are different organizational units with the same purpose: to control a set of capabilities so as to maximize their return. The control systems of these units differ substantially, as do the way the units combine and upgrade their capabilities. In a given competitive context, these differences give one organizational form or the other an advantage.

Modern competitors thus take on a variety of shapes. Two examples will help make these ideas more concrete; both will be discussed extensively in later chapters.

In copiers and laser printers, the competition between Xerox and Canon was not one on one, firm against firm. Instead, a constellation of firms around Xerox competed with Canon, which operated as a single firm. The Xerox constellation is complex, but at its core is a pair of allied firms—Xerox Corporation and Fuji Xerox. Together this pair develops products, penetrates markets, manufactures hardware, and so on—all the things that Canon does on its own. Fuji Xerox is thus much more than a hybrid organization on Xerox's boundary: the two firms are comrades-in-arms. The Xerox constellation has enjoyed some powerful advantages as well as suffered some serious disadvantages because of this structure.

Mips Computer Systems provides another example; this tiny start-up company took the constellation idea to an extreme.[11] It too competed together with allies, but this constellation grew to include over two hundred firms. This large group competed against Intel—a single firm—as well as against other groups. In fact, the strategy of forming alliance groups was contagious. Partly as a response to Mips, Sun Microsystems, Hewlett-Packard (HP), IBM, and Motorola all formed large constellations in the same field as Mips. Here, too, each group had specific strengths and weaknesses that grew out of its structure and composition.

The single firm is thus only one among the many shapes of competitors in modern industry. Some competitors in an industry may be single

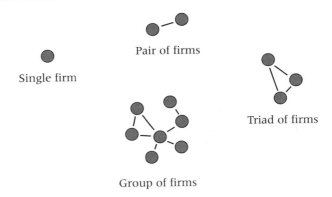

Figure 2 The shapes of competitors. Circles indicate firms; lines indicate alliances between firms.

firms, others pairs, others triads, and still others groups of various sizes (see Figure 2). Single firms also have relationships with other firms, of course, but the partners in constellations are tied together through relationships that involve much greater degrees of joint decision making.[12]

The number of firms in a constellation is only one of the characteristics affecting how the unit competes. In addition, the type of firms in the constellation affects the range of capabilities on which the unit can draw. Group composition may also influence who plays leadership roles and who is more peripheral to the operation of the group. Moreover, the members of some constellations work better together than do members of others; often the effectiveness of a group depends on the degree of internal competition and on the governance structures of the constellation. These and other internal characteristics of constellations will be examined in depth in the chapters to come.

The main messages of this book are closely related to this idea of differently shaped competitors. The first message is that constellations behave differently from single firms, because they are loose collections of firms with disparate interests and capabilities. The second message follows from the first; it is that the competitive behavior of a constellation is driven by the nature of collaboration among members inside the group. The third message is that the rise of constellations reshapes rivalry in an industry, creating what I call collective competition. In this new environment, the structure and dynamics of competition depend on the collective behaviors of allied firms.

COLLECTIVE COMPETITION IN PERSPECTIVE

Collective competition refers to the economic behavior of competitors consisting of more than one firm, and which operate in market environments containing more than one player. One way to think about this new type of competition is by adding collective competition to the simple classification scheme that economists sometimes use to distinguish among different market environments (see Figure 3).

The horizontal axis in this figure indicates the distinction that economists have traditionally made between markets having one, a few, and many competitors. The market with one player—called monopoly—is readily defined, but the distinction between "few" and "many" is not usually quantified. Rather, it refers to the nature of the competitive interaction between the players. When the actions of one competitor affect the environment facing the others, we have "few" players, or oligopoly. When these actions do not affect the environment, and every player takes the environment as given, then we have "many" players, or pure competition.13

In the traditional approach to market structure, the internal composition of the players does not matter. The firms are "black boxes" that

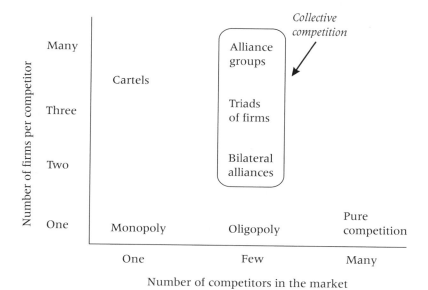

Figure 3 The domain of collective competition.

are either identical or differ only along a few simple, technical dimensions. The rich ideas from the economic theory of the firm seldom condition the ideas concerning market behavior generated by theories of industrial organization.[14]

In this book the internal structure of competitors matters a great deal. But our competitors are not always single firms; as we have just seen, they can be pairs, triads, or larger groups of firms. And, most important, the shape of these competitors affects their competitive behavior. To reflect these ideas, therefore, we need to add another dimension to the traditional scheme of market structures.

The vertical axis in Figure 3 measures the number of firms per player. In the traditional approach, this number is always one—each competitor is composed of one firm. In reality, however, not only do constellations of allied firms exist but they differ from single-firm players in the way they compete. Only by distinguishing among these different shapes of competitors can we understand these new behaviors.

In this two-dimensional classification, the collective competition examined in this book is a variant of oligopoly—it represents competition among "a few" constellations and firms. In practice, purely competitive markets ("many" players) seldom give rise to alliances. One reason is that in purely competitive markets a firm need not tie up with another to gain access to its capabilities—it can usually acquire the inputs it needs from one of the multiple suppliers in the market. Furthermore, the special conditions that give rise to alliances also create barriers to entry that limit the number of competitors.

To see how the vertical dimension in Figure 3 matters, consider how alliances modify the traditional classes of market structure. At the left-most end of the horizontal spectrum (one player), alliances give rise to a cartel—a collection of firms that tries to act as a monopolist. Cartel behavior does not represent collective competition, because the element of competition is missing. In fact modern alliances have seldom led to market dominance, let alone pure monopolies. Still, the long-standing debate about the effectiveness of cartels provides important antecedents to the argument here.

There is ample evidence that cartels cannot act like true monopolists, because of conflicts of interest among the cartel members. They are more fragile and are frequently torn apart by internal conflict.[15] The internal structure of the monopolist, therefore, is critical to its behavior in the market. Related arguments have been made regarding "coalitions" of oligopolists that try to act as single, dominant players. In this situation, too, the internal structure of a player matters. Some have argued, for example, that such a coalition cannot act exactly as would a dominant firm with an equivalent market share, because of the costs of controlling the coalition.[16] This argument, however, has not been examined in great depth, in part because of the almost exclusive emphasis in traditional economics on the horizontal axis in Figure 3.

Even though this figure is useful for roughly indicating the domain of collective competition, it is obviously an oversimplification of the world. In particular, each axis only measures one dimension of, respectively, market and competitor structure. We already saw that the number of firms per constellation—the vertical axis—is only one variable in collective competition. This book is also concerned with other important characteristics of internal structure.[17]

By the same token, the number of players—the horizontal axis—is only one element of market structure; taken by itself, it is a poor predictor of the degree of competition in a market. Some of the analysis will relate directly to the horizontal axis in Figure 3; for example, I will consider whether alliances increase or decrease the number of competitors in a market. But that is not my prime concern. With the exception of the extreme cases of monopoly and pure competition, the number of firms in a market may have little effect on the pattern of competition. Many other factors play a role in the middle ground of oligopolistic competition, including the relative sizes of the players, their history and goals, the extent of barriers to entry and exit, and so on.[18]

Furthermore, even these added variables give only a static snapshot of the degree of competition in a market—they say little about the pattern of change in an industry. An alternative view of competition holds that dynamic variables are more important. Joseph Schumpeter conceived competition as a process of "creative destruction," in which new technologies, markets, and institutions arose to supplant older ones.[19] In this view, what matters in business rivalry are races among competitors to introduce new products and technologies, to expand production, to improve service and quality, to enter new markets, and so on. Much of my discussion of how alliances reshape business rivalry relates precisely to these dynamic aspects of competition.

The puzzle described at the opening of this introduction obviously did not reflect the richness of forms of collaboration and competition sketched so far and treated in depth later. It stated in simple terms the paradox of sustained competition despite increasing cooperation. But the world is more complex and the puzzle more nuanced. The central themes that will emerge from the evidence can now be restated.

Alliances between firms have reshaped business rivalry in at least four ways. First, the alliances link firms into constellations, which then act as new units of economic power. Second, the competitive behavior of a constellation depends on its internal structure and differs from the typical behavior of a single firm. Third, the evolution of constellations and the spread of collaboration have restructured the way capabilities are controlled in an industry. Fourth, the distinctive pattern of rivalry that has emerged—collective competition—is in many ways more intense than traditional models of rivalry among single firms suggest.

Studying Collective Competition

The subject of this book is new and slippery. Our experience with constellations is short, and many of the concepts and measurements required to analyze them are ill defined. Existing theory is helpful in understanding elements of collective competition, but we have as yet no comprehensive model to explain alliances, let alone one that describes the complex interaction between alliances and rivalry. These conditions have shaped the research methods and the type of evidence used here.

This book grew out of my observation that the proliferation of alliances was transforming the way business was conducted. In an earlier study of the computer industry, I traced how alliances affected the industry's evolution, and also learned that emerging industry conditions made further alliances inevitable.[20] In separate case studies of Fuji Xerox and Mips, I examined how collaboration could affect a firm's competitiveness.

These observations suggested that a study of the interaction between collaboration and competition would be worthwhile, but they did not provide strict hypotheses to be tested. Consequently, I pursued an inductive research strategy—gathering data from selected cases and developing concepts as needed to interpret these data. This work yielded three results.

First, I produced rich descriptions of how collective competition works in certain cases and industries. Second, I developed a set of concepts and arguments that help us understand the logic of the phenomenon. Third, I came to the conclusion that the alliance revolution requires us to extend and modify our traditional views of business economics and strategy.

This research was thus grounded in both evidence and theory, but it was not an attempt to test pre-set ideas against data. Instead, it aimed to generate ideas that would stand up to the twin tests of rigor and relevance. The concepts and logic of the arguments are rooted in economic theory, but they were developed with specific applications in mind. The evidence is used to illustrate ideas and show their applications, rather than to provide a proof of my assertions.

In sum, the intent of this book is to stimulate new thinking in the reader and open new avenues of inquiry. It is aimed at an audience of business academics, especially those who think in terms of concepts from the fields of economics, organizational science, and strategy. At the same time the book is accessible to a broader field of social scientists and to general readers interested in business and economics. It requires no technical knowledge of economics; interested readers will find ample discussion of the technical literature in the notes.

Although the book draws liberally on economic theories of the firm and of industrial organization, it does not develop formal models in the traditions of these fields. Still, I hope that economists will find ideas that are worth pursuing with more formal methods. Similarly, the book does not emphasize the "how to" aspects of managing alliances; yet I hope that managers will distill lessons for practice from the argument and the cases.

SCOPE OF THE EVIDENCE

Groups consisting of many allied firms already shape competitive battles in many industries, but they are not universal. Even so, the experience of these groups provides us with a new lens with which to view the conventional—and much more common—alliances between two or three firms. Conversely, our long experience with simpler, bilateral alliances yields basic lessons about collaboration and competition, which are important for understanding the more complex interactions in larger constellations. I shall therefore use evidence on bilateral alliances to examine in detail how firms collaborate, and then use the data on the new alliance groups to analyze the emerging pattern of collective competition.

The main field sites in this research were selected with three criteria in mind. First, I chose companies and industries in which alliances were common; these sites promised to provide the richest evidence on how collective competition worked. Second, I searched for cases that were closely comparable along many dimensions, yet different on a few critical ones. Third, I collected evidence on two different questions: how firms managed collaboration in simple, bilateral alliances; and how large, complex constellations competed with each other. These criteria produced two samples of five firms each; one sample contained bilateral U.S.-Japanese alliances, and the other contained complex alliance groups in the field of reduced instruction-set computing (RISC), a rapidly growing segment of the computer industry.[21]

The data are drawn from the experience of American, Japanese, and European electronics firms from the 1950s to the early 1990s. Altogether, I conducted interviews with roughly 140 executives in forty companies over a period of five years (see Appendix A). Ten of these companies were selected for detailed analysis. Two cases were studied in depth—those of Fuji Xerox and Mips. Eight shorter cases were developed to compare with these two. The Fuji Xerox case is compared with four other cases of U.S.-Japanese joint ventures: Yamatake-Honeywell, Yokogawa-Hewlett-Packard, Amdahl and Fujitsu, and IBM and Toshiba. The Mips case is compared with four other alliance groups operating in the same industry segment as Mips: the groups of Sun Microsystems, Hewlett-Packard, IBM, and Motorola.

In addition to these samples of in-depth cases, I also developed a database of 646 alliances of twenty-four large computer firms from the United States, Europe, and Japan; these data (described in Appendix B) were used to place the case studies in a wider context. Finally, after the broad conclusions of this study were clear, a colleague and I conducted a separate study of collective competition in the field of personal digital assistants (PDAs), an emerging segment of the multimedia industry. Some of the data from this project are reported here, mostly in the case study preceding Chapter 5.

Even though all this evidence concerns alliances in high-technology industries, it leads to many conclusions that should be applicable elsewhere. Likewise, although many of the cases are of international alliances—those with partners from different home countries—most of the conclusions also apply to domestic alliances. In an effort to develop an argument that is broadly applicable, the text does not stress the international and high-technology aspects of the evidence. Where these aspects lead to conclusions that are not likely to be broadly applicable, this is noted explicitly; otherwise, the arguments are meant to apply broadly.

ORGANIZATION OF THE BOOK

This book is organized around two different types of segments. Traditional chapters, which are numbered, contain conceptual and empirical analysis and present the unfolding argument of the book. In between these chapters, there appear the most important case studies; these segments are not numbered. The issues raised by each case are generally dealt with in the chapter that follows. Often, data from a case are used in several subsequent chapters. Three additional cases are presented in Appendix C, and data on all the primary cases appear in Appendixes D and E. Finally, some case evidence is woven into the text. In particular, empirical analysis that compares various cases is usually presented in the main chapters.

To see how the alliance revolution transforms business rivalry, we must first understand the basic logic of collaboration. The question of why firms create alliances is by now standard fare in the literature, and I do not retrace this ground. Instead, I seek to synthesize and extend the existing knowledge with a new purpose in mind: to map out the complex interactions between collaboration and competition. This is the purpose of the first chapter, which develops the conceptual framework applied in the rest of the book.

This framework revolves around the idea that the process of competition between constellations depends on the processes of collaboration within them. The two sides of this coin are examined in the next two chapters. Chapter 2 analyzes the interaction between competition and collaboration in alliances. Chapter 3 then examines how constellations compete and, in particular, how their designs yield group-based advantages. Put differently, Chapter 2 emphasizes strategies for collaboration, and Chapter 3 emphasizes strategies for competition.

These early chapters show how the alliances in my data transformed relationships among a few firms. In Chapters 4 and 5 we see how this transformation spread to engulf a whole industry. The proliferation of alliances was driven by reactive strategies of constellations, in which each tried to outdo the other. The evidence shows that the alliance rage led to diminishing returns for some groups, but not before competition in the industry was transformed. And, contrary to the received wisdom, the spread of alliances in the industries studied increased the intensity and pace of competition, as Chapter 5 documents. The last chapter outlines the main findings and sketches their implications for theory and business practice.

How Fuji Xerox Saved Xerox

The history of Xerox and Fuji Xerox illustrates how collaboration between firms can help them compete. Over the thirty-plus years of its existence, this constellation has evolved into a tight pair of partners, each with a unique role and contribution. This division of labor has allowed the pair to benefit from specialization and to combine the best in Japanese and American business practices. At the same time, collaboration between the companies has not been without friction; but the partners have successfully managed these frictions to face external competitors such as Canon.

The origins of this constellation go back to the 1960s, when the revolutionary Xerox 914 took the industry by storm and the name Xerox became synonymous with photocopying. The company's revenues grew at a record pace for an American business—doubling every ten months, from $40 million in 1960 to $1.2 billion in 1966. Xerox patents on plain-paper copier technology and the company's extensive sales and service network sustained its virtual monopoly in the field.

Beginning in 1970, however, new competitors started chipping away at the Xerox empire. Many of these competitors came from Japan and produced high-quality, low-cost machines. Some developed new technologies that circumvented Xerox patents; others benefited from U.S. antitrust pressure on Xerox that led the company to license its key technologies.[1] Over twenty plain-paper copier vendors operated worldwide in 1975; by then the Xerox share of worldwide copier revenues had plummeted to 60 percent from 93 percent in 1971. Ricoh, the traditional leader in the Japanese market, became the top seller in the U.S. market in 1976. David Kearns, who was then Xerox's chief executive officer (CEO), recalled the crisis his company faced at the end of the decade: "We dominated the industry we had created. . . . Our success was so overwhelming that we became complacent. . . . The Japanese were selling products in the United States for what it cost us to make them. We were losing market share rapidly, but didn't have the cost structure to do anything about it. I was not sure if Xerox would make it out of the 1980s."[2]

Initially, Xerox had done little to respond to the rising tide of Japanese competitors in the low-volume end of the business. Company executives had been more concerned with the entry of IBM and Eastman Kodak into the copier industry, as these companies targeted the more lucrative mid- and high-volume segments of the market.[3] But the crisis forced Xerox managers to change their thinking. They also realized then that they had been ignoring a unique competitive asset in Japan—their joint venture with Fuji Photo Film.

Fuji Xerox was a 50/50 joint venture established in 1962 to market xerographic products in Japan and certain other countries in the region. Xerox had already used an alliance to expand internationally in the 1950s, when cash constraints led it to create a joint venture with the United Kingdom's Rank Organization.[4] Because it had acquired the rights to make and market xerographic products outside of North America, Rank Xerox became Fuji Photo's partner in Fuji Xerox. Figure 4 indicates the complex ownership relationships between these partners as of 1992.

Fuji Photo Film was a manufacturer of photographic film and second only to Kodak in that field. With sales of $90 million in 1962, it was roughly the size of Xerox, although not growing as fast. The company was trying to diversify its business away from silver-based photography, and had already begun experimenting with xerography. Still, under the agreement with Rank Xerox, Fuji Xerox—not Fuji Photo—received the exclusive rights to xerographic patents in its territory.[5]

Fuji Xerox was destined to become much more than a marketing outlet for Xerox products—it helped save Xerox from the demise that Kearns had feared. No one could have predicted this outcome. For a long time, Xerox executives treated Fuji Xerox with a benign neglect that sometimes bordered on condescension. This attitude changed dra-

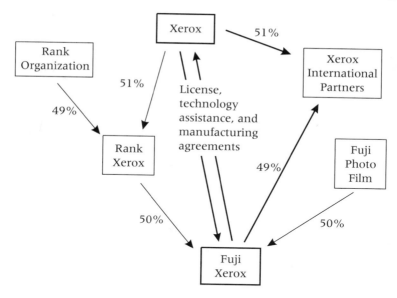

Figure 4 Structure of the Xerox constellation, 1992. Percentages indicate ownership shares. Darker arrows and boxes indicate the more important relationships and parties.

matically in the 1980s, as Fuji Xerox came to the rescue of Xerox. By 1990 Fuji Xerox had become "a critical asset of Xerox," as Xerox CEO Paul Allaire called it.[6]

The Separate Interests of Xerox and Fuji Xerox

The reasons behind the transformation of Fuji Xerox lay in that company's unique relationship with Xerox. By the early 1970s, Fuji Photo and Rank Xerox had each become passive partners in Fuji Xerox. Although they still held nominal decision-making powers, they were not involved in day-to-day activities and they did not continue to supply technology and expertise to the joint venture.[7] For technology and business advice, as well as for certain products, Fuji Xerox turned directly to Xerox.

Xerox did not control Fuji Xerox, however, and was only entitled to a minority share of the profits generated by the joint venture. As a result, Fuji Xerox benefited from a flow of technology from Xerox, but also enjoyed an exceptional degree of autonomy. Yotaro "Tony" Kobayashi, Fuji Xerox's president and CEO from the late 1970s to the early 1990s, ascribed a good deal of the company's success to this autonomy. "The degree to which Xerox let us run was very unusual," he recalled.[8]

The autonomy of Fuji Xerox also stemmed from sheer neglect. To many in Xerox, Fuji Xerox seemed a faraway outpost in a tiny market. Furthermore, it had no technical capabilities to speak of, particularly not when compared with IBM and Kodak, the two giants breathing down Xerox's neck. When Fuji Xerox engineers proposed to develop an indigenous line of copiers tailored to local Japanese conditions, therefore, Xerox executives first tried to dissuade them and then turned a blind eye when they went ahead anyway.

The Rise of Fuji Xerox

The Japanese engineers had always aimed to develop an indigenous expertise in xerography. In the early 1960s, Fuji Photo engineers began modifying Xerox designs to the needs of the local market; Japanese offices, for example, used different paper sizes. Later, Fuji Xerox managers wanted to go beyond adaptation to developing their own products. In particular, they envisioned a high-performance, inexpensive, compact machine that could copy books.

By the late 1960s the Fuji Xerox development group had produced four experimental copiers, each with projected manufacturing costs approximately half those of the smallest Xerox machine. When engineers at Rank Xerox and Xerox first heard of these machines, they doubted their commercial viability. But developers at Fuji Xerox persisted, and in 1970 they took a working prototype to London, where its performance amazed Rank Xerox executives. The machine was slow (5 copies per minute [cpm]), but substantially smaller and lighter than comparable Xerox models. This demonstration boosted the technical reputation of Fuji Xerox. For the first time, Xerox allowed Fuji Xerox to have a small R&D budget. In 1973 Fuji Xerox introduced the FX2200, the world's smallest copier, with the slogan "It's small, but it's a Xerox!"

Fuji Xerox's product development efforts went into high gear in 1975, when the company launched its Total Quality Control (TQC) program. The focal point of the campaign was the development of *dantotsu*, roughly translated as the "Absolute No. 1 Product." Top management gave the marketing and engineering departments a seemingly impossible task: develop a compact, 40 cpm machine, to be manufactured at half the cost of comparable machines, with half the number of parts of previous models, and do it in two years, instead of Xerox's typical four.

Two years later, this "impossible" product was ready. Kearns, for one, was amazed when he first saw a demonstration of the prototype, and spontaneously broke out in applause. By 1979 the FX3500 had broken the Japanese record for annual sales of a copier. Largely because of its effort to develop the FX3500, Fuji Xerox won the Japanese government's prestigious Deming Prize, awarded annually to a company achieving outstanding quality, in 1980.

The FX3500 was Fuji Xerox's "declaration of independence,"[9] but it was an independence born of necessity. The project came after Xerox had canceled a series of low- to mid-volume copiers on which Fuji Xerox was depending. Code-named SAM, Moses, Mohawk, Elf, Peter, Paul, and Mary, each was canceled in mid-development, even though Fuji Xerox needed models of this type in its product line. Jefferson Kennard, the Xerox director of Fuji Xerox relations, recalled that when Tony Kobayashi was told about the cancellation of Moses, he was also asked to stop work on the FX3500 project. According to Kennard: "Tony refused, and said, in effect, 'As long as I am responsible for the survival of this company, I can no longer be totally dependent on you for developing products. We are going to have to develop our own.'"[10]

Fuji Xerox to the Rescue

The growth in the technical capabilities of Fuji Xerox took place in what was for Xerox a "lost decade."[11] This was not a coincidence. The threat to Xerox's monopoly came from Japan, where new technologies, domestic demand, and rivalry among producers generated a unique environment for product innovation. Xerox competitors like Ricoh, Canon, and Minolta benefited from this environment, but so did Fuji Xerox. The joint venture also had the additional advantage of direct access to Xerox technology coupled with autonomy. Paul Allaire later explained:

> The fact that we had this strong company in Japan was of extraordinary importance when other Japanese companies started coming after us. Fuji Xerox was able to see them coming earlier, and understood their development and manufacturing techniques. . . . If Fuji Xerox were within our organization, it would be easier, but then we would lose certain benefits. They have always had a reasonable amount of autonomy. I can't take that away from them, and I wouldn't want to.[12]

But it took a while for Xerox executives to recognize the competitive value of Fuji Xerox. In 1978 Fuji Xerox offered to sell low-end copiers to Xerox and Rank Xerox to help them counter Japanese competition in their markets. At the time, Xerox did not yet see the need to do so. But Rank Xerox purchased 25,000 of the machines for sale in Europe.[13] The success of this transaction led Rank Xerox to import more of the Fuji Xerox machines. With this product—and a delay in Kodak's entry to Europe—Rank Xerox was able to defend its market, while the position of Xerox in the United States continued to decline.

A year later, Xerox too began to import the FX2202 and related machines into the United States. At first these products were assembled by Fuji Xerox. Then, acceding to the demands of American unions, Fuji Xerox exported them as knock-down units (kits of parts) to be assembled at Xerox. Over time, Fuji Xerox exported more and more finished products, disassembled kits, and copier components to Xerox units worldwide, as trade figures reflect (see Figure 5).

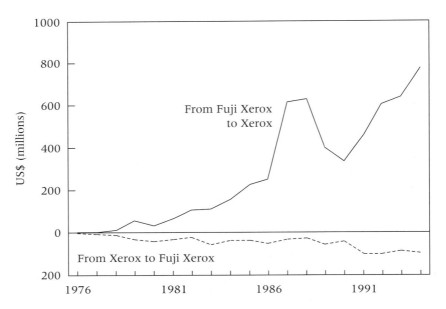

Figure 5 Trade between Xerox and Fuji Xerox, 1976–1994. Data for Xerox include data for Rank Xerox.
(Source: Internal company reports.)

The Fuji Xerox exports to Xerox helped stem the advance of the competition, but they did not change how Xerox itself developed, manufactured, and marketed its own products. Fuji Xerox's quality control program eventually served as a model for Xerox that led to deep changes in these areas as well. Xerox acquired management ideas, subcontracting approaches, and product development techniques, and competitive data from Fuji Xerox. Through this reverse flow of technology, Fuji Xerox helped Xerox get back on its feet.

The Transformation of Xerox

The Xerox turnaround can be traced to about 1979, when David Kearns took a close look at the strategies and products of Fuji Xerox and other Japanese companies. Xerox engineers were amazed by the Fuji Xerox reject rate for parts, which was a fraction of the American rate, and by the substantially lower manufacturing costs at Fuji Xerox. Visits to Fuji Xerox facilities introduced Xerox executives to the practice of "benchmarking," which systematically tracked costs and performance in all areas of operations against those of the best in the field. Xerox's own benchmarking studies helped fuel Kearns's efforts to infuse his organization with new vision and determination.

In 1981 Kearns announced a companywide initiative for "business effectiveness," and two years later he formally launched the Leadership Through Quality program, based partly on the experience of Fuji Xerox. Throughout the effort, Kobayashi and others at Fuji Xerox were called on for help. Xerox hired Japanese consultants recommended by Fuji Xerox, and some two hundred high-level Xerox and Rank Xerox managers visited Fuji Xerox in later years to learn directly about its quality management program.

The rallying point for the Xerox quality movement was the development of the 10 Series, a new family of copiers. Dubbed the "Marathon" family, this became the most successful line of copiers in Xerox history and served to restore the company's finances and morale. The flagship Xerox 1075 became the first American-made product to win Japan's Grand Prize for Good Design. Altogether, some fourteen models were introduced between 1982 and 1986, six of which were still sold in 1990. Fuji Xerox designed and produced the low-end models in the series— the 1020, 1035, and the 1055, the latter drawing on basic technologies from the FX3500, the first machine that Fuji Xerox developed internally.

Because Xerox's Japanese competitors were not strong in mid-volume copiers at the time, the 10 Series forestalled their move into that segment of the market and helped Xerox win back market share. On the strength of the 10 Series family, Xerox regained 2 to 3 percentage points of market share in 1983, and 12 points in 1984. By the end of 1985 more than 750,000 of the new machines had been rented or sold, accounting for nearly 38 percent of Xerox's worldwide installed base.

Xerox continued throughout the 1980s to change the way it did business. Taking another leaf from the Fuji Xerox book, the company reduced its supplier base, bringing the cost of purchased parts down by 45 percent. Average manufacturing costs at Xerox were reduced by 20 percent and the time-to-market for new products was cut by 60 percent. This progress was recognized by the U.S. Commerce Department in 1989, when the company won the Malcolm Baldrige National Quality Award.

Fuji Xerox Gains Greater Independence

Fuji Xerox continued to grow and mature through the 1980s. Its dollar revenues grew faster than Xerox's, and by the end of the decade represented a more significant portion of the Xerox group's worldwide revenues than ever before. Fuji Xerox's financial contribution to Xerox's net earnings in the form of royalties and profits had also grown sharply—from 5 percent in 1981 to 22 percent in 1988. And throughout the decade, Fuji Xerox had been an important source of low-end copiers for Xerox. Between 1980 and 1988, Fuji Xerox's sales to Xerox and Rank Xerox grew from $32 million to $620 million.

The technological capabilities of Fuji Xerox continued to broaden and deepen in the 1980s. One measure of these rising capabilities was the increasing number of patents granted to Fuji Xerox in Japan and the United States (see Figure 6).[14] Fuji Xerox's increased technological strength is also reflected in the technology fees it received from Xerox for designs it supplied to Xerox (see Figure 7). These fees were first introduced when the technology agreements between Xerox and Fuji Xerox were renegotiated in 1983. The new agreement also called for a gradual decline in Fuji Xerox royalty payments to Xerox, in anticipation of a declining value of xerography.[15]

Yet a third measure of the growing capability of Fuji Xerox was the proportion of models developed in-house. In the 1970s, the majority

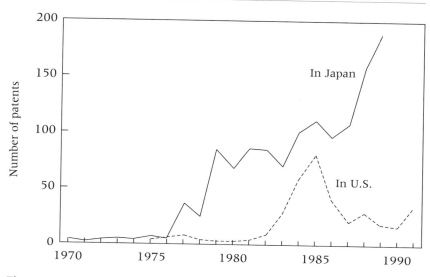

Figure 6 Patents granted to Fuji Xerox, 1970–1991.
(Sources: Japan data from Fuji Xerox; U.S. data from Chi Research, Inc.)

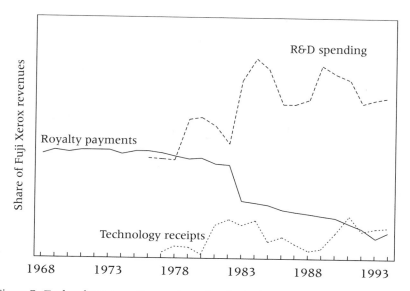

Figure 7 Technology spending and receipts by Fuji Xerox, 1968–1994. "Technology receipts" are payments to Fuji Xerox for development work done on machines sold by Xerox.
(Source: Internal company reports.)

of models sold by Fuji Xerox had been developed by Xerox. Although Fuji Xerox continued to rely on Xerox for basic research in new technologies, by the late 1980s few of its models had been designed by Xerox. For the most part, these were high-end copier models, working at speeds of above 120 cpm. By the late 1980s Fuji Xerox had produced many low-end models, and even a few in the 60–90 cpm range.[16] Many of these were exported to or manufactured by Xerox and Rank Xerox. In 1980, 70 percent of the low-volume units sold by Xerox and Rank Xerox were of their own design, and 30 percent were of Fuji Xerox design; by 1987, 94 percent were of Fuji Xerox design. Xerox and Rank Xerox continued to design and make their own mid- and high-volume copiers, however.

Closer Collaboration to Meet New Challenges

By the 1990s, Xerox and Fuji Xerox faced new competitive challenges and were determined to meet them together. One challenge was the rising capabilities of Canon. Although Xerox's precipitous decline in the 1970s had been stemmed and many of its competitors from that decade had faded away, Canon's copier business continued to expand. From 1980 to 1989 Canon's total sales grew from $2.9 billion to $9.4 billion, a growth rate of 14 percent per year. Canon's R&D spending grew even more rapidly at 24 percent per year, from $77 million to $525 million. By 1989 Canon was no longer primarily a camera company—40 percent of its revenues came from copiers, and 20 percent from laser printers.

In the second half of the 1980s, Canon developed a dominating presence in the low-end laser printers that were becoming ubiquitous companions to microcomputers. Laser-printing technology was closely related to plain-paper copying technology, and as digital copying systems were introduced, the importance of laser printing in the PPC market was bound to increase. Canon's laser-printing engines were the core of the highly successful Hewlett-Packard Laserprinter series, which accounted for about 50 percent of laser printer sales in the United States. This OEM (original equipment manufacturer) business was thought to yield Canon $1 billion in revenues. In the rest of the world, Canon sold printers under its own brand name.

In copiers, Canon was strong in the low end of the market, and the company had recently developed a growing business in color copiers, where it held 50 percent of the market by 1989. Analysts pointed out that Canon was introducing twice as many products as the Xerox group, although it spent less than $600 million on R&D annually, compared with Xerox's $800 million and Fuji Xerox's $300 million. Canon's goal was to become a $70 billion company by the year 2000, which would require a 22 percent annual growth rate in the 1990s. A significant portion of this growth was projected to come from Xerox's heartland of high- and mid-volume copiers and printers.

Xerox, however, was determined to be aggressive in its response. The company's strategists now saw the relationship between Xerox and Fuji Xerox as a critical element in competing worldwide against Canon. Canon had a strong presence in all major world markets, as did the Xerox companies. But Paul Allaire highlighted a major difference in the two firms' global networks: "When we negotiate with Fuji Xerox, we can't just represent ourselves. We need to find what is fair and equitable to essentially three partners. Canon is 100 percent owned by one company."[17]

Tony Kobayashi saw the difference between Canon and Fuji Xerox in this way: "We often compare our situation with that of Canon or Ricoh, companies that have a single management organization in Japan. Are we as efficient and effective in the worldwide management of our business as we could be?"[18]

In addition to this potential scale advantage in manufacturing, Canon appeared to gain from its centralized research. In the late 1980s, therefore, the Xerox partners began to work more closely together. In research, they launched their first joint projects, in which they agreed on "lead" and "support" roles and eliminated overlapping activities. Research collaboration between the companies was reinforced by exchanges of personnel and by an evolving communication process. Personnel from Fuji Xerox spent time as residents at Xerox, and engineers from both companies frequently crossed the Pacific to provide on-the-spot assistance. These personnel exchanges were also an important channel for the transfer of technology between the companies.[19]

There were also efforts to intensify cooperation in product development, manufacturing, and planning. Kennard and William Glavin, vice chairman of Xerox, worked together to launch "strategy summits." These top management meetings, held about twice a year during the 1980s, led to further meetings between the functional organizations on each side. The personnel exchanges and summit meetings contributed to a constructive relationship. "Whenever a problem came up, we established a process to manage it," explained Kennard. "The trust built up between the companies has been a key factor in the success of this relationship. It enables one to take on short-term costs in the interest of long-term gains for the group."

Uniting Separate Interests

In the context of the recognized need for closer collaboration, Allaire and Kobayashi commissioned a "Codestiny Task Force," charged with developing a framework for cooperation between the two companies for the 1990s.[20] One of the issues addressed by the team was how the Xerox group should manage the low-end laser printer business in the United States.

Most laser printers were assembled by OEM customers using image output terminals (IOTs) produced by vendors such as Canon, Matsushita, Oki, and Fuji Xerox. These IOTs were the hardware innards of the printer, that is, the drum, photoreceptor, laser, and paper-handling mechanism. OEMs added their own electronic and software subsystems. Dependence on OEM customers and high volumes of production made for competition in the IOT business. "The margins in this business are razor-thin," commented Julius Marcus, vice president for strategic relations at Xerox. "And the business is very different from any with which Xerox or Fuji Xerox was familiar. You need to sell it before you have it, and price it before you know what it costs."[21] Furthermore, production costs for IOTs were highly sensitive to scale.

In 1990 Bill Lowe was Xerox's executive vice president for development and manufacturing. He explained how Xerox and Fuji Xerox failed to work together effectively in this business:

> Both companies were trying to get full profit out of it, even though the margins were slim. Fuji Xerox's policy was to mark up costs; Xerox's was to get an acceptable gross profit. Furthermore, each product had a different mark-up scheme, and many sideline deals confounded the issues. This fostered sharp dealings between the partners. So, most of our energy was focused on each other, not on Canon. We were pointing fingers and frustrating ourselves.[22]

Xerox and Fuji Xerox devised a creative response to the challenge of selling low-volume laser printers in the United States. In 1991 they established Xerox International Partners (XIP), a joint venture to market Fuji Xerox printer engines outside of Japan. Xerox holds a 51 percent ownership share in XIP, and Fuji Xerox 49 percent; the first president of XIP was an experienced Fuji Xerox executive and the first chairman was a senior Xerox executive. XIP had a staff of fewer than sixty people, mostly in sales, but the new joint venture would also get help from Fuji Xerox engineers. The new venture was licensed to sell in Xerox territory via certain specific OEM customers outside of Japan, but most of its business was in the United States, where most global OEM customers were headquartered. XIP would handle only low-end laser printers.

Executives from Xerox and Fuji Xerox felt that this new alliance gave them a better chance at competing in a tough market. They traced their earlier difficulties in that market, in part, to the lack of an appropriate organization for the business. Although Xerox had an existing OEM business, which it contributed to XIP, the business had lacked a competitive array of low-volume products. Fuji Xerox sold to Japanese OEM customers, but was not licensed to sell in the United States; furthermore, the competitive environment in Japan was less fierce. The new alliance would give Fuji Xerox more direct contact with U.S. customers and align the two companies behind a common business strategy for this specialty market.

Perhaps because of the need to get the "right" structure for the alliance, it took the companies a year to negotiate the XIP agreement. From the beginning, the aim was a structure that would create incentives for collaboration. Marcus, who was the Xerox executive in charge of these negotiations, stated his philosophy: "I am not a believer in management, but rather in organization. An agreement needs to be self-policing." The negotiating teams left no stone unturned, as he described: "A lot of bright people argued down all the alleys looking for potential future problems. We spent our time going through all the 'What if . . .' questions. We took the agreement apart and put it back together. Because of this searching, things should be pretty smooth. Throughout all these arguments, we maintained a long-term vision."[23] Toshio Arima, chief negotiator for Fuji Xerox, agreed with this assessment. "It remains to be seen if we will survive in the business," he said in 1993, "but XIP is already a success in terms of the strategy and the arrangement."[24]

Among other things, the new arrangement aimed to alleviate friction over how profits from the business would be shared. The joint ownership of XIP helped to align the interests of Xerox and Fuji Xerox. In addition, the negotiators practiced "mathematical gymnastics to create a seamless company with all the right incentives to succeed. Now it is only us, not we and they," explained Marcus. The seamless company reached all the way to Japan, where Fuji Xerox created a separate unit for the low-end printer business. This unit transferred products to XIP, which then sold them to the OEM customers. The agreement also set the ratio at which profits from the whole business would be shared between Xerox and Fuji Xerox; the level of transfer prices would not affect this ratio.

The new arrangement also helped Fuji Xerox upgrade its capabilities more rapidly. Fuji Xerox planner Tommy Tomita summarized the impact of this venture in 1993: "Through XIP, Fuji Xerox was thrown into a new arena. Today, we can take on Canon because of the discipline we learned from the U.S. market. XIP helped us see the need for low-cost engineering and showed us how to fill the needs of our customers."[25]

To fill these needs, Fuji Xerox completely changed the way it designed and built laser printer engines. It created a business unit dedicated to the development of IOTs and made the engines in a factory specializing in high-volume production. Even more important were the changes in management. Fuji Xerox engineers were involved, for the first time, in direct discussions with OEM customers in the United States. Marcus described other changes: "They made a huge commitment to turn things around. They changed suppliers, inventory management practices, design processes, sourcing, and so on. You name it, they changed it—everything in the food chain. The organizational learning was tremendous."[26]

The changes at Fuji Xerox paid off. Between 1989 and 1993, the company developed and marketed three generations of printer engines, each one better and more cost-effective than the previous one. Xerox managers estimate that, in 1990, the Fuji Xerox IOT was technically inferior to the benchmark set by Canon, and 25 percent more expensive to produce. Their 1993 offering, however, was fully up to par technically, and almost at the benchmark level in terms of production cost.

XIP's early results were encouraging. On the strength of the new Fuji Xerox products, XIP gained major customers in Digital Equipment Corporation (DEC), Compaq, Apple, Star, and other companies, in addition to supplying Xerox itself. The printer engine business remained dominated by Canon, which held about 80 percent of the global market. Fuji Xerox, however, was starting to make inroads. By 1993 its share of various market segments had risen considerably.

The formation of XIP was only the latest in a long series of adjustments that Xerox and Fuji Xerox had made in their relationship. In the 1960s, Xerox penetrated and dominated world markets with its revolutionary copier technology. When it was first set up, Fuji Xerox was intended to represent Xerox in Japan, but no more. During the 1970s, as Xerox battled in vain against a rising tide of Japanese competition, Fuji Xerox redoubled its efforts and developed unique technologies and management strategies. With these, Fuji Xerox helped save Xerox in the 1980s. By the end of that decade, the two companies—now almost equal partners—faced a new competitive threat together.

In the 1990s, therefore, Xerox and Fuji Xerox competed as one unit against Canon. To succeed, Fuji Xerox's traditional autonomy—which had been so instrumental in that company's success—had to be replaced by tighter integration and closer coordination with Xerox. The outcome would turn partly on features that distinguished a constellation of two allied firms from a single firm. In Chapter 1 we will identify these features and examine why constellations have arisen in so many modern industries.

Firms, Alliances, and Constellations

The battle between Xerox and Canon is a microcosm of collective competition. For years, Xerox and its semi-independent venture in Japan benefited from the loose coupling between them—the alliance facilitated learning, product flows, and marketing in disparate regions. Yet in the 1990s, competition from Canon forced Xerox and Fuji Xerox to coordinate their operations more tightly to address a global market that was becoming increasingly integrated. In short, in order to compete more effectively, the Xerox constellation needed to intensify the collaboration among its members.

In future chapters we shall examine more complex versions of collective competition. Many of the constellations studied later will be larger and have members with more divergent goals than does the Xerox pair. Many of these groups are new to the market and still growing; they have not had the long history of collaboration of Xerox and Fuji Xerox. Often, these constellations have contained members from disparate industries and with different capabilities; in comparison, Xerox and Fuji Xerox look like a pair of clones. Finally, the constellations examined later have competed not only with single firms but also with other constellations; the rivalry of group versus group has led to distinctive competitive behaviors.

But to understand these complex versions of collective competition, we need to start with the basics. The Xerox story is a fitting introduction. In this chapter, I will introduce a simple framework for understanding this and other cases of collective competition.

My framework highlights the role of three sets of factors: capabilities, control, and context. By *capabilities,* I mean the set of tangible and intangible assets that enable an organization to develop, make, and market goods and services.[1] *Control* stands for the authority of a decision maker in using and deploying these capabilities. And *context* refers to the environment that places demands and creates opportunities for the organization. These three factors are critical in defining constellations, in identifying their strengths and weaknesses, and in explaining how they behave in the market.

In this framework, firms and constellations are different ways of controlling a set of capabilities. The single firm can be thought of as having full control over all its capabilities; in the constellation, control over the set of capabilities of the group is shared among separate firms. Furthermore, constellations typically differ in the way they control capabilities; the pattern of alliances inside a constellation determines the allocation of control.

Some simple relationships among the three concepts are indicated in Figure 8. As we will see in the coming chapters, the context of an organization often determines which capabilities it needs to be successful (arrow 1). If a firm has these capabilities internally, it can go it alone; if not, it may seek an alliance. In either case, therefore, the set of capabilities needed influences the structure of control in the resulting organization (arrow 2). This structure of control, in turn, influences the way the organization's capabilities are managed and the degree and type of investments made to upgrade these capabilities over time (arrow 3). As the organization's capabilities change in response to investments, the unit may offer new products and services; this may transform the pattern of competition and the context facing other players in the industry (arrow 4).

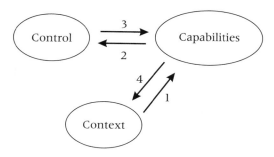

Figure 8 Context, control, and capabilities.

For example, the Xerox group and Canon each had the set of capabilities needed to develop, make, and sell copiers and laser printers worldwide. But these two rival organizations controlled their capabilities in different ways. At the risk of oversimplification, we may say that Canon had full control over its capabilities, because it owned 100 percent of its laboratories, plants, and marketing organizations in Asia, Europe, and the United States. In the Xerox group, however, control over the capabilities was split—Fuji Xerox owned some assets and Xerox owned others; Fuji Xerox had rights to the Japanese market and Xerox to the U.S. market. And Xerox did not have full control over the capabilities of Fuji Xerox, even though it owned part of the venture's equity. Indeed, the tradition of Fuji Xerox autonomy gave Xerox even less effective control than the 50/50 ownership structure of Fuji Xerox might indicate.

How will such a constellation fare in competition with traditional single firms? The answer depends on the competitive context. As a general matter, the relative advantages of an organization depend on how well its structure meets the demands of the competitive context.[2] This applies to constellations as well as to firms.

As we have seen, the Xerox constellation was well suited to the context of the 1970s, because it allowed Fuji Xerox to strike out on its own and benefit from the technological and market trends in Japan. But by the late 1980s and early 1990s, the global context demanded greater integration; Canon's way of controlling capabilities seemed better suited to this new environment.

To understand better how different control structures can favor one organization over another, we must delve deeper into the meaning of control and the organizational alternatives available for managing capabilities.

The Control of Capabilities

Capabilities do not produce economic value by themselves—they have to be put to use in a productive activity. They have to be allocated to a project and consciously combined with other resources. Over time, every valuable capability will need to be upgraded through investments of capital and effort. All these activities require managerial decisions, and so are shaped by the structure of control in the organization. Control over a set of capabilities thus determines how these capabilities will be used and developed over time.

THE FIRM AND THE MARKET

Ever since the work in the 1960s of the Nobel Prize winner Ronald Coase, economists have seen the firm and the market as the two principal mechanisms for governing the allocation of resources. For example, a maker of computer systems can choose to buy the semiconductor chips it needs from other firms, or it can make the chips internally; in the first case, the mechanism of the market will govern the transaction, in the second, that of the firm.

In our framework, these two mechanisms are, again, different ways of controlling capabilities. In the market, the capabilities are owned by separate parties—the computer maker and the semiconductor maker each decides on its own how to deploy its assets. In the firm, all capabilities are controlled in unison—the computer maker, in this case, controls both sets of capabilities.

These two ways of controlling capabilities have different costs and benefits. In market transactions, buyers and sellers have to find each other and negotiate a contract. After that, each party must monitor whether the other is living up to the contract, and, if needed, enforce the contract. In short, each side has to devise mechanisms to guard against opportunistic behavior by the other side. These and related issues generate the costs of using the "arm's length" contracts that are typical of market transactions.[3]

A parallel set of costs arise when transactions take place inside a firm. Some of these costs, such as direct production and overhead costs, would have to be incurred by someone whether or not the transaction occurs inside one firm. But sometimes bringing a transaction in-house generates new costs. For example, the computer maker may find that an efficient semiconductor business requires a huge scale and a wholly different set of capabilities than the rest of its business. Forcing the two businesses under one roof would create diseconomies of scale and divert the focus of management.

One of the insights of this approach to economic organization is that the relative costs of using the market or the firm for a transaction determines the "boundary" of the firm—that imaginary line that separates what is done inside and outside the firm. Because these costs and benefits are thought to depend on the nature of the transaction, it will be cheaper to conduct some transactions in the market and others in the firm. To the extent that contracts are costly to negotiate, monitor, and enforce, transactions will be carried out within firms.[4] And to the extent that centralized decision making and bureaucracies generate distortions and high overhead costs, transactions will be carried out in the market.

For any given transaction, however, these two propositions can only yield an extreme solution: either the firm or the market is superior. By this reasoning, both solutions cannot be optimal, nor can anything in between. But alliances occupy precisely this middle ground. They are neither firm nor market, and yet share features with both. That is why alliances have always been a puzzle to standard economic theory.

ALLIANCES BETWEEN FIRMS

In this book, an alliance is any governance structure involving an *incomplete contract* between *separate firms* and in which each partner has *limited control*. Because the partners remain separate firms, there is no automatic convergence in their interests and actions. As a result, to deal with unforeseen contingencies the partners need to make decisions jointly.[5]

A contract is termed incomplete when, despite the fine print, it does not specify fully what each party must do under every conceivable circumstance.[6] Lawyers generally try to avoid writing incomplete contracts, because these arrangements typically end up in court or arbitration when an unforeseen controversy arises. Even so, legal experts would be the first to recognize that many contracts are incomplete in one way or another.

For many economists, the prevalence of incomplete contracts yields the basic rationale for the existence of the firm. Market transactions work well when the parties can write complete contracts, they argue. But when this is not possible, it is usually more efficient to "internalize" the transaction within a firm; this firm can then make optimal decisions when unforeseen circumstances arise. If such an incomplete contract is left to the market, the parties—each acting in its own best interest—are likely to haggle over how to handle the "gaps" in the agreement. At the extreme, the very prospect of such ex-post haggling and opportunistic behavior might deter the parties from concluding an agreement in the first place. Integration is thus many economists' favorite way of governing incomplete contracts.

But an alliance is also a way to manage the execution of an incomplete contract. Alliance agreements are typically open-ended and contain "gaps" typical of incomplete contracts. But, in contrast to full integration, alliances use some form of joint decision making to deal with unforeseen circumstances.[7]

Alliances thus involve a mix of features of firms and of markets.[8] They resemble markets in that the partners remain separate parties, driven by their own interests. Each partner thus runs some risk that the other will act opportunistically, as traders might in the open market. Alliances resemble firms in that the partners agree to coordinate their actions and participate in joint decision making. In this sense, the partners practice mutual forbearance: they forgo short-run opportunistic actions in the interest of maintaining the relationship, which they expect will yield long-run benefits.[9] Like firms, alliances involve some degree of "trust" between transacting parties.

Although all alliances share these basic attributes, they come in a myriad of different structural forms. These different structures affect the pattern of decision making and the control of capabilities. Jointly owned ventures, licensing relationships, joint R&D programs, co-marketing programs, and partial equity investments are all alliances by my definition.[10] The relationship between a buyer and supplier of an intermediate product, too, may represent an alliance, provided that the contract between the two is in some substantial sense incomplete.[11]

Alliances also differ according to the operational relationship between the partners. Some alliances represent what economists call vertical relationships—between suppliers and buyers—and others represent horizontal relationships—between companies selling the same or similar products. Some alliances combine one firm's technological capabilities with another firm's marketing organization; other alliances pool similar capabilities from different companies.

The differences between these alliance forms need not be dwelled upon, as we already know much about them.[12] More important, the analysis in this book is not restricted to one type of alliance. Every type of alliance is represented in our sample, and the analysis is applicable to the full range of relationships just described. These differences do matter for some purposes, of course. But the questions addressed and the conceptual framework developed here are usually not affected in a substantial way by the differences among alliance forms.

CONSTELLATIONS OF ALLIED FIRMS

The alliance itself is not the unit of competition we have been calling a constellation. Rather, alliances are the links between firms in a constellation—the firms are the building blocks, and the alliances are the mortar that holds them together. In most instances, the alliances inside a constellation are bilateral, that is, they link one firm to another.

But sometimes a subset of the firms in a constellation may join in a common, multilateral agreement. The constellation itself can consist of any number of allied firms, from pairs to triads to groups of various sizes.

The number of member firms in a constellation affects how the constellation competes. Having more members, for example, may give the constellation access to a broader range of capabilities; but a larger size also tends to make it harder for the group to unite behind a common strategy. In the chapters to come, we will explore these and other advantages and disadvantages of group size. In addition, we will see how other group characteristics affect the way a constellation competes. For now, it is useful to keep in mind that constellations come in many forms and flavors. Table 1 surveys some of the constellations we will examine.

This sampling illustrates the breadth of the concept of a constellation. Aside from the different sizes of the constellations, their internal structures are different. In many cases ownership ties help cement alliance relationships, but sometimes only contractual agreements are used. Often all the firms in a constellation have an alliance with a "central" firm (such as in the Mips example); but sometimes all members are allied to each other (the IBM-Motorola-Apple example); or all adhere to a common, overarching agreement (the ACE example). Sometimes a constellation consists of one firm that invests in another (the Honeywell and Amdahl examples), and sometimes two or more firms invest in a separate joint venture (the Xerox example). The degree of involvement of the partners in a constellation also varies widely, from those that remain as "silent" financial investors to those that continually provide technology, production capacity, and market access to their partners. These nuances in internal structure matter, but they do not define the basic concept of a constellation.

These differences in the make-up of constellations are variations on one theme: the firms have joined in various arrangements to compete collectively, as one entity. Every constellation in this book has faced other constellations or single firms in the market. None of these networks of firms has covered the whole industry—they have always been subgroups in the industrywide web of relationships. None include all major players in a market, as would a cartel aiming to monopolize the industry. Like cartels, the constellations often suppress competition among member firms. But in the collective competition studied here,

Table 1 Selected constellations

Constellation	Description and competitive context
Xerox and Fuji Xerox	Long-lived constellation based on extensive ownership and contractual ties; some influence from Fuji Photo and Rank. Competed with global firms such as Canon and Kodak in copiers and printers.
Honeywell and Yamatake-Honeywell	Long-standing ownership tie was modified and augmented by broad contract. Competed with global firms, such as Johnson Controls and Omron, in electronic controls.
Fujitsu and Amdahl	Long-standing ownership and contractual ties. Competed with IBM and Hitachi in IBM-compatible mainframe computers.
Mips group	Over 20 firms tied to Mips through contracts and ownership; members from all branches of computer industry. Enabled Mips to compete with HP, Sun, and other large firms in the RISC field.
Advanced Computing Environment (ACE)	A loose group that began with core Mips allies and expanded to include over 200 firms with the intent to follow a common RISC standard. Competed with Intel and other constellations.
IBM-Motorola-Apple	Core of the constellation competing with Mips and Intel over microprocessor standards for PCs. Based on contractual and ownership ties.
Apple Newton group	Apple and allies that developed, made, and marketed the Newton and competed with other vendors of personal digital assistants (PDAs).

the suppression of internal competition has often translated into fiercer rivalry among constellations.

The analysis so far suggests that three conditions must obtain for a constellation to be an optimal form of organization, or what economists call "efficient." First, there must be an advantage to combining the capabilities of two or more firms. For this to occur, each firm must be unable to develop internally the capability offered by the other firm; for example, it may be constrained in doing so by its resources, by its skills, or by time. Also, the combination of capabilities must yield a total value that is greater than if the capabilities were used separately. This type of "synergy" is common in modern businesses, particularly in high-technology fields.

The second condition required for an efficient constellation is that it be costly or impossible to combine the capabilities through pure market transactions (that is, using complete contracts). For example, each owner may need to "tailor" or upgrade its capability through investments or invisible efforts that are specific to the transaction; this creates a threat that one firm will hold the other "hostage" after the investment is made, and try to extract a greater share of joint profits. Complete contracts under such circumstances are costly to negotiate, monitor, and enforce, as each firm will have an incentive to cheat. The firms then have to find an alternative way to govern the incomplete contracts that result; this, too, happens often in high-technology fields.[13]

Complete ownership would be a way to govern such incomplete contracts. So, the third, and final, condition for a constellation to be optimal is that a full merger between the firms must be costlier than a series of alliances as a way to govern the incomplete contracts. This condition does not occur as commonly as the other two, with the result that we often see full integration as a mechanism for combining capabilities. But when there are limits to the size and complexity of the firm—that is, when integration generates high costs—then an alliance is a more efficient solution.

These conclusions are consistent with the evidence on why firms choose alliances in some situations and integration in others. Early research on this question found that the choice was driven by a trade-off between a need for external resources and a need for control.[14] Dominant firms, in consequence, seldom use alliances, because they don't need help and they value full control highly. Conversely, firms seeking to catch up with leaders use alliances to acquire new capabilities and to learn faster. For example, IBM in its heyday shunned alliances, but second-tier computer firms like Fujitsu and Amdahl used alliances to close the gap with IBM. Later, when IBM lost its dominance—owing largely to a change in the technological context—IBM, too, started using alliances to complement its internal capabilities.

Organizational Advantage

The structural differences that exist among constellations affect their competitive advantages in the marketplace. A constellation may have the edge over a single firm in certain contexts; in others, the reverse is the case. Furthermore, the way a constellation is structured and managed may affect its advantage relative to other constellations and to single firms.

Firms and constellations each have distinct advantages stemming from their internal organization. Their organizational advantage revolves around their effectiveness in combining and upgrading capabilities. Which is a more effective way to control a set of capabilities? The answer depends on the particular context in which the systems operate. Certain contexts may favor constellations, and others, single firms. To see that, we must first define the unique characteristics of each form.

UNIFIED CONTROL

The modern theory of the firm argues that when an actor needs to exert special effort or make an investment[15] to maximize the returns from an asset, it will have a greater incentive to do so if it has full control over the asset than if it has partial control.[16] Partial control leads to shirking and underinvesting, because the actor will receive a lower share of profits than if it had full control.

This argument would seem to give single firms an organizational advantage over constellations, all else being equal.[17] Because members of a constellation share control over the pooled capabilities of the group, each may have a lower incentive to invest than if these same capabilities were owned by a single firm. Firms thus have the advantage of *unified control.*

Complexity and decentralization. Unified control over capabilities does not always confer an advantage. In a complex business context, for example, the capabilities that need to be combined may be diverse and best managed separately. Even though the outputs from these capabilities may be complementary, the inputs and investment decisions required to upgrade each may be different. The British economist G. B. Richardson was an early proponent of the idea that alliances provide linkages between firms which make products that are complementary, but that are produced by dissimilar activities.[18] In such situations, the assets required in production are often best held by separate owners, each of whom has maximum incentives to invest in its own special capabilities.

Is a firm as well equipped as a constellation to address such diversity? The answer depends partly on the degree to which the firm can forgo using its unified control in a centralized fashion and instead create a decentralized system of control. If we assume that a firm can fully mimic the control system of a constellation through decentralization, then it has an advantage over the constellation. The firm can choose when and where to decentralize control; the constellation cannot. Some scholars see theoretical limits to the ability of the firm to do this, and there is much evidence suggesting that there are practical limits to the complexity that firms can handle efficiently.[19]

The problem for the firm mimicking a constellation becomes even more daunting if we consider how "dual-use" capabilities exponentially increase the complexity of such a firm. Assume that a given business requires a set of capabilities, each of which also has other uses in a vast network of applications. A constellation would organize these capabilities by leaving each in a member's control; it can then be used in that firm's wholly owned business as well as in other constellations in which the firm is involved.[20] If a single firm were to control fully this same set of capabilities, it would either have to forgo controlling another part of the chain of applications or internalize the whole network, which may be uneconomic or impractical.[21]

Constellations, in contrast, can exploit synergies in parts of such a network without internalizing the whole chain.[22] Each firm in a constellation typically also has relationships outside the constellation, perhaps in a different line of business. The interlocking pattern of constellations further raises the costs of mergers. In 1993, for example, a proposed merger between Swissair and KLM was canceled because each had deep ties to rival U.S.-based airlines (Delta and Northwest, respectively).

The case of IBM and Toshiba illustrates the governance trade-offs facing two firms in a complex transaction. Both firms had some of the key technologies required for developing and making flat-panel displays, and each had potential applications for the displays. Sharp and other companies had been leading this field in investment and product performance. IBM and Toshiba saw an opportunity to catch up by combining their capabilities. But these capabilities were deeply embedded in both firms, that is, they were required for other operations in each firm. A full merger of IBM and Toshiba, however, was clearly not justified by the synergy in this narrow field.[23] The companies therefore formed an R&D alliance that later grew into a 50/50 manufacturing joint venture.

Evidence from dominant firms. Unified control is a powerful advantage of single firms. As a result, managers on the whole prefer to compete as single firms, not in pairs or groups. A firm will thus only use an alliance when it must—when a weakness in its internal capabilities makes collaboration attractive, or when it is forced by governments or powerful rivals. Either way, the firm seeks help because it cannot go it alone.

Broad evidence on the behavior of dominant firms supports this view. Dominant firms are those that consistently win competitive battles with their rivals because of their size, market position, technology, or access to key resources. Eight such firms are listed in Table 2; each dominated its industry during the periods indicated, and none used alliances to do so. In fact, most explicitly shunned alliances.

IBM's reasoning in avoiding alliances in the 1960s and 1970s was typical of the thinking of dominant firms then and now.[24] IBM avoided alliances because of the loss of control inherent in joint decision making. Like many other dominant global firms, IBM followed integrated global strategies with heavy reliance on international trade, common marketing policies, and the use of cross-subsidies among national markets.[25] Partners at the local level would likely interfere with such efforts, because policies that maximize global profits may conflict with those maximizing local profits.[26]

As always, there are exceptions to the rule that dominant firms shun alliances. Xerox dominated the plain-paper copier business in the

Table 2 Dominant firms with few alliances

Firm	Field and period of dominance	Attitude toward alliances
IBM	Mainframe computers, 1960s and 1970s	Owned 100% of all foreign subsidiaries Emphasized control of global strategy Left India in 1978 rather than give in to government demand for joint venture
DEC	Minicomputers, 1970s and 1980s	All major foreign ventures 100% owned All technology developed internally; Mips alliance (1988) was exception
Intel	Microprocessors, early 1990s	CEO is vocal skeptic of alliances Poor record with alliances IBM only licensee of 80386 and 80486 chips
Sony	Audio and video equipment, 1970s	All technology developed internally Refused to license Betamax VCR system until forced by VHS alliance strategy
General Motors	Autos in U.S., 1950s and 1960s	Owned 100% of major foreign subsidiaries Less willing than Ford and Chrysler to enter into joint ventures abroad
Du Pont	Chemicals in U.S., 1950s to 1970s	Most technology developed internally No major joint ventures until rise of biotechnology industry
American Airlines	Air travel in U.S., early 1990s	Only major U.S. carrier without alliances with European carriers

Table 2 (continued)

Firm	Field and period of dominance	Attitude toward alliances
Gillette	Razor blades, 1960s to present	No major joint ventures abroad Foreign joint ventures were either controlled by Gillette or did not carry Gillette brand names

Sources: For IBM, see Joseph L. Badaracco, Jr., *The Knowledge Link: How Firms Compete through Strategic Alliances* (Boston: Harvard Business School Press, 1991), and Benjamin Gomes-Casseres, "Computers: Alliances and Industry Evolution," in *Beyond Free Trade,* ed. David B. Yoffie (Boston: Harvard Business School Press, 1993); for DEC, see AnnaLee Saxenian, *Regional Advantage* (Cambridge, Mass.: Harvard University Press, 1994); for Intel, see *Business Week,* February 8, 1993, p. 102; for Sony, see Michael A. Cusumano, Yiorgos Mylonadis, and Richard S. Rosenbloom, "Strategic Maneuvering and Mass-Market Dynamics: The Triumph of VHS over Beta," *Business History Review* (Spring 1992): 51–94; for GM, see Badaracco, *The Knowledge Link,* and Gomes-Casseres, "Multinational Ownership Strategies," D.B.A. dissertation, Harvard University, 1985; for Du Pont, see David A. Hounshell and John Kenly Smith, Jr., *Science and Corporate Strategy: Du Pont R&D, 1902–1980* (Cambridge: Cambridge University Press, 1988); for American Airlines, see "Swissair's Alliances," in David B. Yoffie and Benjamin Gomes-Casseres, *International Trade and Competition: Cases and Notes in Strategy and Management* (New York: McGraw-Hill, 1994); for Gillette, see Gomes-Casseres, "Multinational Ownership Strategies."

United States in the late 1950s and early 1960s, but still formed major alliances in Europe and Japan. Why? First, the young, fast-growing company simply did not have the financial resources for a major expansion abroad. Second, in Japan the government forced it to form a joint venture. Although Xerox thus dominated its rivals technologically and had a dominant share of the market in the United States, it was not dominant in Europe and Japan.

The example of Intel today also demonstrates why dominant firms sometimes form alliances. In microprocessors, where Intel dominated the market worldwide, it shunned alliances. But in memory chips, where Japanese producers had much stronger positions, it collaborated with Sharp and other Japanese firms. Even more striking, for new products that were not yet accepted in the market, Intel used alliances like any other firm. When the company introduced its ProShare Video System for videoconferencing in 1994, it disclosed marketing and development agreements with no fewer than twenty telecommunications, computer, and software firms.[27]

Constellations have a different advantage from single firms. Even though they lack unified control over their capabilities, they have more freedom in assembling, managing, and upgrading these capabilities. This is the advantage of *flexible capabilities*.[28]

The flexibility of constellations comes in two forms—static and dynamic. First, they are better equipped than firms to combine inputs from a diverse set of capabilities, as already discussed. This is the static advantage of constellations. Second, constellations are often better equipped than firms to pursue changing opportunities by adjusting their set of capabilities over time.

The division of labor. The static advantage of a constellation stems from the principle of the division of labor. Adam Smith explained over two centuries ago that a factory could attain higher productivity if it divided up the production task so that workers could specialize and deepen their expertise in making components of the whole product.[29] In a constellation, individual member firms can specialize in parts of the business, so that the group as a whole can attain a higher level of performance.

The alliances in the field of personal digital assistants (PDAs) illustrate this argument. Developing, making, and selling these devices required use of capabilities from at least four different fields—computer hardware, computer software, telecommunications, and consumer electronics. These capabilities were so dissimilar that they were in practice held and managed separately. The PDAs introduced in the mid-1990s were therefore all creations of constellations of firms. For example, Apple teamed up with ARM and Sharp; AT&T with Eo and Matsushita; and IBM with BellSouth and Mitsubishi. No single firm mastered the complexity involved, and all used their alliances partly as options in an uncertain market.

The challenge for such a constellation lies in how best to coordinate the inputs and decisions of various firms. In Adam Smith's factory, the ultimate owner or overseer could determine who should produce what, in which quantities, and at what quality. The activities of firms in a constellation, however, are by definition not controlled by a single entity—decision making and control are shared among members. This sharing of control encourages specialization, but makes it harder to coordinate and integrate inputs. Indeed, one observer noted that many of the PDAs sold by large constellations suffered from a lack of coherence—they had excellent components and functions, but the products as a whole did not work well.[30]

The static advantage of a constellation, therefore, depends on the balance between the need for specialization and the need for integration. In some products and services the specialized ownership of capabilities will be more valuable than in others; this gives constellations an advantage over single firms. In other fields of business, systemwide integration and coordination is more critical, perhaps because the components are standardized; the constellation's advantage will be lower here.

Learning through alliances. The modern theory of the firm argues that firms are bundles of capabilities that are fixed in the short run and slow in changing; radical departures from the historical paths of these capabilities are not possible without losses in efficiency.[31] Constellations, in contrast, can assemble new capabilities quickly by forming new alliances, and can develop new capabilities more quickly and cheaply by using alliances for learning. They are freed somewhat from the inertia created by their heritage. This is their dynamic advantage.

Alliances can serve as channels for the transfer of technology and enable other kinds of organizational learning.[32] In seeking drastic transformation, organizations incur what one organizational economist has called transition costs—the costs of learning and of restructuring the business.[33] Alliances help lower these costs by facilitating learning. In addition, they may reduce the transition time, that is, the time it takes for the firms to change. Alliances help shorten this time, and reduce what another economist has called "the costs of not having the capabilities you need when you need them."[34] In rapidly changing environments, this ability of alliances to facilitate change can be critical to competitive performance.

Could a firm mimic the learning characteristics of the constellation? The answer lies not in static limits to the size of the firm, but in limits to the growth of the firm. Scholars agree more on these dynamic limits than on the static ones. Among the limits to the growth of firms are the inability of management teams to grow rapidly[35] and various cognitive sources of inertia.[36] In addition, alliances have a unique advantage in dynamic contexts—they can be used as options on future expansion. Particularly when the direction of change is uncertain, it may be cheaper for the firm to "buy" some of these options than to invest heavily in every direction, only to find out later that several of these investments were dead ends.

The history of Xerox and Fuji Xerox illustrates the learning advantages of a constellation. In its first decade, Fuji Xerox learned a great deal from Xerox; this process was facilitated through the peculiar mix of autonomy and access to technology that Fuji Xerox enjoyed. Had the Japanese venture been controlled more directly by Xerox, it would probably not have struck out on its own to develop the new technologies that proved so valuable later. Alternatively, had the venture been wholly independent from Xerox, it would not have gotten access to Xerox technology and expertise.

In later years, it was Xerox that benefited from its alliance with Fuji Xerox. The Japanese firm had specialized in a different set of skills and products than had the American firm. Xerox then used products and management ideas from Fuji Xerox to break away from its traditional methods and long-standing focus on expensive, high-volume products. It is doubtful that a wholly owned Xerox "clone" in Japan would have been able to help its parent company transform its business as Fuji Xerox did.

BALANCING UNITY AND FLEXIBILITY

Even though firms generally are characterized by unified control and constellations by flexible capabilities, each organizational form exhibits some characteristics of the other. Firms can be unified to a greater or lesser degree, and can have more or less flexible capabilities. Decision making in a firm like General Electric, for example, is fairly decentralized, and individual businesses can often be more flexible in responding to market pressures than if they were subject to a stronger central authority.

By the same token, control in some constellations is more widely dispersed than in others; we shall see that the Sun group was more centralized than the Mips group. And some constellations are more flexible than others; the division of labor in the Xerox alliance, for example, changed more dramatically over time than did that in the Japanese alliances of Honeywell and Hewlett-Packard.

Unity and flexibility, in other words, are not mutually exclusive features of firms and constellations but characteristics that may appear in differing proportions in every organization. The dividing line between the behavior "typical" of firms and of constellations is fuzzy. Usually, firms tend to have the edge over constellations in terms of unity; the reverse is usually the case in terms of flexibility. But this is not a hard and fast rule. And even when the rule does apply, the extent of one organization's advantage can vary. For example, Xerox may have certain advantages over Canon stemming from its ability to draw on both Japanese and American practices; but Canon might narrow this advantage by investing in the United States and decentralizing certain decisions.

The balance between unity and flexibility is also important in another sense. When a constellation competes with another constellation, the internal structure of one can provide an advantage over the other, as we shall see in Chapter 3. One constellation may exploit flexibility better than the other, and one may be hurt by divided control more than the other.

The Role of Context

The trade-off between unified control and flexible capabilities also varies depending on the *context* of the organization. By "context" I mean the set of external conditions that shapes the competitive behavior and performance of an organization.

The evidence already reviewed suggests that three elements of context tend to be critical in shaping organizational advantage. The first is the *market environment* of the organization, including markets for both inputs and outputs. These markets shape product requirements and determine the sources of components. The second element of context is the *technological environment,* which includes both product and process technologies. These technologies determine which capabilities the organization needs to master or draw on. The third important element of context is the *competitive environment,* which refers to the set of rivals and potential rivals facing the organization. The advantage of the organization is measured against these rivals, which are typically both firms and constellations.

ALLIANCES IN THE COMPUTER INDUSTRY

The computer industry provides a good example of the ways in which the competitive environment influences the relative advantages of firms and constellations. In the late 1970s and early 1980s this industry saw dramatic shifts in the pattern of competition. Earlier, U.S. firms, and IBM in particular, had been the global leaders in technology, production, and market share. The gaps between them and non-U.S. firms began to narrow in the late 1970s, and the relative decline of IBM signaled growing rivalry in the industry. Compounding this trend was the rise in the early 1980s of new U.S. computer firms focused on microcomputers, such as Apple and Sun Microsystems.

Together, the appearance of new technologies, the rise of new competitors, the interpenetration of markets by firms from different nations, and the growing technical capabilities of non-U.S. firms led to a dramatic increase in interdependence among firms. Established and new firms used alliances as a way to manage this interdependence.

In response to these new competitive pressures, IBM abandoned its earlier stance against sharing control of subsidiaries and entered into alliances with local firms. In 1982–1984, IBM Japan formed only 4 alliances with local firms involving some equity investment; in 1987–1989, it formed 25 such alliances. The company's reliance on externally sourced components also increased during these years, as IBM purchased more semifinished products from other firms; the share of all such components rose from 20 percent of all components in 1982 to over 50 percent in 1989.[37] Following the example set by IBM Japan, IBM Europe expanded its stock of equity-based alliances from 6 in 1987 to 150 in 1990.

In the United States, too, IBM's personal computer (PC) business came to depend heavily on a partnership with Microsoft and on close relations with Intel. As the decade progressed, IBM acceptance of alliances grew to the point, in the early 1990s, where it billed itself as a "spectrum of businesses"—a collection of more or less autonomous businesses, many jointly owned with other firms. In all, IBM's alliances numbered in the hundreds, and it regularly topped lists of those firms most active in interfirm collaboration. A major alliance with Apple launched in 1991 served only to underscore this new philosophy.[38]

IBM was not alone in these changes—all major computer firms increased their use of alliances in this period.[39] Furthermore, the data demonstrate that the national origins of these firms influenced the division of labor in alliances. Computer firms from different countries had different strengths and weaknesses. On the whole, the U.S. firms were the technological leaders and the Japanese firms were best at manufacture and export of capital-intensive products; the European firms were weak on both counts, but generally held on to their local customer base.[40] As a result, computer firms chose to use international alliances for distinctly different purposes (see Table 3).[41]

American computer firms tended to use international alliances to gain access to markets; 49 percent of all their alliances were for this purpose. These firms were typically strong in technology and production, and so needed less help in that area. But this did not mean that they could easily extend these advantages into foreign markets, where they faced high barriers to entry. Jacques Maisonrouge, CEO of IBM World Trade, observed in 1973: "Political power is stronger than economic power when the two collide."[42] When they did collide—as in countries like India, Mexico, and Japan—U.S. firms were sometimes forced by government regulations to take on local partners.[43]

Japanese computer firms also sought access to markets (38 percent of their total), but European firms did not (20 percent). The latter used alliances more often for sourcing products (37 percent) and for gaining access to technology (43 percent). Japanese firms were less interested in sourcing products (28 percent), but were stronger than European firms in supplying products (29 percent for the Japanese as compared

Table 3 Motivations for international alliances in computers, 1975–1994

Home country of firm	Access to			Total	
	Products	Technology	Markets		
A. What Firms Seek					
United States	45 (25%)	47 (26%)	89 (49%)	181 (100%)	
Japan	28 (28%)	33 (34%)	37 (38%)	98 (100%)	
Europe	45 (37%)	53 (43%)	24 (20%)	122 (100%)	
Total	118 (29%)	133 (33%)	150 (38%)	401 (100%)	
B. What Firms Offer					
United States	56 (36%)	61 (39%)	40 (25%)	157 (100%)	
Japan	28 (29%)	27 (27%)	43 (44%)	98 (100%)	
Europe	17 (18%)	35 (38%)	40 (44%)	92 (100%)	
Total	101 (29%)	123 (35%)	123 (36%)	347 (100%)	

Source: Database described in Appendix B.

Note: The absolute numbers do not represent individual alliances, because some alliances had more than one goal. Also, because there were partners from other countries, the totals in panel B are less than in panel A. See also note 41.

with 18 percent for the Europeans). These striking differences among firms from different nations are consistent with the general strengths and weaknesses of the firms and their home countries. While Europe's trade deficit in information technology deepened in the 1980s, Japan's trade surplus widened; and while Japanese firms narrowed the gap with the American industry leaders, European firms continued to struggle.[44]

Finally, when foreign firms sought out Japanese partners, it was usually to gain access to the Japanese market (44 percent). This, too, is consistent with the strong position of Japanese firms in their local market, which represented a barrier to entry to foreign firms. Japanese and European firms faced much lower barriers in entering the U.S. market, so that they seldom needed American partners for this purpose (25 percent).

The distribution of strengths and weaknesses among computer firms thus dictated the pattern of collaboration among them. The changes in the global context of these firms created new advantages for constellations, which supplanted the advantage previously enjoyed by single firms.

DIMENSIONS OF CONTEXT

Not all environmental changes favor constellations. In fact, in the late nineteenth century, the emergence of scale and scope economies in production and marketing promoted the consolidation of networks of semi-independent firms into huge, integrated firms. The changes in technology, markets, and competitors in this earlier period increasingly favored firms over constellations.[45]

How, then, does context affect the relative advantages of an organization? The overall evidence points to two characteristics of the context: the degree of *complexity* and the *rate of change*. High degrees of complexity and rates of change in the environment tend to favor constellations. Furthermore, a third characteristic—uncertainty—often grows out of and compounds the other two. Together these characteristics go a long way in explaining the current alliance revolution in high-technology businesses.

Complexity. The complexity of modern business is one fundamental reason for the formation of constellations. By "complexity" I mean that many businesses are composed of separate but interrelated parts.[46]

Examples of these parts are represented in the components of an assembled product, the different technologies required for production, the distinct segments in a value-added chain, and geographical markets linked through trade and investment. The computer industry has always exhibited these characteristics, but the complexity of that industry increased in the 1980s as new technologies, markets, and competitors emerged. Electrical and electronic goods, information technology, automobiles, and airlines also share these characteristics.

Business complexity influences the organization of firms. A firm may be strong in one part of a business while being weak in the others; the assets and skills required for success in one part may not apply elsewhere. Is it better then to engage in all these activities at once, or to specialize in a few?[47] In the industries studied here, complexity led to increased specialization, and firms used alliances to manage their interdependence. Complexity thus shifted the relative advantages of unified control and flexible capabilities, favoring the rise of constellations.

Rapid change and uncertainty. The competitive environment of high technology changes continually, rapidly, and often in unpredictable ways. From one month to the next, new products are introduced by rivals, new technologies are developed, and new markets appear. Environmental change can raise the demand for collaboration by generating a need for new capabilities. Indeed, in two recent cross-industry studies, high-technology businesses had the highest numbers of alliances, although these businesses ranked lower in an earlier study covering the 1970s.[48]

Why does rapid change in the environment increase the potential benefits of a constellation? In fast-changing environments, the very need for a transaction may be subject to uncertain variation. A firm may be faced with an apparent need for an external resource today, but the competitive situation might change to make this resource useless tomorrow. Or firms may lack a capability today, but later develop it internally. Or, alternatively, a firm may suspect that one of three different resources may be needed, but it will only find out later which of the three that is.[49] In these situations, a firm's need for a new capability may appear or vanish overnight.

Under such conditions, the governance benefits of using a constellation are high. As already noted, complete contracts that account for all the possible contingencies that may arise over time are costly to write.[50] Worse yet, full integration in fast-changing environments would be disruptive to the firm. If the need for a capability were uncertain, for example, and the firm internalized this capability by buying another firm, it would run the risk of having to spin off the acquisition after the uncertainty was resolved. Given a large number of such uncertain external transactions, the firm that used a merger each time would be continually buying and selling businesses. Aside from the transaction costs of this activity, the firm's evolution is likely to be pushed and pulled in different directions as each new capability is first integrated and then de-integrated.

A constellation, in this context, provides a buffer between the firm and the changing environment. The notorious "instability" of alliances is, in this sense, one of their benefits. Firms may use alliances as a temporary stopgap while they develop their internal capabilities. Or the alliances may be used as options in uncertain environments, with firms expanding or dissolving relationships in response to future developments.[51] In addition, constellations may be more amenable to periodic adjustment and restructuring than the internal hierarchies of a firm. In each case, the transaction costs of entering into, changing, or breaking an alliance are likely to be lower than the costs of a string of mergers, spinoffs, and internal company reorganizations. Constellations, therefore, are a unique way for firms to manage transitions.

The conditions that favor constellations over firms or the reverse also influence the relative advantages of different types of constellations. To see this, we need to examine explicitly the choices available to firms in designing constellations.

The Design of Constellations

As we move along the spectrum from single firm to large alliance group, we encounter several distinct organizational shapes—pairs, triads, groups of various sizes.[52] Constellations consisting of more than two or three firms are often referred to as "alliance networks."[53]

Confusingly, the term "network" is also often used to refer to the structure of connections among all the firms in an industry. For example, if all the linkages among firms in the computer industry were to be mapped, we would see that every firm is either directly or indirectly connected to every other firm. In this view, all the firms in the industry are part of one network.[54] This use of the term is different from what is meant by alliance network in this book. Our definition refers to identifiable subgroups in the industrywide network; these subgroups compete as collectives against other such subgroups and against traditional single firms.[55]

In short, the alliance networks studied here are collections of firms aligned in specific formations to pursue specific goals. Like firms, the most effective networks have a competitive strategy and a structure to match that strategy. Many, of course, do not have such a grand design, and are looser agglomerations with less unified aims. Still, to understand the competitive behavior of a constellation, we need to examine two elements of its design—its strategic rationale and its structural form.

STRATEGIES OF CONSTELLATIONS

The evidence from a broad spectrum of industries and companies shows how varied are the motivations behind the formation of alliance groups. Common drivers of constellation formation are (1) globalization of competition, (2) deepening industry convergence, (3) standards battles, and (4) positioning strategies of individual firms. These varied motivations share a common theme—the exploitation of economies of scale and scope.[56] Each motivation for group formation can be seen as a way for the allies to take advantage of such economies.

Rising global competition. The rising importance of global scale provides strong incentives for the creation of alliance groups. Cross-border networks can help a firm spread its costs over larger volumes or give it access to skills and assets in different nations. Furthermore, crossing borders by means of wholly owned subsidiaries is often stymied by regulatory barriers, as in the case of Xerox in Japan.

Alliance networks in the airline industry illustrate the pattern. Deregulation in the United States, the rise of the hub-and-spoke system, and the economic integration of Europe increased the value of scale and scope in this industry during the 1980s and 1990s. Large carriers like American Airlines and British Airways might survive on their own in this environment, but smaller carriers like Swissair had little choice but to link with a collection of other airlines.[57]

Deepening industry convergence. Alliance groups are also common when new technologies create linkages between formerly separate industries. These groups allow leaders from each field to exploit new opportunities faster than if each were to develop the capabilities of the others.

Convergence can appear in any industry, but in the 1980s and 1990s the phenomenon has revolved around electronics and information technologies. Digitization of information, combined with new ways of storing, transmitting, and manipulating it at ever-decreasing costs, has affected many sectors of the economy and created new fields of business.[58] In these new businesses, competitive advantage often stems from how well a firm can assemble the disparate capabilities needed. Because the capabilities of firms depend on the areas in which they have specialized in the past,[59] they are unlikely to have all these disparate capabilities in-house. For the same reasons, it is often difficult, costly, and time-consuming for firms to develop the capabilities they need. Alliance groups, as well as bilateral alliances and mergers, have become popular strategies for gaining access to the needed capabilities.

Battles over technical standards. Technical standards have become critical elements in modern competition, in part because of the spread of digital electronics technologies. These digital electronics technologies are inherently complex systems, in which specific pieces of hardware, software, and content have to be compatible with one another. Technical standards govern the interfaces between these components, and determine whether or not two components are compatible. Because digital technologies have come to be applied in every industry and field, issues of compatibility and standards now arise in a wide range of industries.

When a technical specification of the interface between two components is fully standardized and available for all to use (the standard is then said to be "open"), suppliers of the parts can usually operate without an alliance. They simply produce their part to the standard specifications. But when these specifications are not yet well developed, not generally accepted, or not available for all to use, then the suppliers need to coordinate their designs to ensure compatibility. Alliances are then useful mechanisms for managing this interdependence.

The importance of standards in emerging businesses also means that some firms might gain an advantage by producing a widely used standard.[60] In the reduced instruction-set computing (RISC) industry, Sun, Mips, IBM, HP, and DEC each strove to have its design accepted by more users. To do that, each had to convince enough "sponsors" to join its group.[61] Each also counted on a snowball effect: the more machines sold with its technology, the more software would be produced, which in turn would help sell more machines, and so on. The alliance networks created by JVC and Sony in the battle over standards in the videocassette recorder (VCR) industry provides another example, as do the networks created by stereo equipment vendors when quadrophonic sound technology was introduced.[62]

Positioning strategies. Not all alliance groups are formed in response to industrywide changes. Some alliance networks develop from strategic decisions of individual firms to, for example, diversify or reposition the company in other ways. When these new strategies cannot be accomplished internally or through one or two alliances, a series of alliances may be used.

For example, the Japanese firm Kubota used an alliance network to diversify into computers. Kubota's core businesses were steel and farm machinery. In the early 1980s the company began a program of investing in American computer start-ups, with the intention of acquiring technology and entering the computer business. These start-ups included Mips (RISC computers), Rasna (CAD/CAM software), Exabyte (tape drives), Maxoptics (optical storage), Akashik Memories (magnetic storage), and Ardent (graphics workstations). Olivetti provides another example of the use of a network of alliances to reposition a business. When Olivetti's traditional office equipment business was threatened by the rise of computers and digital technologies, it launched an aggressive campaign to acquire technology, source products, and gain access to markets in information technology.

Firms also use alliance groups to achieve positioning aims other than diversification. IBM Japan expanded its network of local partners as a defense against Fujitsu and NEC in the early 1980s. Alliance groups are also used by newcomers as a way of attacking incumbents. The RISC groups are good examples of this use, particularly Mips's ACE group and IBM's PowerPC group. Although these groups competed against each other in a battle over standards, they also aimed to unseat Intel as the dominant producer of microprocessors for desktop computing.

STRUCTURES OF CONSTELLATIONS

Pairs of firms linked through bilateral alliances are the basic building blocks—the atoms, so to speak—of all other constellations. In larger constellations, member firms are typically linked to each other through a series of bilateral alliances, although there may also be multiparty alliances. These linkages are never random—we can usually discern patterns that are distinct for each constellation. This internal structure matters a great deal: it shapes the overall advantage of the constellation as well as the relative power of individual members, as we will see.

A group always takes on characteristics that supersede those of its component pairs,[63] because the bilateral alliances interact with each other. Two relationships can either reinforce or detract from each other. Sometimes the synergy among alliances is managed through collective governance, or through the coordinating decisions of a central firm. But even when groups have no mechanism for collective governance and the pattern of linkages is more decentralized, the whole is often greater than the sum of the parts. The overall design of an alliance network, therefore, affects its results.[64]

Several design elements differentiate one group from another and affect the advantages of constellations. Among these are the size of the group, its mix of members, and the degree of internal competition. Group size influences how members relate to one another; for example, the larger the group, the more likely it is that members will need common governance mechanisms to manage their interactions.[65] Even so, the effectiveness and even the survival of a group often depends on its not being too large, as Chapters 3 and 4 will show.

The structure of the group also shapes the relative influence of individual members. Some group members may be more centrally located than others, in the sense that they are directly connected to many members.[66] The characteristics of these central firms are usually critical in influencing the structure and impact of the group.[67] Furthermore, the presence of a strong central member can aid in coordinating the decisions of the constellation. Sometimes these central firms may intentionally create duplication and competition among members, so as to increase their own options and bargaining power.

COMPETITION AMONG CONSTELLATIONS

The evidence from high-technology industries and other fields suggests that there is often more than one alliance group in an industry. Although there may be some firms that have alliances with firms in more than one group, the firms within each group usually have more extensive and intensive collaboration with one another than they have with firms from other groups. The battle between two or more alliance networks is referred to here as *group-based competition*.

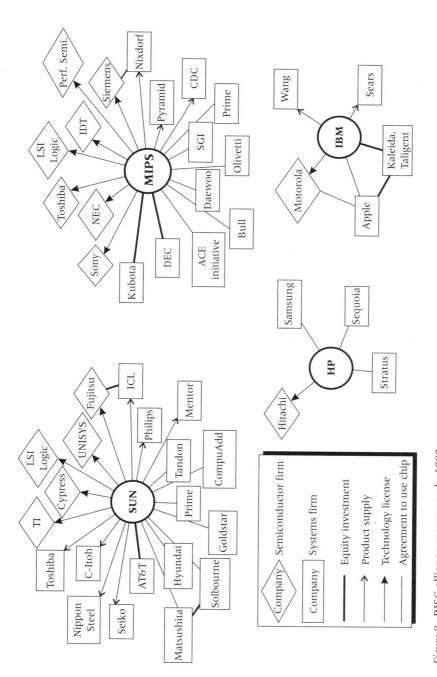

Figure 9 RISC alliance groups, early 1992.
(Sources: Survey of press reports—see Appendix B—and company interviews.)

The RISC groups led by Mips, Sun Microsystems, Hewlett-Packard, and IBM illustrate this concept. Over time, each of these firms built a network of alliances to develop, make, sell, and promote its chip or system. The most important alliances in each network, as of early 1992, are shown in Figure 9. Here each alliance group is composed of a mix of firms producing semiconductors, reselling systems, and making their own systems. The firm at the center of each network designs the RISC technology, licenses the semiconductor firms to produce chips, and supplies completed systems to the original equipment manufacturers and to the resellers. The link between the central firm and the systems manufacturers is often less formal; the latter simply commit to using the RISC design in their systems (a "design win"). Some firms are also linked to each other through equity investments.

COMPARISONS WITH OTHER GROUPS

The idea that firms can gain from banding together is not new. A comparison with other types of collectives will help refine our understanding of modern alliance groups.

Japanese *keiretsu*, for example, are collections of firms with long-standing and broad-based relationships with one another; they tend to help one another in various ways and in multiple fields of business.[68] The alliance groups examined here are more focused; they were created for specific strategic purposes, and the roles of their members are narrowly tailored to these purposes. Even so, in some ways these groups resemble vertical *keiretsus* that are composed of one large firm and many smaller partners.

Business groups, common in Latin American and Asian developing countries, are another form of alliance network. These groups often arise as family businesses expand into related fields, using capital from one business to finance another and drawing on members of the family to head individual operations. Their internal "markets" for capital, managerial talent, and goods bypass external markets. A shared culture, trust in family members, and existing business relationships often facilitate the internal transactions. Again, the alliance groups discussed in this book, operating in a closely related set of businesses, are more focused than these business groups. Furthermore, our constellations do not rely on the social, familial, and cultural affinities that often tie together the firms in business groups.[69]

Interwar cartels were another type of group; they too differed from modern alliance groups in their basic purposes.[70] When American and European firms in the sugar, rubber, nitrogen, steel, aluminum, magnesium, incandescent lamp, and chemical industries banded together in cartels, they aimed to allocate world markets and restrict competition. Usually this goal meant that all the major competitors in an industry joined together in one cartel. Although the ultimate competitive effects of today's alliance group are not always clear, there is usually more than one group in each industry, a situation that leads to fierce competition. Each of the groups studied has aimed to combine assets, technologies, and markets in ways that enhance its ability to compete against others. Despite the dense network of intercompany linkages in RISC and PDAs, I found no evidence of industrywide cartelization.

Notwithstanding these differences between different types of networks, all have to manage competition among their members. This challenge is most acute in cartels, where there are constant incentives for members to cheat on each other. But *keiretsu* and business groups also need to find ways to moderate internal frictions. The same is true for every constellation included here.

In Chapter 2 we will look at the mechanisms through which allies manage the often confusing mix of rivalry and cooperation. But instead of studying this mix in the large constellations portrayed in Figure 9, we will begin in the next case study by examining a simpler constellation of two firms. Later these findings will be extended to the case of more complex groups.

Conclusion

Economists and managers now realize that the old dichotomy between firms and markets no longer applies; perhaps it never did. Alliances fill the wide gap between these two extremes—they are a unique way to govern incomplete contracts between separate parties.

At the same time, these alliances are more than a convenient governance mechanism. By tying firms together—however loosely—they create the new units of competition I have called constellations. In an increasing number of fields, constellations compete with other constellations as well as with traditional single firms. In these battles, the groups have distinct advantages and disadvantages that depend on their design and on the external context of the battle.

In the case study preceding this chapter, we saw how Xerox benefited from its alliance with Fuji Xerox. But we also saw that the context of this constellation was changing in the 1990s, requiring new structures and strategies. In future chapters, we will follow this story for the lessons that it teaches about how constellations adapt to address the demands of their environment. We will see how the two firms drew closer together and intensified their collaboration in an effort to compete more effectively against Canon.

Not all constellations react to new challenges in this way; some are torn apart by changing circumstances. But to succeed, a constellation must find mechanisms to manage internal rivalry among member firms. The following case of Honeywell and Yamatake-Honeywell illustrates just how delicate the balance is between cooperation and competition.

Did Honeywell Create a Competitor?

Honeywell's relationship with Yamatake-Honeywell exemplifies the old dictum that trust is hard to build and easy to destroy. The same is true of successful collaboration. A long history of harmonious relations in this alliance was threatened in the early 1990s after Honeywell reduced its investment in Yamatake-Honeywell. This move raised the possibility that the alliance might break up; if that happened, Honeywell would face a new global competitor of its own making.

For almost forty years, the relationship between Honeywell and Yamatake-Honeywell had been a model of U.S.-Japanese collaboration. Before World War II, Honeywell had licensed technology to Yamatake, a family-owned Japanese company making process control systems for industrial plants. In the early 1950s Yamatake's owners came to Honeywell with a detailed accounting of the license fees they thought they owed because of their use of Honeywell technology during the war. Impressed by the sincerity of this offer, but preferring a stake in Japan over cash in its pocket, Honeywell offered to buy a 50 percent share in Yamatake instead. Some years later, the Yamatake family sold its shares on the Tokyo stock exchange. Honeywell, with its 50 percent share, was by far the largest shareholder in the company after that point.

Yamatake-Honeywell, as the company was renamed, prospered in Japan's postwar boom. It established a dominant market share in electrical controls for buildings and residences, a position it maintains today. Even though the American parent transferred technology to the Japanese venture during these years, it developed a distinct "hands-off" approach to Yamatake-Honeywell. This approach—which continued well into the 1980s—originated with Edson Spencer, Honeywell's representative in Japan between 1958 and 1962.

The Rise of Yamatake-Honeywell

Edson Spencer represented a new type of Honeywell executive. Although the Minnesota company had sales of $210 million in 1953, it had little business outside the United States. In contrast, Spencer was an internationalist. He had a degree in political economy from Williams College in Massachusetts, had been a Rhodes Scholar at Oxford, and had worked for Sears & Roebuck in Venezuela.

As Spencer understood it, his role in Japan was to oversee—not manage—Honeywell's equity interest in Yamatake-Honeywell. Early difficulties in transferring American technology to Japan, however, forced Spencer to take a more active role. He ushered out the existing generation of Yamatake-Honeywell managers and promoted a new one. Then he gave them free rein, believing that Yamatake-Honeywell would do best if managed by the Japanese and left alone by the Americans.

Spencer left Japan in 1962, but he continued to oversee Honeywell's relations with Yamatake-Honeywell. As Honeywell's vice president for international operations (1965 to 1973) and then as CEO (1973 to 1989), he protected Yamatake-Honeywell's autonomy and ensured the company's access to Honeywell's technologies. Disagreements between Honeywell and Yamatake-Honeywell managers surfaced from time to time, but these were usually resolved smoothly through Spencer's personal attention and his relationships with the Japanese. More than any other alliance in this book, the alliance of Yamatake-Honeywell relied on trust and the power of a single personality.

All of Yamatake-Honeywell's major business lines—industrial controls, components, and home and building controls—trace their origins to an injection of Honeywell technology. Although Yamatake may have been capable of entering some of these fields on its own, the company's alliance with Honeywell expedited the process. Honeywell maintained loose restrictions on its technology, consistent with the hands-off policy it had maintained earlier. For a long time the company's managers believed that personal relationships, rather than legal documents, would steer the alliance; territories, dispute-resolution mechanisms, and conditions for access to technology remained undefined. This arrangement affected the flow of technology and subsequent competition between the partners.

Honeywell first transferred technology to Yamatake in the 1930s, when it licensed the Japanese company to make some of its industrial controls. By the 1960s Yamatake-Honeywell was suffering from several difficulties. Its management seemed slow to adopt modern ways, and the company was under a sustained attack from Yokogawa Electric. Honeywell responded by taking charge of the operation and by transferring more technology. This time the technology was in home and building controls, a business that Honeywell dominated throughout the world.

According to Spencer, the new transfers had a major impact on Yamatake-Honeywell: "Yamatake-Honeywell was the first company, by a decade, to enter Japan's building control business. That decade—the first of the Japanese miracle—saw an explosion of local commercial construction and demand for building controls. Yamatake-Honeywell's headstart proved difficult for competitors to beat."[1]

Although the infusion of Honeywell expertise and technology opened new businesses for Yamatake-Honeywell, it did little to ensure close collaboration between the partners. In fact, economic realities almost guaranteed that the partners would head off in separate directions. In contrast to industrial systems, home and building controls are highly sensitive to national code requirements; thus products must often be custom-designed for individual national markets. Jean-Pierre Rosso, head of Honeywell's home and building control division, explained what this meant for collaboration: "Yamatake-Honeywell has a complete product line of its own with its own architecture and protocols; this line is essentially incompatible with our own line. So it's very difficult to bring the two together."[2]

Honeywell's third product line, the components of its Micro Switch division, was also transferred to Yamatake-Honeywell. This technology transfer, however, was accomplished reluctantly.

Honeywell management had prodded Micro Switch in the 1950s to take advantage of Yamatake-Honeywell as a distributor for components, and perhaps even as a manufacturer. But Micro Switch refused, fearing that this action could turn Yamatake-Honeywell into another Japanese competitor.[3] During World War II the Japanese firm Omron had copied the Micro Switch technology, thereby generating the ap-

prehension exhibited by Micro Switch managers. The delays in transferring technology to Yamatake-Honeywell, however, only made Omron stronger.[4]

In the late 1960s Honeywell succeeded in persuading Micro Switch
to work with Yamatake-Honeywell. The licensing agreement implied—though did not spell out specifically—that Yamatake-Honeywell
would not venture outside the territorial confines of Japan in pursuit
of Micro Switch customers or sales. Still, Raymond Alvarez, head of
Micro Switch, explained that this technology transfer was "a very
guarded type of exchange. The Yamatake-Honeywell people wanted
more interchange and access, but they were really not treated as a
partner."[5]

Honeywell Rocks the Boat

On October 24, 1989, Honeywell sold 16 percent of Yamatake-Honeywell to a group of Japanese investors led by the Fuji Bank. Over the
next three months, it sold another 9.8 percent. These transactions
yielded $400–$500 million in cash for Honeywell and left it with a 24.2
percent stake in Yamatake-Honeywell. Ostensibly the equity sale had
nothing to do with the alliance itself, but was entirely motivated by the
need to fend off a hostile takeover of Honeywell.

Honeywell's business was in transition in the second half of the
1980s. Its computer business was being sold off to Groupe Bull and
NEC. Its defense business had suffered as military contracts began to
dry up. Wall Street's confidence in the company declined. By 1989
Honeywell had become a prime takeover target, as investors saw its
stock as undervalued. Yamatake-Honeywell was a big part of CEO
James Renier's takeover defense.[6]

Honeywell's decision to reduce its ownership in Yamatake-Honeywell was thus driven by circumstances outside the alliance itself. Honeywell senior management hoped that building a credible takeover
defense could be accomplished without threatening its good relationship with Yamatake-Honeywell.

REPLACING EQUITY WITH CONTRACTS

At the same time that it reduced its equity stake in the Japanese
venture, Honeywell signed a Strategic Alliance Agreement (SAA) with
Yamatake-Honeywell. In the late 1980s Honeywell had already begun

to look for ways to strengthen the structure of the alliance, so that it relied less on personal relationships. According to Michael Bonsignore, who succeeded Renier as Honeywell chairman and CEO, "as the markets became more complicated and the competition more intense . . . we felt it was time for Honeywell and Yamatake-Honeywell management to sit down and find ways in which the relationship could be formalized."[7]

The new agreement was described as "balanced, bi-directional, mutually beneficial, and one that will perpetuate the Alliance in a disciplined and predictable manner."[8] Lasting for ten years, with an option for restructuring or termination of the agreement at the midway point, the SAA aimed to reduce areas of potential conflict, to better define partner roles, and to steer the alliance into a new era.

The agreement specified, for the first time, definite rules for collaboration in the alliance. It called for global product leadership teams that would define common product needs, designate which locations would become centers of excellence, and determine how technology and product transfers would be managed. The new blueprint reaffirmed the concept of coordinated research and development (R&D) and manufacturing and tried to reduce points of conflict.[9]

The SAA dissolved earlier transfer price arrangements, which it called "no longer relevant in this new arm's length, intercompany environment."[10] With respect to intellectual property, it established a policy whereby "all licensing, transfers of technology and joint developments are . . . to be pursued on a case-by-case basis"; nor did the agreement encompass any broad cross-licensing.[11] In addition, primary developers of new technology and secondary contributors would henceforth be clearly defined.

THE EFFECTS ON COLLABORATION

Honeywell managers believed that their thirty-six-year working relationship with Yamatake-Honeywell could continue relatively undisturbed after the change in the formal alliance. One reason for this belief was that Honeywell would remain by far the largest shareholder in Yamatake-Honeywell. Honeywell had also ensured that the buyers of its shares were "silent" investors not interested in daily management. The American partner emphasized, moreover, that the sale of ownership was precipitated solely by a takeover threat looming over Honeywell in the United States and did not reflect a declining commitment to Yamatake-Honeywell. Finally, the new SAA was supposed to encourage future collaboration between the firms.

Despite Honeywell's best efforts, however, the mutual trust that had characterized its relationship with Yamatake-Honeywell was shaken. Edward Hurd, head of Honeywell's industrial controls business, described the sale of equity as "dropping a bomb"; Bonsignore's analogy was "picking a scab."[12] Alvarez saw the sale as a true turning point: "We had been making a lot of progress in collaboration throughout the mid-and late 1980s. Things were really starting to cook for us. Personnel exchanges were accelerating; product specializations were being carved out; mutual understanding was deepening. And then we sold the stock. I think it was the right decision, but the relationship suffered. It generated bitterness at Yamatake-Honeywell."[13] Spencer underlined the importance of the intangible factors in the relationship: "You've got to have management teams that trust each other. If they don't, it doesn't make any difference what the percentages of ownership are, or what agreements are signed. It can take decades to build up, and just moments to destroy."[14]

It is difficult to quantify this loss of trust and to determine its impact on collaboration. To evaluate these questions, we can look at some of the tangible and intangible issues that the equity sale raised for Yamatake-Honeywell:

- *Implications for cash position.* Forced to follow the Japanese practice of reciprocal share purchases, Yamatake-Honeywell took an equity interest in Fuji Bank, the major buyer of Honeywell's unloaded shares. Short of cash, Yamatake-Honeywell had to borrow $250–$300 million to fulfill this corporate obligation.

- *Loss of face in local community.* Newspaper stories in Japan painted the sale as a humiliating one for Yamatake-Honeywell. Even the American press questioned Honeywell's motives, speculating that the company was signaling a declining interest in international business.[15] Reports circulated that morale was plummeting among Yamatake-Honeywell employees.

- *Thoughts of abandonment.* Despite Honeywell's assurances to the contrary, fears persisted that Honeywell would sell its remaining interest in Yamatake-Honeywell. According to Honeywell's Rosso,

"Many people concluded that this was the first step toward a complete divorce. Down in the ranks of both companies, people began thinking 'Do I really want to do this? Do I really want to share? Are these guys going to steal my technology?' "[16]

The changes in the relationship between Yamatake-Honeywell and Honeywell thus had far-reaching implications. Spencer recalled: "On the one hand, the equity sale contributed, in a very substantial way, to Honeywell's maintaining its independence. But on the other hand, it created long-term strategic problems for the company since the relationship with Yamatake-Honeywell no longer stood on the same basis."[17]

From Collaboration to Competition in Global Markets

The change in the relationship between the two companies was most striking in the global market for industrial controls. Industrial controls was the largest and most global of Honeywell's business lines. Industrial-control systems are specific to an industry rather than to a country or customer, unlike, say, home and building controls. Once a system is developed for an Exxon oil refinery in Indonesia, for example, that product can be sold to any oil refinery in the world.

Global product applicability creates both opportunities and threats for an alliance. For more than two decades, Yamatake-Honeywell and Honeywell took advantage of opportunities for shared research. About one-quarter of the members of Honeywell's global design teams for industrial control systems were from Yamatake-Honeywell. Hurd explained: "We looked at technology and applications around the world and synthesized the best product for the world market."[18]

But conflict, too, can arise from globalization, and it can threaten the success of collaboration. For example, when alliance partners jointly develop products in response to global demand, they often end up with product lines that mirror each other, increasing the likelihood of conflict.

The 1989 SAA agreement between Yamatake-Honeywell and Honeywell specified that each company would be responsible for selling in particular countries and regions. But it left open the question of which company would serve an area called "Other Asia."[19] This loose end in the agreement was a sure source of future conflict, which first manifested itself in China. This market had been left for both companies to pursue "independently," on the theory that the vast opportunities there made it unlikely that the two companies would bid for the same sales. But this is exactly what happened.

Yamatake-Honeywell and Honeywell both entered China with joint ventures and ended up in direct competition. Honeywell tied up with the state-controlled petrochemical giant Sinopec, and Yamatake-Honeywell allied itself with the Sichuan Industrial Corporation. In 1993 the two companies found themselves bidding to sell identical industrial systems to the same customer, Shanghai Petroleum. Yamatake-Honeywell believed that because Shanghai Petrochemical had been its customer in the past, it should remain so in the future. Honeywell argued that because its new joint-venture partner (Sinopec) had close corporate affiliations with Shanghai Petrochemical, it should get the sale.

"The last thing we can afford," commented Bonsignore, "is to have the customer caught in the crossfire between Yamatake-Honeywell and Honeywell."[20] In October 1993 Bonsignore went to Asia to search for a solution, where he discovered that the problem went deeper than the sale to Shanghai Petrochemical. Yamatake-Honeywell and Honeywell sales reps were approaching the same Chinese, Taiwanese, and Korean companies doing business in China.

Concerned with what he discovered, Bonsignore took several steps to remedy the situation. He created a task force to investigate the problem; he reaffirmed Honeywell's equity commitment to Yamatake-Honeywell;[21] and he proposed that Yamatake-Honeywell serve the Japanese companies operating in China, while Honeywell serve the American and European companies operating there. He also warned that, if frictions did not diminish, Honeywell might reach the point of telling the Japanese, "We don't want you to come over here and help us co-invent something which we're then going to use against each other in the marketplace."[22]

The conflict arose for two fundamental reasons. The first was the vague territorial division of labor in the SAA. The second was Honeywell's own global strategy. Beginning in the second half of the 1980s, Honeywell began to take Asia more seriously. The company opened a Hong Kong regional office, which by the early 1990s was aggressively engaged in Asia. This region became the fastest growing in Honeywell's global business. Suddenly areas of the world that Yamatake-Honeywell had traditionally counted as its territory—even though there was no contract stating this—became fair game for both firms.

Honeywell had effectively created a competitor in Asia. Yet the new rivalry was embedded in a long history of cooperation, and both companies saw future benefits in continued cooperation. The new rivalry, therefore, did not completely destroy the old alliance. Cooperation was indeed strained during the two years after Honeywell's sale of equity; but it gradually improved. Hurd described the impact of the sale on collaboration in the industrial controls field: "We went through a period of a year and a half where we were floundering. Things came to a grinding halt and had to be redefined. We then reached an agreement which was similar to one we had reached before the ownership change. But now it had to be more formal, especially from a legal point of view."[23]

By 1994 it appeared that the two sides had learned how to cooperate within the new framework. And Yamatake-Honeywell came to see that Honeywell was not planning on abandoning it. "In terms of collaboration, we are finally back to the point of just before the equity sale," explained Alvarez.[24]

At the very least, valuable time had been lost. More important, the reservoir of goodwill accumulated over the years had been drained. The Honeywell constellation survived, but it was weaker and more fragile than before. The pair was still confronted by powerful global competitors such as Omron, Yokogawa Electric, Siemens, and Johnson Controls. To face this external competition, the Honeywell partners would need to strengthen their alliance and reduce the rivalry between themselves.

Allies or Rivals?

In the span of a few years, the relationship between Honeywell and Yamatake-Honeywell turned from close cooperation to head-to-head competition. This had not been Honeywell's intent when it sold off a share of its equity in the Japanese venture. But this move, combined with Honeywell's new push into Asian markets, precipitated a crisis that threatened to destroy the forty-year alliance between the companies. If the relationship had fallen apart, Honeywell might well have found itself competing globally against a rival that it had created.

The line between competition and collaboration is a thin one. Honeywell and Yamatake-Honeywell had traditionally not competed in Asian markets and had cooperated in the development of new technologies and products. But the division of labor between the companies was not based on formal commitments or agreements; it was built on personal understandings and trust. The unilateral changes that Honeywell made in this relationship rocked this informal agreement and blurred the thin line that had kept the allies from becoming rivals.

In today's collective competition, it is often hard to distinguish rivals from allies. Managers often report that they are forced to compete with a firm in one instance and then collaborate with it in the next.[1] Some have seen this as a sign that the dividing line between collaboration and competition is vanishing, or that a new process is emerging out of the mix of the two—a process of "coopetition."[2] But this neologism implies a mixture of cooperation and competition that may well confuse more than it helps. It is true that competition and collaboration are inextricably intertwined in the web of relationships surrounding modern businesses. Precisely because of that, it is important for us to separate the two forces in our thinking. I propose an approach that decomposes a relationship into separate collaborative and competitive parts and maps out the effects that each part has on the others. Such an analytical map helps us to see how collaboration and competition sometimes reinforce each other and sometimes conflict.

The Web of Business Relations

Separating the effects of competition and collaboration in the web of business relationships requires carefully defining where, when, and how each process occurs. It seldom happens that a firm competes with another firm in precisely the same place, at the very same time, and in the same activity in which the firms are also trying to collaborate. Usually firms will compete in one market and collaborate in another, or in one stage of the business but not in others; sometimes the two processes are separated by time; often firms collaborate with each other in order to compete against a third party. In one sense, therefore, the traditional view is correct: like oil and water, competition and collaboration do not mix. Instead, they operate side by side, one after the other, or layered one on top of the other.

PATTERNS OF COLLECTIVE COMPETITION: A PREVIEW

The essence of collective competition is that alliances inside constellations influence rivalry among constellations, and the reverse. Alliances thus create aggregations that compete with other such aggregations, or with single firms, at a "higher" level. This notion of multilevel competition applies to simple bilateral alliances as well as to large groups. Xerox and Fuji Xerox, for example, collaborated at one level and competed at a higher level with Canon; the same can be said for the many members of the Mips group, which collaborated with one another in order to compete with other RISC groups at a higher level. Collaboration within constellations thus occurs in tandem with competition between constellations.

Collective competition does not eliminate rivalry among the firms inside the constellations. But because intragroup rivalry is "nested" in a larger competitive process, the incentives generated by that larger process can moderate rivalry inside groups. Conversely, competition between groups is driven by the effectiveness of collaboration inside the groups.

This chapter and the next focus on the interactions between rivalry and alliances in multilevel competition. In the rest of this chapter, we will explore how intra- and intergroup competition affects the degree of collaboration in a constellation. In Chapter 3, we turn to the ways in which collaboration among members affects the competitive advantage of a constellation.

Because these two chapters examine the two sides of the same coin, it is useful to keep in mind how one side affects the other. The following propositions summarize the general findings of these chapters:

- Collaboration within a constellation tends to enhance the group's competitive advantage, because it allows the group to marshal its internal resources more effectively.

- By the same token, competitive friction within a constellation usually dulls its competitive edge, by diverting and duplicating internal efforts.

- Competition between constellations tends to enhance collaboration within them, because it draws members closer together behind a common goal.

- Conversely, forces that reduce rivalry between groups—such as common standards or common allies—tend to hurt the unity of each group by generating split loyalties.

- Finally, rivalry among members of a constellation, while usually reducing the effectiveness of the group as a whole, sometimes benefits individual members by increasing their bargaining power over other members.

INTERACTIONS BETWEEN COMPETITION AND COLLABORATION

The process of collaboration in an alliance often depends on an absence of competition between the partners. This view is consistent with traditional economic theory, which sees collaboration and competition as inextricably opposed. But this is only the simplest form of interaction between alliances and rivalry, as we shall see.

In the case of a single, direct relationship between only two actors (for example, firms) operating in only one arena (for example, a market), collaboration and competition are indeed polar opposites. The direct effect of one is to counteract the other. Collaboration between the actors is reduced whenever competition between them rises, and the reverse. Adam Smith was right about the simple case of meetings between "people of the same trade"; but his conclusion cannot be generalized to the intricacies of collective competition.[3]

In more complex situations, the interaction between competition and collaboration depends on the indirect effects of all contacts between the actors. The following situations generate these indirect effects: (1) multipoint relationships between the actors; (2) repeated relationships through time; and (3) third-party relationships.

Multipoint relationships. In a multipoint relationship, the two actors encounter each other in more than one arena. Collaboration at one point can then enhance collaboration in another; the same is true for competition. Furthermore, competition at one point curtails collaboration at another, and the reverse. The reason for this linkage is simple. When a firm benefits from collaboration with another firm in one particular project, it will be less likely to cheat in another project with the same partner, for fear of destroying the beneficial relationship in the first project. Conversely, a firm is less likely to collaborate with another if it suspects that such collaboration will help the other firm compete with it in a second market or project.[4]

Such effects are important because multipoint relationships are widespread. All the long-lived alliances in this book—Xerox and Fuji Xerox, Honeywell and Yamatake-Honeywell, Hewlett-Packard and Yokogawa-Hewlett-Packard, and Amdahl and Fujitsu—were multipoint relationships in which collaboration on one project enhanced collaboration on another. In the Xerox relationship, the partners served separate markets and so avoided the emergence of competition. Table 4 provides other examples of multipoint relationships among the alliances studied.

In every case shown, the areas of competition tended to cast a negative influence on the collaborative projects. But in no case was the competition so severe as to break the relationship. The benefits of collaboration in these cases exceeded those of competition, particularly because there were often several areas of collaboration.

Long-term relationships. One of the reasons why many of the alliances in this book survived despite some internal competition was that the partners expected future benefits from collaboration. A *repeated relation-*

Table 4 Examples of multipoint relationships

Alliance	Areas of collaboration	Areas of competition
Xerox and Fuji Xerox	Most copier technology Marketing copiers in U.S. and Asia Printer technology and global sales	Certain copier technologies[a] Production of some components[a]
Honeywell and Yamatake-Honeywell	R&D for industrial controls Building controls sales in Japan	Marketing in certain Asian countries
HP and Yokogawa-HP	Computer sales in Japan R&D on semiconductor testing equipment	
Fujitsu and Amdahl	Plug-compatible machine (PCM) sales in U.S. Development of mainframe technology	Shares of production[b]
IBM and Toshiba	R&D on flat-panel screens Production of flat-panel screens	Sale of notebook computers
Sun and Fujitsu	R&D on microprocessors Design of SPARC architecture	Production of microprocessors[c] Workstation sales in Japan
HP and Hitachi	R&D on microprocessors Technology transfers	Microprocessor production Workstation sales in Japan
IBM and Apple	PowerPC architecture	PC sales and operating systems
IBM and Motorola	PowerPC architecture R&D on microprocessors	Microprocessor production and sales

a. From time to time, the partners had overlapping R&D projects and production.
b. Early in every computer generation, the partners negotiated and set the allocation of production.
c. Sun had a close relationship with Texas Instruments, which competed with Fujitsu for Sun's business.

ship is a variant on the multipoint relationship—the multiple encounters between the actors here occur over time.

The promise of future benefits from cooperation is a classic reason why two potential rivals might suppress opportunistic behavior in the short run. In the study of game theory, this effect is known as the "shadow of the future." In a typical game theoretic experiment, two actors are given a choice of cooperating on a transaction or cheating on each other. The payoff structure they are given is such that each could gain once from cheating, but at the loss of any chance of future gains from cooperation. If this game is played only once, the parties will cheat, as there is nothing to lose. But if they know that the game can be played repeatedly, they will forgo the immediate gain in return for cooperation in the future. Collaboration is thus enhanced by the prospect of future collaboration[5] and eroded by the prospect of future competition.[6]

Aside from expectations about the future, the weight of history, too, tends to affect the likelihood of collaboration between potential rivals. Past rivals often find it difficult to overcome ingrained suspicion, and past allies will have a mutual understanding that enhances collaboration. In other words, cooperation and competition have a tendency to perpetuate themselves. But sometimes past collaboration may also heighten future competition, particularly if the allies have developed similar skills and market positions. This lack of differentiation can lead to fierce competition.

The successes and failures of collaboration between Honeywell and Yamatake-Honeywell illustrate the role of repeated relationships. A history of successful collaboration came to a halt when Honeywell suddenly reduced its equity investment in Yamatake-Honeywell—the latter felt betrayed, and the companies began competing in several Asian markets. Because of their past coordination in R&D, the companies' product offerings were almost identical. The prospect of continued competition in the future reduced the willingness of Honeywell to continue to share technology with its Japanese partner.

Like multipoint alliances, repeated relationships are also becoming more common as firms develop a history of using alliances. All the constellations studied showed variable performance over time. Most were generally successful, but each experienced failures and mixed results from time to time.[7] Table 5 provides an overview of these episodes. When a constellation went through a difficult phase, a past record of success and expectations of new gains helped partners

Table 5 Performance of selected constellations over time

	Results and tasks	Period
Pairs of Firms		
Xerox and Fuji Xerox	Success in transferring xerography to Japan	1960s
	Success in Xerox defense in low-end copiers	1970s
	Success in improving Xerox quality management	1980s
	Success in penetrating Asian markets	1980s
	Mixed results in development of laser printer business	1990s
HP and Yokogawa-HP	Success in developing semiconductor equipment	1970s
	Success in selling HP computers in Japan	1980s–1990s
	Failure in penetrating other Asian markets	1990s
Honeywell and Yamatake-Honeywell	Success in dominating building controls market in Japan	1950s–1980s
	Success in joint R&D for industrial controls systems	1970s–1980s
	Mixed success in leveraging Japan component business	1970s–1980s
	Success in returns to Honeywell through equity sale	1980s
	Failure in penetrating China and other Asian markets	1990s
Fujitsu and Amdahl	Success in launching Amdahl plug-compatible machine (PCM) business in U.S.	1970s
	Success in developing Fujitsu technology and scale	1970s–1990s
	Failure in expanding business beyond PCMs or abroad	1980s–1990s
IBM and Toshiba	Success in developing technology jointly	1980s
	Mixed results in production efficiency	1990s
RISC Groups		
Mips (and SGI)	Success in Mips's survival at start-up	Mid-1980s
	Success in spreading Mips architecture	1980s–1990s
	Mixed results in technology leadership	1980s–1990s
	Failure in leapfrogging Intel in personal computers (ACE)	Early 1990s
	Failure in Mips's survival as separate company	Early 1990s

Table 5   (continued)

	Results and tasks	Period
Sun Microsystems	Success in penetrating new markets	1980s
	Success in creating sourcing options for Sun	1980s–1990s
	Failure in developing clone business	1980s
	Failure in technology leadership	Early 1990s
Hewlett-Packard	Success in high-end markets	1980s
	Mixed results in joint development	1980s
	Failure in penetrating low-end markets	1990s
IBM	Success in technology leadership	1990s
	Success as credible threat to Intel in personal computers	1990s
	Failure in penetrating Japanese market	1990s
Motorola (88K)	Success in creating common standards in group	1980s
	Failure in promoting adoption of chip	1980s

weather the storm and improve their collaboration. Lackluster performance during the start-up phase or sinking expectations would have likely led to the dissolution of these alliances.

Third-party relations. The balance between cooperation and competition between two parties can also be affected by outside parties. When two actors have separate relationships to a common third party, the indirect effects can be complex.

Collaboration between two actors is likely to be enhanced when they both collaborate with a third party; this third party can then act as a sort of policeman or mediator. But collaboration can also be enhanced when the two parties compete with the common third party; here the mutual "enemy" is likely to encourage greater cooperation. In both of these cases, the two firms agree on how to treat the third party.

The situation becomes more complex when the two allied firms have different attitudes toward the third party. When one of the two competes with the third party and the other cooperates, there are likely to be frictions in the triad.[8]

The effects of third-party relations are critical in today's collective competition. The collaborative relationships between IBM, Apple, and

Motorola around the PowerPC, for example, are mutually reinforcing. Triad relationships within larger constellations also shape the degree of internal competition in the group. Sun, for example, promoted competition among the several chip suppliers within its group. Such competition influences the competitive advantage of the group as a whole as well as the relative bargaining power of individual members inside the group. Triad relationships are also important in relations between constellations, or simply between firms, because all firms are now embedded in an industrywide network of relationships. This network can support or detract from collaboration between any two parties.

Technology Alliances and Market Rivalry

The combinations of competition and collaboration described so far appear in many concrete forms. One form of multipoint relationship is particularly common in high-technology industries: technological collaboration between firms that are potential rivals in the market. All the constellations studied included alliances of this type. As a general matter, the success of technological collaboration in these alliances depended on the suppression of market rivalry among the partners.

Three types of technology collaboration were common among the firms studied. In cases of technology transfer, one partner absorbed existing technology from its alliance partner. In cases of learning by experience, one partner accumulated experience by supplying products to the other. Finally, shared innovation occurred when both partners combined resources and capabilities to develop new products or processes. Table 6 summarizes the evidence on these types of technology collaboration among five long-lived bilateral alliances.

TECHNOLOGY TRANSFER

The evidence from these five cases and others suggests that technology transfer between two firms is inhibited by market competition. The cases of Honeywell and Xerox are instructive examples.

Honeywell freely transferred technology for building controls to Yamatake-Honeywell, but was more hesitant to transfer technologies for Micro Switch components. One reason for this difference lay in the potential the American firm saw for creating a competitor in its own market. The building controls industry was strongly influenced by local regulations, standards, and connections; Yamatake's strength in Japan

Table 6 Varieties of technological collaboration in five cases

Case	Technology transfer	Learning by experience	Shared innovation
Xerox and Fuji Xerox	Basic xerographic technology to FX in 1970s Total Quality Control (TQC) methods to Xerox in 1980s	FX development and manufacture of low-end copiers (1970s and 1980s) and printers (1990s) for sale in U.S.	Increasing joint work in 1980s and 1990s on color copying and low-end printers
HP and Yokogawa-HP	Instrumentation technology to YHP in 1970s TQC methods to HP in early 1980s Computer technology to YHP in late 1980s	HP experience with quality control owing to sales in Japan	Increasing joint work in 1990s in basic sciences in HP lab in Japan
Honeywell and Yamatake-Honeywell	Building controls, industrial process, and Micro Switch technology to YH		Joint development of industrial control systems in 1970s and 1980s
Fujitsu and Amdahl	Computer architecture technology to Fujitsu in early 1970s	Fujitsu development and manufacture of computer components for Amdahl	Joint development of successive generations of computers
IBM and Toshiba	Both IBM and Toshiba transferred technology to joint venture	Toshiba builds experience via joint venture production in Toshiba plant	Joint R&D projects develop advanced color display technology

would therefore not be a threat to Honeywell in the United States. But the Micro Switch business had the potential for global economies of scale; indeed, Omron had started in Japan and competed worldwide in this business. This potential reduced Honeywell's incentive for transferring Micro Switch technologies to Yamatake-Honeywell.

The technologies transferred by Xerox were also applicable to global markets. But the license of Xerox to Fuji Xerox determined strict territories that effectively eliminated market competition between the two firms. Furthermore, the agreement also blocked Fuji Photo from using the transferred technology in its own operations—another safeguard against creating a competitor. To this day, Xerox executives continue to believe that "good fences make good neighbors."[9]

LEARNING BY EXPERIENCE

When partners learn by experience, the potential for market rivalry tends to have less of an effect on technological collaboration. This type of learning is often incidental to the main purpose of the alliance. Product supply, not technology development, is usually the primary motive. And, typically, the supplier is in a different industry—and gains experience in a different field—from the buyer. The nature of the buyer-supplier relationship, therefore, insulates one firm from the other and may encourage each to specialize and accumulate experience in its own field.

The relationship between Fujitsu and Amdahl is a case in point. The collaboration between the companies began as an effort to develop a line of IBM-compatible mainframe computers, or plug-compatible machines (PCMs). Amdahl contributed technical expertise and patents to this effort, but did not license Fujitsu to sell PCMs in the United States. This provision served the same function as the territorial license of Fuji Xerox: it encouraged technology transfer by reducing the potential for market rivalry.

Amdahl also sourced key computer components from Fujitsu; at the same time, Fujitsu benefited from the increased scale of production for these components, which the company used in its own computers. This supply relationship became the most important aspect of the Amdahl-Fujitsu collaboration. The companies took care to see that, even though each specialized in one part of the value chain, their machines could be manufactured through the same processes. Fujitsu thus gained scale and experience in component production and was continually pushed by Amdahl to advance its process technology.

SHARING INNOVATION

The third type of technology collaboration—shared R&D—is also influenced by market rivalry, although this is not always recognized. The increasing costs of R&D have driven many companies into alliances intended to share in the expense and risks of innovation. In some instances, government programs have encouraged such cooperation under the banner of "precompetitive" R&D.[10] The idea in these programs is that companies can cooperate on technology innovation and then compete in the market. The evidence suggests that this is a misguided notion. In shared innovation, as in technology transfer, the potential for rivalry discourages collaboration.

The case of IBM and Toshiba provides an example of effective shared innovation. The companies joined in research on flat-panel displays because they thought that together they could develop a better product more quickly than if each tried to do so alone. They probably considered the costs of collaboration, too; IBM in the mid-1980s was still wary of sharing technology with unaffiliated firms. But pressure from competitors and the rapid pace of technical change in the industry heightened the urgency of the task. So the firms became partners, not just for a joint research project, it turned out, but also for a subsequent joint venture that made the screens. Even this thumbnail sketch of the IBM-Toshiba alliance illustrates two lessons on shared innovation that also emerge from the other cases.

First, the partners faced a common technological threat—rival firms appeared likely to beat both of them with new technology. This threat created an incentive for cooperation, just as such threats generally have for other alliances. Fujitsu and Amdahl faced the threat of IBM, which dominated the mainframe business that the allies were trying to enter. Xerox and Fuji Xerox faced a continuous stream of new products from Canon. Yamatake-Honeywell and Honeywell faced global competitors such as Yokogawa and Johnson Controls.

Does this mean that joint research is always a defensive strategy? Not necessarily, but competitive pressures do induce companies to seek ways to accelerate or reduce the costs and risks of research. Sometimes companies collaborate to develop new products in emerging markets where there are as yet no incumbents or clear threats. Still, these companies usually do so because they see other groups or other alliances as potential threats.[11]

The second lesson on shared innovation is that the prospect of shared commercialization of a technology encourages collaboration, and the likelihood of market conflict discourages it.

In the case of IBM and Toshiba, there was no advance promise of continuing collaboration when laboratory research was begun. But much of the development work took place later, when the two agreed to invest in the production joint venture. The venture would not market the product independently of the parents, and it did no R&D by itself. Each partner in this 50/50 venture was expected to buy half the output, but there was no guarantee that they would not use the screens in competition against each other. The 50/50 arrangement did not eliminate competition between IBM and Toshiba in notebook computers. But it moderated and contained this rivalry by enabling the partners to keep up with each other's latest screen advances.[12]

The promise of future collaboration, or at least of a moderation of future rivalry, is important, because technology can often be a fundamental input to development and production. Once technology is transferred to a rival or, more likely, once a former partner turns into a rival, there is no stopping the damage. When technological advantage is based on a firm's ability to continually develop new generations of a product, such "leaks" may be less damaging.[13]

THE MYTH OF PRECOMPETITIVE COLLABORATION

Both technology transfer and shared innovation, I have argued, are discouraged by competition between partners in downstream markets. This issue highlights an obstacle to collaboration in precompetitive R&D. The experience of European research programs in information technology is telling.

European governments have sponsored several efforts to encourage national computer firms to collaborate on precompetitive R&D, such as the Esprit and Eureka programs. The idea in each case was to subsidize company research if the companies agreed to collaborate and to disseminate the results of their research broadly.

By most accounts, these programs have had mediocre results in terms of incremental innovation. Among the reasons for this failure is the lack of complementarity among the European participants—the programs were focused on a small group of firms from similar countries suffering similar problems. More seriously, the Esprit projects in particular did little to improve returns to investment in R&D. On the contrary, by requiring licensing to all the Esprit members, they reduced such returns. Because of that, firms were hesitant to invest substantial amounts in these projects, preferring to pay only what was needed to get matching, even if small, government subsidies. These same firms were more willing to invest in Eureka projects, which allowed greater restrictions on diffusion of results and also enabled collaboration in activities more closely related to production and marketing.[14]

The histories of other precompetitive consortia, such as Sematech in the United States and the Very Large Scale Integrated (VLSI) Technology Research Program in Japan, provide further evidence of how difficult it is for competitors to collaborate. Sematech set out to develop new manufacturing processes that would help American semiconductor firms compete more effectively with Japanese firms. It soon found, however, that it was difficult to get cooperation among rivals on issues that could grant competitive advantage. Instead, Sematech refocused its efforts on supporting the growth and development of U.S. semiconductor equipment manufacturers; all Sematech members benefited from a strong domestic base in equipment manufacturing. The VLSI Project and other Japanese R&D consortia were reportedly adept at selecting research agendas that benefited all members and at using governance structures that generated incentives for collaboration among members.[15]

This example underlines a paradox: precompetitive research works only if it is not precompetitive. When the firms engaged in the research are likely to compete with each other using the very fruits of this research, they will not invest in shared learning. In contrast, when the postresearch competition is moderated, either by the companies themselves or by market and regulatory conditions, then firms are more likely to share costs and capabilities in joint research.[16]

The evidence on technology alliances demonstrates the ways in which collaboration in one project or aspect of a business can be influenced by competition in another arena. In every case studied, the threat of market competition tended to reduce the effectiveness of technology collaboration. Transfers of technology, learning by experience, and shared innovation were most successful when the partners either were not competitors or found ways to suppress their market rivalry.

The Evolution of Cooperation

Effective alliances depend not only on the structure of relationships among partners but also on the history of these relationships. Collaboration and competition are not single acts but processes that unfold over time. The very incentive to create an alliance revolves around the efforts and investments required to tailor and combine the capabilities of the partners. Furthermore, the control system of an alliance itself evolves as capabilities and market contexts change.

Some of the drivers of change are internal to the constellation and some are external. The role of the external drivers is straightforward. Changes in context—that is, in technology, market pressures, or in the other businesses of the alliance partners—change the relative advantages of different systems of control. Organizations that adjust to new circumstances survive, others suffer deteriorating performance and decline. All the alliances studied experienced external pressures for change at one time or another.

VICIOUS AND VIRTUOUS CIRCLES OF CHANGE

The effects of internal drivers of change are more complex and less deterministic. The initial allocation of control determines the investments that the partners make in upgrading capabilities. For example, the distribution of control affects the distribution of labor, the accumulation of experience, and the incentives for technology transfer in an alliance. Through these processes, the capabilities of the partners are transformed. The new capabilities of the partners are then likely to require a new round of investments to maximize their potential. This, in turn, will call for a new allocation of control that creates the proper incentives.

This process of internal change is thus a circle of causation: initial capabilities require a structure of control; this structure transforms capabilities; the new capabilities require a new structure of control; and so on. It is easy to see how such a process could appear as a vicious circle to the partner who sees its relative capabilities decline and control slip away, and as a virtuous circle to the other party.[17]

This circle of causation is evident in several of the long-lived alliances examined here. The relationship between Xerox and Fuji Xerox, for example, was set up to help the latter learn xerography and adapt it to local market conditions. As Fuji Xerox did that, it became increasingly capable in developing and manufacturing low-end copiers. Gradually the division of labor between the firms shifted, and Fuji Xerox acquired more and more responsibility in the Xerox global strategy. Decision-making structures were adjusted accordingly, until Fuji Xerox became—for all practical purposes—an equal partner to Xerox in selected businesses. The steady series of adjustments in response to new capabilities in this constellation is summarized in Table 7.

The sequence of strategies adopted by Xerox and Fuji Xerox was not planned beforehand; instead, one thing led to another. This feedback process led to continual change in the form and substance of collaboration. The Xerox case is not unique in this sense: alliances seldom end up as they started. Although some aspects of their evolution may be predictable, many others are not. Strategic shifts in partners or changes in the competitive environment clearly cannot be predicted; neither can the repercussions of feedback processes within the alliance.

This conclusion highlights one of the key underlying differences between single firms and constellations. Single firms, too, evolve and are subject to feedback processes. But in firms there are more forces against change—bureaucracies with ingrained interests, established ways of doing things, loyalties among employees, and so on.[18] As a result, their evolution is more predictable than is the evolution of a constellation—it adheres more closely to a common theme and path. Constellations typically have fewer of these forces and loyalties that resist change.

All the long-lived alliances studied experienced changes in the division of labor and renegotiations of contracts. This is not surprising. As an alliance ages, underlying conditions are likely to diverge more and more from what they were at the formation of the alliance, causing pressures for change. Another reason is that the powerful feedback processes take time to develop. Finally, with time, a new factor begins to drive collaboration: the deepening of the relationship itself.

THE ACCUMULATION OF RELATIONSHIP CAPITAL

The passage of time changes the requirements and mechanisms of control by clarifying goals, shaping expectations, building reputations, and generating "trust." Even without changes in capabilities and with-

Table 7 Evolution of the relationship between Xerox and Fuji Xerox

Changes in capabilities	Changes in relationship
	Transfer of plants from Fuji Photo to Fuji Xerox (1970)
Fuji Xerox develops manufacturing capability	
	Technology agreements and R&D reimbursement plan between Xerox and Fuji Xerox (1976–1978)
Fuji Xerox designs and manufactures machines for sale in U.S. and Europe by Xerox	
	Fuji Xerox allowed to fund own R&D; becomes major supplier to Xerox and Rank Xerox
Fuji Xerox learns from experience and through own R&D; institutes Total Quality Control (TQC) program	
	Xerox adopts TQC ideas; uses Fuji Xerox as window on Japan
Fuji Xerox's product line is increasingly independent from Xerox's	
	New technology assistance and product acquisition agreements lower royalties and institute manufacturing license fees for Fuji Xerox (1983)
Fuji Xerox's ambitions in Asia and U.S. markets grow	
	South Pacific Operations sold to Fuji Xerox (1990); Xerox International Partners created in United States (1991)
Fuji Xerox develops new expertise in low-end printers	

Source: Interviews at Xerox and Fuji Xerox; see case study preceding Chapter 1.

out changes in the formal structure of control, this process can affect the way joint decisions are made. As a result, success in collaboration tends to build on itself, allowing a given formal control structure to handle more challenging tasks over time. Although control is split, the relationship between longtime partners becomes "solidified" with success, allowing them to act in more unified fashion and with less shirking and opportunism.[19]

The forces behind alliance formation and evolution discussed thus far revolve around economic factors. Often, what matters most is how these factors are perceived by managers; this perception is shaped by the managers' experience with collaboration. This subjective experience accumulates in the practices and outlook of the partners, and shapes the "relationship capital." This relationship capital is the set of understandings and practices that facilitates collaboration.[20] It includes the following:

- The depth of personal relationships between counterparts in each firm[21]

- An understanding of the other firm's mode of operation and culture[22]

- Lessons drawn from experience about what does and does not work in the relationship[23]

- The reputation of each partner in fulfilling commitments made to the other[24]

- Increased reliance in decision making on a notion of "fairness" based on past practices[25]

- Trust among the partners, defined as their expectation of mutually assured reciprocity[26]

- Mutual forbearance, defined as a commitment to accept short-term costs in the pursuit of long-term benefits[27]

These factors affect the partners' expectations of each other.[28] In other words, each develops greater confidence in predicting whether the other will deliver on its promises, whether there will be future opportunities for gainful collaboration, whether the information provided by the other is accurate, and so on. The history of collaboration between partners refines their judgments about these expectations; that is why the influence of this process grows with the age of the alliance.

Experience with collaboration can be either positive or negative—it can either build or destroy relationship capital. Long-term collaboration does not automatically lead to mutual confidence; it merely improves each partner's ability to forecast the future behavior of the other. For example, repeated failure by one partner to fulfill commitments is likely to lead to a breakup, as the other partner loses trust. Or a radical change in previously stable behavior may trigger a similarly deep change in expectations. Nevertheless, a long-standing alliance often indicates a mutually beneficial working relationship that reinforces each partner's positive expectations about the other and about the future.

The history of Yamatake-Honeywell demonstrates how relationship capital can influence the process of collaboration. Honeywell's original investment in Yamatake grew out of a long-standing technology license relationship. Over the years, this relationship was expanded and solidified through the personal intervention of Edson Spencer. First as Honeywell's representative in Japan and later as its CEO, Spencer guarded Yamatake-Honeywell's autonomy and ensured its access to Honeywell's technology. During these years, most conflicts between the companies were ironed out informally, with Spencer's intervention if needed.

The foundation of this relationship was rocked in 1989 when Honeywell decided to sell half of its equity in Yamatake-Honeywell. The companies also created an extensive contractual agreement to formalize much of what had previously been informal understandings between them. Shortly before, Spencer had retired as Honeywell's chairman.

These moves almost destroyed the alliance. Honeywell's unilateral decisions were an embarrassment to Yamatake-Honeywell and raised suspicion about Honeywell's future commitment. Yamatake struck out on its own in certain Asian markets—China in particular—and the companies were unable to agree formally on who should serve which markets. Collaboration on technology came to a halt. Honeywell was still the largest shareholder, but the informal basis of joint decision making had changed dramatically. It would take years for the companies to rebuild the relationship capital that had been destroyed.

This case shows that history matters a great deal in alliances. The balance of competition and collaboration in a constellation often evolves according to its own logic. History shapes the decision-making process and generates expectations about the future. In addition to formal structures of control, therefore, the practice of collaboration among partners influences the competitive behavior of a constellation.

Triad Tensions

The balance of collaboration and competition between two partners also depends on the relationships that each has with third parties. The relationships among three firms are inherently more complex than those between two. Still more complex are the relationships in groups of over three firms. This evidence on the differences between single firms, bilateral alliances, triads, and groups supports the fundamental insights of the nineteenth-century sociologist Georg Simmel. Simmel studied the significance of numbers in social relations and argued that only four numbers mattered: one, two, three, and many. He found that when an individual formed a bilateral relationship with another individual, his or her social behavior would change, and that other changes would follow when this pair of individuals added a third party to the relationship; thereafter, however, additional parties would not substantially change social behavior, until there were many in a group. Simmel also made a distinction between small and large groups, admitting that the boundary between "small" and "large" was fuzzy.[29]

More modern concepts from sociology are also useful in examining webs of relationships among three or more firms. Sociologists have defined two types of triangular social relationships. In "balanced" triads, the relationships between the three parties reinforce each other; in "unbalanced" triads there is a constant tension that detracts from the cooperation among the parties.[30] The difference is illustrated in Figure 10, where collaboration between the parties is indicated by a plus sign and conflict by a minus sign.

In the balanced triad on the left, each party collaborates with each of the others; each instance of collaboration is then likely to be reinforced by the others. In the middle, A collaborates only with B, and C is in conflict with both A and B. This triad, too, is balanced, because the conflicts with C do not detract from the collaboration between A and B; the common enemy may even strengthen this collaboration. The

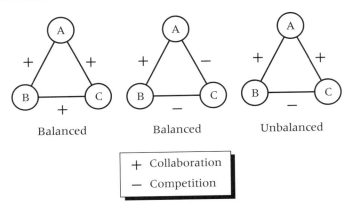

Figure 10 Balanced and unbalanced triads.

cluster on the right, however, is unbalanced: the collaboration between A and B and between A and C will suffer under the strain of the conflict between C and B.

These are, in the abstract, relationships that may arise among any three parties. If we take the pluses to represent alliances, then only the configurations on the left and on the right represent alliance groups, because there are more than two alliances in each; the configuration in the middle is a bilateral alliance. The alliance group on the left, however, has mutually reinforcing alliances; the one on the right has internal competition that detracts from the cohesion of the group.

Balance can affect relationships between firms.[31] Partners in balanced triads are more likely to agree on common strategies and to transfer sensitive technology to each other than are partners in unbalanced triads.

In 1991, IBM, Apple, and Motorola formed a set of alliances that constituted a balanced triad. The alliance between IBM and Apple aimed, among other things, to develop a new personal computer standard based on IBM's PowerPC RISC chip.[32] At the same time IBM agreed to develop a new version of this chip jointly with Motorola, and to grant Motorola a license to make and sell the new product independently. Apple had been one of Motorola's chief customers, using Motorola microprocessors in all of its computers. This established relationship between Apple and Motorola thus reinforced the new relationships between IBM and the others. Furthermore, Apple probably would not have agreed to adopt the IBM chip were it not for the assurance that there would be a second source of the product, preferably Motorola. Standing alone, therefore, none of these alliances would have been as strong as when it was part of the triad. Two plus two here equaled five.

But even this triad was not without friction. IBM and Apple remained competitors, and their software operating systems were incompatible. Apple and IBM agreed in 1994 to develop a common hardware platform for the PowerPC, but they failed to agree on a common software platform. Many observers felt that, without a common hardware and software architecture, the constellation would fail in its battle against Intel.

In unbalanced triads, the firm in the "middle" (firm A in the rightmost diagram in Figure 10) can play several roles. It may try to mediate between the two conflicting firms; it may dominate the group because the others are split; or it may actively play one partner off against the other in a divide-and-rule strategy. Each of these situations occurs in business triads.[33]

Sun Microsystems had relationships with several firms that competed with each other, and sometimes Sun seemed to use a divide-and-rule strategy. Sun developed the architecture for its SPARC microprocessors, but left it to suppliers to produce the chip. And from one SPARC generation to the next, Sun chose different suppliers. Fujitsu produced the first working chip by following Sun's designs, but it did not become a major supplier for Sun's first-generation SPARCstation machines. The processors for that machine, introduced in 1987, came from LSI Logic, Cypress, and Weitek, each of which developed the chip on its own. The second-generation SPARCstation (introduced in 1988) used a chip developed independently by Fujitsu and Weitek; Fujitsu became a major supplier to Sun for this product.

For the third-generation SPARC chip (introduced in1992), Sun followed a different strategy. It hired its own team of semiconductor designers and worked with Texas Instruments (TI) to develop the SuperSPARC chip. TI was to be the vendor for this chip. Still, Cypress also began to work on its own design (HyperSPARC), as did LSI (Lightning) and Fujitsu. Cypress finished the development of the HyperSPARC chip, but Sun did not adopt it, choosing the TI chip instead.[34] LSI and Fujitsu both dropped their development efforts when it became clear that Sun would adopt the TI chip.

This issue of balance only arises after a group grows to include three or more firms. Groups larger than three firms, of course, will contain more than one triad, every one of which may be either balanced or unbalanced. These third-party effects mean that the benefits of groups are not simply the sum of the benefits of the bilateral alliances within the group. The presence or lack of balance in the triads that compose a group can either reduce or increase total group benefits.

In a large group, the tensions around triad imbalance are reflected in the degree of internal competition.[35] Some groups have more internal competition than others, leading to some of the same effects already described. The level of internal competition in a group influences the competitive advantages that members can draw from a group. We will see in Chapter 3 how internal competition in a constellation affects the competitive advantage of the group and the relative position of individual members.

Collaboration and Competitive Performance

The balance of competition and collaboration in an alliance would be little more than a curiosity if it did not also affect the competitive performance of the constellation. Sometimes a little internal competition does not damage the constellation; but at other times, it can doom the group. As might be expected, the difference lies in the context. A requirement for large scale in R&D and manufacturing, for example, often creates a strong incentive for greater integration. In order to benefit from these economies, partners in a constellation often have to find ways to reduce internal competition.

But managing internal competition is inherently more difficult for constellations than it is for a single firm. When subsidiaries or divisions of a single firm compete, there is always a tie-breaking authority higher up and a common ownership interest by which to judge which side provides the greatest contribution to the firm. Not so in constellations of allied firms. These firms remain separate entities with separate economic interests; to align their interests, they often have to modify their alliances or forge wholly new structures of control.

The difficulty of integrating the separate interests in an alliance can thus handicap constellations when they compete against single firms. Xerox and Fuji Xerox came to recognize this in the early 1990s and developed an instructive response to the problem.

In the 1970s, Fuji Xerox benefited from its semiautonomous status within the Xerox group. Not only did it develop a strong technical capability, but it grew faster than its single-firm Japanese counterparts. But after the late 1970s Canon and other competitors developed important new technologies. Canon's copier sales then grew rapidly to match those of Fuji Xerox in 1980 and surpassed them after 1988 (see Figure 11).

If Fuji Xerox gained so much from its relationship with Xerox, why did Canon come to surpass it? The evidence suggests that this might have happened because the nature of competition changed dramatically with the rise of global competition and the demands of new technologies.

By most accounts, Canon was getting more out of its centralized R&D than was the loose combination of Xerox and Fuji Xerox. By the end of the 1980s, Canon was introducing twice as many products per year as the Xerox group. In round numbers, Canon spent less than $600 million on R&D annually, compared with the $800 million spent by Xerox and $300 million by Fuji Xerox. The two Xerox companies combined thus spent almost twice as much as Canon. Roughly speak-

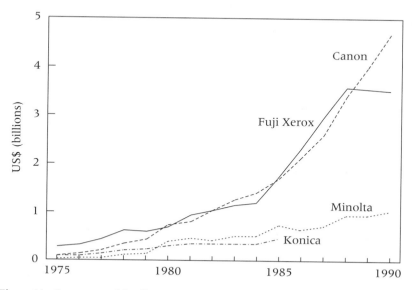

Figure 11 Revenues of leading Japanese copier producers, 1975–1990. (Sources: Based on data from Donaldson, Lufkin & Jenrette, Inc., and company annual reports.)

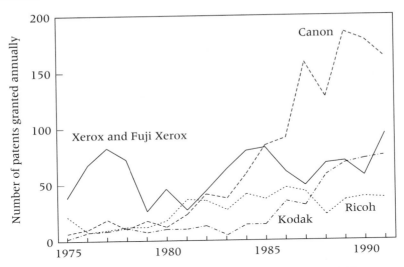

Figure 12 U.S. office equipment patents to copier firms, 1975–1991.
(Source: Based on data from Chi Research, Inc.)

ing, this suggests that Canon's R&D was four times as productive as that of the Xerox–Fuji Xerox constellation.

Canon's higher rate of innovation is also evident from its U.S. patents for office equipment technology. Before 1985, it received fewer patents annually than did Xerox and Fuji Xerox; after that, Canon surpassed the Xerox group by a ratio of almost two to one (see Figure 12).[36]

The data in Figure 12 suggest that the collaborative arrangements that helped launch Fuji Xerox in the 1960s and 1970s were not as effective in the fierce battle to develop new technologies in the late 1980s. Instead of relying on technology transfer and experience as the vehicles for learning, Xerox and Fuji Xerox were forced to start doing more joint R&D. The managerial autonomy that served Fuji Xerox so well in the 1970s had to give way to greater coordination and integration between the partners.

The Xerox handicap in comparison with Canon was most severe in the low-end laser printer business. Canon benefited from large-scale production and dominated the market worldwide. It supplied the laser printer engines that were at the heart of the Hewlett-Packard Laserjet series and other popular machines. Despite years of trying, Xerox and Fuji Xerox could not make a dent in Canon's position.

One reason for this failure lay in Xerox's poorly coordinated approach to the business. In keeping with the pattern in low-end copiers, Fuji Xerox was in charge of development and manufacturing, and Xerox marketed the printer engines in the United States, home of the largest customers. This split approach to the business led to numerous frictions and delays and to poor communication. For one, Fuji Xerox and Xerox quibbled over transfer prices and profits; given the razor-thin margins in this business, the dual claims on profits were costly. In addition, Fuji Xerox only received "second-hand" feedback from the market through the Xerox agents who had direct contact with customers. At the same time, Xerox salespeople had only indirect contact with the engineers and units that developed and manufactured the product.

In response to these frictions, Xerox and Fuji Xerox forged a new alliance—Xerox International Partners. This marketing unit for low-end laser printer engines was jointly owned by Xerox and Fuji Xerox, and encouraged a greater alignment of interests between them. For the first time, Fuji Xerox gained a direct stake in marketing operations in the United States. In parallel, Fuji Xerox created a new business unit in Japan that was focused exclusively on developing and making the printer engines. This structure enabled the partners to monitor costs along the whole value-added chain, thus minimizing disagreements over transfer prices.

In short, the structure of the XIP alliance determined how effectively the companies could exploit the scale economies inherent in their business. The competitive advantage of this pair derived from the way in which the firms organized themselves to build common strengths. Facing fierce competition from a single firm—Canon—the Xerox constellation had to restructure itself to enhance internal cooperation.

Conclusion

Collective competition requires that firms walk a fine line between rivalry and collaboration. More so than single firms, constellations have within them sources of conflicts that can tear them apart. At the very least, internal frictions can reduce a constellation's ability to exploit benefits from collaboration. And lacking these benefits, the group stands little chance in the competitive marketplace.

Firms have several mechanisms at their disposal with which to manage the balance of competition and cooperation. Multiple projects, long-term relationships, and mutual allies can be used to enhance incentives for collaboration within a constellation and to reduce internal rivalry. Most of the constellations studied used several of these mechanisms. Still, because of the added burden of managing internal frictions, constellations often operate at a disadvantage when facing strong single firms. Overcoming these disadvantages usually requires greater integration among members of a constellation.

In many modern businesses, constellations do not face all-powerful single firms. Instead, the battle is one of group versus group. In this context, all competitors share the basic handicap of internal friction, even though some might manage to overcome this handicap more effectively than others. Furthermore, differences in the composition and structure of the constellations are likely to provide one group competitive advantage over another. Competing in constellations, therefore, calls for effective design and management of collaboration.

The managers at Mips Computer Systems tried to exploit these ideas. They used a large constellation of allies to take on the giants in their industry. Their story shows both the promises and the pitfalls of collective competition, as we shall see next.

Tiny Mips Takes On the Giants

Mips Computer Systems began as a Stanford University research project led by three professors, who went on to found the company in 1984. The professors intended to develop and commercialize the first microprocessor based on reduced instruction-set computing (RISC) principles. Their story is a striking example of how a constellation can create the scale and scope necessary to compete against large single firms.

RISC was a streamlined approach to computer design. This approach challenged the traditional design—called complex instruction-set computing (CISC)—which was at the heart of every computer in the market at the time.[1] Like other RISC designers, the founders of Mips saw performance, cost, and time-to-market advantages in their approach. With simpler instruction sets, RISC chips required less circuitry; hence, a shorter design and initial-testing phase, as well as lower manufacturing costs. As with CISC, however, the manufacture of RISC chips required a high level of capital investment and volume production.

The Odds against Mips

Notwithstanding these apparent technical advantages, there was much debate in the late 1980s about whether RISC would ever become commercially viable. Ten years after its invention at IBM in 1975, not one major chip manufacturer or computer firm had introduced a RISC-based product.[2] The two major U.S. microprocessor makers—Intel and Motorola—were slow in developing the new technology, being reluctant to cannibalize their existing CISC-based product lines. HP, DEC, and IBM all had established RISC R&D programs, but lack of confidence in the market's acceptance of RISC kept these projects on a wait-and-see status.

The major drawback to RISC was that software developed for traditional CISC systems was incompatible with RISC systems. IBM was said to have dropped its early RISC efforts in the late 1970s because it estimated that to write the software programs needed to attract customers to RISC would require a thousand employee-years.[3] This lack of software, many believed, would keep RISC a theoretical concept or, at best, a niche technology with a narrow range of applications.

The three Stanford professors thus entered a business that had already been examined and rejected by the giants of the computer industry. Furthermore, the success of RISC in the market would depend on the establishment of an operating system standard.[4] Nearly every RISC architecture under development used UNIX, an operating system originally developed by AT&T and prevalent in the workstation segment of the industry. The greatest penetration of RISC-based computer systems was therefore in this segment.

Originally purchased for scientific and engineering applications, workstations gained popularity in much larger commercial markets such as electronic publishing and business graphics during the late 1980s.[5] Workstations were the fastest-growing segment of the computer industry. But here too there were established giants. In 1990 the workstation market was dominated by four vendors—Sun Microsystems, HP/Apollo,[6] IBM, and DEC.

And there were other barriers to entry. Sales of U.S.-based workstation vendors in 1990 hit $8.5 billion, up from $4.5 billion in 1988; this 40 percent annual growth rate was expected to continue.[7] Despite 50–75 percent annual gains in performance expected from RISC architectures—compared with 30 percent annual gains for CISC—not all end-users found switching feasible or desirable. Large CISC customers, such as banks, department stores, and airlines, had invested billions of dollars in software over the years. For smaller customers, the selection of available third-party software was much greater for CISC than for RISC, thereby making a strong case for staying with CISC. In addition, in the face of the RISC threat, CISC developers were increasing the performance of their chips and lowering prices.[8]

The Start-up Sputters

Against all these odds, Mips Computer Systems was instrumental in changing the industry's opinion of RISC technology. In 1985 Mips brought to the market a RISC chip (the R2000) that represented a tenfold increase in processing power at a fraction of the price of a CISC chip. This demonstration of RISC's commercial feasibility caused other firms, including Sun Microsystems, HP, IBM, Motorola, and DEC, to launch full-blown RISC development programs.

But by early 1987, despite the adoption of its chip by several computer vendors, Mips had accumulated a deficit of $16 million; less than $1 million of its original venture capital was left. Despite Mips's acknowledged leadership in RISC technology, customers were hesitant to adopt Mips technology because they could not be sure that the young company would survive.

Before Robert Miller joined Mips as president in 1987, the company had no strategy or plan for penetrating the market. Miller brought a vision, and an ambitious one at that. He later explained: "There have only been three successful standard architectures[9] in the computer industry: the IBM 360 in mainframes, the DEC VAX in minicomputers, and the Intel X86 in personal computers. Each company has made a ton of money . . . we had to be on the forefront of the next wave. That is what we are doing at Mips and that is why we need to make the Mips architecture pervasive worldwide."[10]

Miller's first concern was to return the company to a secure financial footing. To do so, he led a crash effort to reduce cash outflows and raised $14 million from the venture capital community. Next, the question of the company's strategic direction was addressed in a four-day meeting of top executives. What emerged was a plan to change the basic business approach of the company. Miller recalled the problem that Mips faced at the time: "Mips had wanted to build semiconductors. It thought it could compete with the likes of Intel and Motorola, but it could not. It was paying foundries on a wafer-by-wafer basis to produce its chips, but with its small volume, it was getting second-class treatment."[11]

The Mips Model

Miller proposed to license Mips technology to semiconductor firms that could use leading-edge process technology to manufacture Mips chips and could also help to market the product. By the end of 1987 he had succeeded in signing on three small California firms—LSI Logic, Integrated Device Technology, and Performance Semiconductor.

Mips executives also agreed to build up a systems business to complement the company's technology revenues. If Mips remained simply a design house for RISC technology, they realized, it would never have the marketing clout needed to convince software developers to write applications. The company thus began to form alliances with computer companies known for their strong marketing and service capabilities. These companies would act as resellers for Mips systems products, either licensing its technology for use in their own systems or purchasing computer systems products from Mips.

The alliance strategy unfolded gradually. First Mips received another infusion of cash from Kubota in exchange for manufacturing and marketing licenses and an ownership share in the company. Then DEC invested in Mips and adopted the Mips chip for its workstations. This alliance boosted the credibility of Mips.

Early on, Mips recognized the importance of a strong international presence. "Companies like to buy locally," explained Miller. "The computer industry is a global business supported by domestic suppliers."[12] In addition, the best technology, process manufacturing, and marketing capabilities for semiconductors were often located outside the United States. To succeed in attracting regional systems vendors and original equipment manufacturers (OEMs), Mips strategists considered a local supply of chips to be critical. To this end they signed on NEC in Japan and Siemens in Europe to produce chips. Nixdorf and Bull were important systems allies in Europe, and Kubota and NEC sold Mips-based systems in Japan.

By 1991 Mips had established itself as a one-stop source for RISC technology, designing RISC microprocessors, compiler and operating system software, board products,[13] and RISC systems. All Mips products were based on a single, compatible RISC architecture. Chip and software designs were licensed for production to six semiconductor partners, who marketed these products. Mips licensed its systems products (including software, board products, and systems architecture) to systems developers, OEMs, resellers, and integrators.

Chester Silvestri, Mips vice president for technology products at the time, summed up this business model: "The foundation of our strategy is that one customer can buy at any level of integration. We attract them at either part of the food chain. Sometimes they begin with a chip and move up, or they begin with a box and move down to the boards. Once we begin a relationship, we build a business strategy around selling to them at all levels."[14]

Mips could never have hoped to offer such a menu of products and services without its network of partners. In 1987, when it started forming its alliance network, Mips had sales of only $14 million. Even by 1990, Mips had revenues of only $152 million and just 775 employees. But its size belied a larger market effect.

Division of Labor in the Mips Group

Between 1985 and 1991 Mips launched four generations of RISC microprocessors—the R2000 (1985), R3000 (1988), R6000 (1990), and R4000 (1991). In addition, Mips designed and introduced to the market seven systems products by 1991. Although Mips was responsible for the design of all of these chips and the accompanying compiler and operating-system software, it had only minor roles in their production and marketing. For these it relied on an extensive network of alliances: technology licenses, OEM arrangements, and relationships with value-added resellers (VARs). The members in the Mips group, as of early 1991, are shown in Table 8.[15]

The major alliances and subgroups of alliances in this network played specific roles in the Mips strategy. Kubota and DEC, for example, helped Mips gain credibility and financial stability when the company was foundering. The Semiconductor Partners, as Mips's semiconductor licensees were known, were responsible for producing and selling Mips chips; often they helped in their development. Systems vendors made and sold systems that incorporated the Mips chip; sometimes they also bought components or complete systems from Mips. The functions and specialties of the members of this alliance group, therefore, complemented each other. In addition, these members are fairly evenly distributed across major geographic regions.

ALLIANCES WITH KUBOTA AND DEC

Ironically, Mips did not actively seek its first ally. Early in the summer of 1987, Robert Miller was approached by Kubota, which had already provided financing to several other U.S. firms, among them Ardent Computer Corporation, a California start-up. Ardent planned to build

Table 8 Main alliances of Mips, 1991

In North America	In Europe	In the Far East
Technology-Licensing Partners		
	Semiconductor Partners	
DEC[a]	Siemens	NEC
Integrated Device		
LSI Logic		
Performance Semiconductor		
	Other Semiconductor Firms	
		Daewoo
		NKK
		Sony
		Toshiba
	Manufacturing License	
		Kubota Computer
Systems Vendors		
	OEMs and Other Manufacturers[b]	
Control Data	Groupe Bull	Daewoo Technology
Evans & Sutherland	IN2 (Siemens)	Kubota Computer
Prime Computer	Olivetti	Sumitomo Electric
Pyramid Technology	Siemens-Nixdorf	
Tandem Computer		
Wang Laboratories		
	Value-added Resellers	
American Airlines	Bachal Telematique	Hitachi-Zosen
Computer Dynamics	Metrologic S.A.	
Dynix Corporation	TIS	
Falcon Microsystems		
Gain Communications		
	Distributors and System Integrators	
Bolt Beranek & Newman	Comparex	Kubota Computer
Sylvest Management Sys.	GEI Rechnersysteme	
Texas Instruments		

Source: Interviews and company reports.

a. DEC had a license to manufacture Mips processors for its internal use, but had not exercised it as of 1991.

b. Original equipment manufacturers (OEMs) and other manufacturers typically also had software licenses from Mips.

a line of supercomputers around the Mips RISC chip, and Kubota thus had a direct stake in the survival of Mips.

Kubota purchased a 20 percent equity stake in Mips, worth $20 million. For an additional $5 million, Kubota helped to fund a high-end systems development program at Mips in return for the exclusive right to sell that product in the Far East. Kubota also agreed to build a $100 million computer factory in Japan. Mips, in turn, agreed to restrictions on its ability to grant additional manufacturing licenses in the territory covered by the agreement, and agreed to source a certain percentage of its sales to OEMs through Kubota.

Later Kubota purchased more nonexclusive manufacturing rights to other Mips products, and Mips appointed the company as a distributor of certain semiconductor products in its territory. The company also began to purchase from Mips components that were difficult to obtain in Japan. By 1991 the alliance between these two companies had grown to the point that one product made up 90 percent of Kubota's manufacturing for Mips, and Kubota products represented 20–25 percent of Mips revenues. Kubota thus functioned as an early and continual source of support for Mips.

If Kubota helped Mips survive, the alliance with DEC gave the fledgling company instant credibility. In September 1988, DEC paid $15 million for access to all current and future Mips architectures, designs, and related systems software. It invested an additional $10 million for a 5 percent equity share in Mips, with the option to purchase another 15 percent, and the right to elect one of the six Mips board members. This agreement gave Mips both credibility and access to the engineering customer base of DEC.

In the fall of 1988, DEC announced plans to design its new generation of workstations around the Mips RISC chip, the first time that DEC had gone to outside technology for its products. DEC did so because its own proprietary RISC project—code-named Prism—was running behind schedule. This internal project was canceled when DEC opted to use the Mips chip.[16]

The credibility that DEC provided to Mips was important in attracting other allies, in particular NEC and Siemens, who signed licensing agreements shortly after the alliance with DEC was formalized. They became members in the important Semiconductor Partners subgroup of the Mips network.

Mips's semiconductor partner strategy was formed when Mips switched from being a chip manufacturer to a chip design house. The first three small U.S. licenses were signed soon after management's off-site strategy meeting in 1987, when it decided to seek a maximum of six partners to make mainline semiconductors.[17] Mips promised these firms that no other semiconductor partners would be added until 1992.

Miller later explained that the "ideal" outcome for Mips would have been "to sign one of the top three semiconductor firms in the United States, one of the top three in Japan, and one of the top three in Europe."[18] Three other U.S. firms—Motorola, Advanced Micro Devices (AMD), and National Semiconductor—were approached by Mips, but all refused. Motorola and AMD were unwilling to give up their own RISC development efforts, a Mips requirement at the time, and National Semiconductor would not agree to marketing and sales obligations.[19]

DEC became the fourth licensee of Mips semiconductor technology in 1988. For DEC, this license was little more than an insurance policy, as it never manufactured the chip. For the two remaining slots, Mips sought international partners. Siemens A.G., of West Germany, had its own RISC project going, but the Mips chip would allow it to reduce to one quarter its previous time-to-market. Also, because Siemens was DEC's largest supplier of semiconductors in Europe, DEC Europe welcomed the deal. NEC, the world's largest semiconductor manufacturer, signed on in Japan. Through a former agreement with Intel, NEC was experienced in making and selling microprocessors, and the company was willing to commit exclusively to the Mips technology.

The terms of these semiconductor licenses, which Mips called Level III licenses, were similar to second-source agreements common in the semiconductor industry, with the exception that Mips would not compete with the licensees. The firms were granted rights to the Mips second-generation RISC chip, the R3000. Mips provided each firm with the RISC instruction set and the precise technical design, or layout, for this chip, as well as licenses to all applicable systems software. Each licensee, for its part, agreed to an up-front payment of about $10 million and royalties of approximately 5 percent based on the selling price of each unit sold. Mips believed that the up-front payment was close to the actual cost for the technology being transferred. These licenses were valid for five to ten years, during which time Mips guaranteed that it would provide access to new generations of its technology for additional fees. Beyond ten years, the licensees had complete rights to continue to use the architecture covered by the license in perpetuity, but Mips guaranteed no access to future technology.

Mips provided exact technical specifications for the R3000 and tested all products for compatibility, ensuring that the chips from different producers were identical in form and function. The Mips "seal of approval" assured customers that chips from different manufacturers were fully interchangeable. Miller explained that, although Sun Microsystems also licensed its SPARC chip widely, its approach differed from that of Mips:

> Mips completely designs its microprocessor, down to the mask level [the full layout of the chip]. So when we sign our semiconductor partners, we give them everything, and they can be in production faster than licensees of other designs. Sun provides only the instruction set and licensees have to do all of the designing themselves; as a result, it can take them up to two years to reach the production phase. For this reason, Mips can command much higher up-front fees and royalty payments.[20] Furthermore, SPARC chips made by different firms are not pin-compatible.[21]

This seemingly technical point about pin compatibility had important implications for competition and for the way the Mips alliance group operated. It meant that there was practically no differentiation between the chips of different producers, a situation that would benefit users. Also, the Mips group was able to exploit economies of scale in design, inasmuch as all the producers used the same specifications.

Mips also created two other types of semiconductor licenses, which allowed it to continue to promote its technology without creating competition for the first six Semiconductor Partners.[22] The conditions in all these technology licensing programs sought a balance between encouraging the spread of Mips technology and avoiding too many overlapping alliances. To spread the technology, Mips actively pursued all alliance opportunities and sought partners who could push its technology in different market niches. At the same time, Mips limited the degree of competition in each market segment and application, so that its allies would not compete away one another's profits. In this way, Mips tried to maximize complementarity among its alliances and to minimize conflicts.

The Mips distribution strategy for systems products grew out of the realization that Mips could not single-handedly create the volume that would make it a major player in the RISC marketplace. Its technical alliances created a portfolio of products for the group; without aggressive marketing, however, these products would not make it into users' hands.

In 1989 the company began to develop sales relationships with OEMs, distributors, VARs, and system integrators. Many of the largest OEM customers of Mips were ailing makers of minicomputers, the segment of the market most directly threatened by the rise of RISC workstations. The company avoided competition with these parties by deemphasizing its direct sales efforts. Direct customer contact by Mips was limited to advanced technical end-users, such as universities.

Systems were marketed under both the Mips brand label and the labels of its OEM customers. Prime Computer, Control Data, Wang, Bull, Nixdorf, and others purchased systems products manufactured by Mips, packaged in various configurations. This approach gave the systems vendors a range of options. They could purchase complete Mips systems, add their company logo, and achieve quick time-to-market advantages. Or they could purchase products at the chip, board, or subsystem level and add their own value to the design before selling them to end-users and resellers. Finally, they could design their own products using a combination of these integration options. Charles Boesenberg, Mips president at the time, described how varied and dynamic these OEM relationships could be: "We often begin working with an OEM to fill a gap in their product line, say, by providing workstations to complement their minicomputers. In time, the more successful they are in reselling our systems, the more likely they are to want to design and build them from the microprocessor up, with the result that our sales to them would decline. So our challenge is to keep replenishing these OEMs with new products."[23]

The resellers typically would purchase complete systems products from Mips and then bundle them with their own application software; they often specialized in specific vertical markets. Because these VARs did not build systems, they were not likely to replace Mips machines with their own. System integrators, still another type of reseller, purchased products from Mips and incorporated them into customer-specific systems and networks. The system integrators provided custom end-user systems design and management. Distributors were mainly used for sales to end-users, often in international markets where Mips had no direct sales presence.

In addition, Mips developed alliance programs to encourage the development of software for its chips and systems. Mips had standard licensing agreements for its operating system (RISC/os) and compiler software. It also allowed licensees to modify the software for their products and applications and, in turn, license these to third parties. As before, however, third parties needed to execute a licensing agreement with Mips for the original software. Mips believed that by optimizing all of a RISC system's components—chip, operating system, and compiler software—and licensing it all, its architecture would maintain technological superiority in the marketplace.

In each part of its business, therefore, Mips found partners—not one, but many. This constellation was essential to whatever commercial success Mips achieved. Without it, the company would probably have gone bankrupt in 1987. Because of it, the start-up not only survived but grew into a serious challenge to the likes of Intel, Sun, HP, and IBM. In time these competitors redoubled their efforts, and many formed their own constellations to counter the Mips threat. In the process, collective competition engulfed the whole RISC industry.

The story of how group-based competition spread in this industry will be told later. In the chapter that follows, we pause to analyze the nature of this new type of competition.

Competing in Constellations

Mips Computer Systems was a peculiar company. It employed fewer than a thousand people, yet chose to take on huge, well-established companies, including Intel and IBM. It adopted this strategy, moreover, in an industry where production scale and market penetration are critical to commercial success. On its own, Mips clearly did not stand a chance.

Mips managers therefore concluded early on that they needed allies. Not one, but many—Mips would compete in a constellation of many firms. The constellation started small, but soon there were six Semiconductor Partners and countless systems vendors in the Mips group. Allies brought production capacity, market presence, technologies, and cash. In return, Mips provided a unique semiconductor design and coordinated the activities of the constellation.

This strategy transformed the unit of competition. Legally, Mips remained a small corporation. But economically it was part of a much larger whole, and it was this larger whole that competed against other firms and groups. Increasingly, the talk in the industry focused on how the Mips "camp" was faring versus the camps centered around other firms.

Alliances can thus reshape rivalry by elevating the battle to a level above that of single firms. As this happens, competition increasingly takes place among constellations of allied firms. In this new style of group-based competition, who wins and who loses depends on the competitive advantages that each group of firms creates through collective action.[1]

Yet even for firms heavily involved in such competition, what counts to their owners is the profits of the firm, not those of the group. Although the game has changed, we still keep score the old way. In the long run, each group member must benefit from the collective effort. Without private gains, or at least the expectation of such gains, the group will fall apart.

What determines the performance of firms competing in constellations? The answer lies in the pattern of collaboration inside the constellations. This chapter explores the ways in which the design of constellations affects the competitive performance of the groups as a whole and of the firms within them.

Competitive Advantage in Groups

We begin our exploration of competitive advantage in groups with a simple but powerful framework. Firms engaged in group-based competition can draw on two sources of competitive advantage. The first is group-based advantage; it is derived from who is in the group and how the group is managed. Competing groups are usually driven by the same underlying economic factors, such as economies of scale and scope. But precisely how the groups respond to these factors differentiates one from the other. This differentiation, in turn, can become a source of potential advantage or disadvantage.

The second source of competitive advantage is firm-based; it is derived from the distinctive capabilities of each firm. This conventional type of advantage takes on a special role in group-based competition. First, the pooling of these distinctive capabilities of firms in a group helps to create group-based advantages; there is thus a kind of spillover effect whereby members of the group benefit from one another's firm-based advantages. Second, firm-based advantages help determine the position and power of each firm within its group.[2]

The distribution of firm-based advantages in a group may in itself be a differentiating element among alliance groups. In some groups, one firm holds the key advantages and makes the bulk of the collective profit. In others, many firms each hold complementary but equally important advantages and share profits more evenly. Because this intragroup balance of power between members may affect how well firms within the group work together, it can influence group-based advantages.

The benefits that each firm derives from participation in a group, therefore, are a function of the total benefits of the group and the firm's share of this total.

GROUP BENEFITS AND MEMBER SHARES

The economic viability of a group depends on the existence of a positive "network effect"—this is the payoff to collaboration.[3] If the network effects were negative—that is, if an alliance between firms led to a reduction of their overall advantage—then there would not be any group surplus to distribute among members, and so no incentive for firms to stay together.[4] With a positive network effect, the surplus created through collaboration is distributed among members.

The extent of the group-based advantages of a constellation depends on the design of the group. Alliances are specific systems for controlling a set of capabilities. The choice of which capabilities the group will contain is thus one critical design decision; the second is how the control system is structured, because that determines whether the potential synergies among the capabilities are realized.

The share of the group surplus that each firm receives also depends on the design of the group, but in a different way. The network effect of a group is generated by the way the group's structure differentiates it from other groups and from single firms. This effect is attributable to the group as a whole and is identical for all members of the group, regardless of their position in the group. But the share that each member in fact receives from the group's surplus does depend on the unique position of that member in relation to others in the network.

The total set of capabilities is not important in determining the share of each member; the crucial consideration is the firm's capabilities relative to those of its partners. Firms can be thought of as bargaining over the spoils of their joint action; their contribution to the joint enterprise is then a prime source of bargaining power. We would expect that a firm contributing a highly valued capability would be able to claim a higher share of the group surplus than one contributing something of lesser value. Furthermore, a firm may improve its bargaining power in the group by changing its position in the group.[5]

BENEFITS FROM GROUP MEMBERSHIP

The combination of network effects and network position is a distinguishing mark of collective competition. The competitive advantage of each member depends critically on who its partners are and on the structure of the alliances among the partners.

The benefits due to each member in a group vary with total network effects as well as with the bargaining power of each firm. As a result, it may appear attractive for a firm to join a group even if the network effects are low, as long as the firm can be enticed by a large share of total benefits. Conversely, a firm in a poor bargaining position may benefit little from participating in a powerful group, even when the total benefits of the network are high.

Network effects and the bargaining power of members are likely to change over time as groups grow and relationships between members evolve. Because of these changes, firms may choose to join constellations even in the absence of immediate benefits if they expect network effects to rise with the growth of the group. Similarly, a member's position in a group may become more or less attractive over time, depending on its relative position. Ironically, the position of some firms may deteriorate as a group grows—their internal bargaining power may decline even while the overall economic power of the group increases.

Collective Competition in the RISC Field

Examples from several industries, especially the RISC industry during the late 1980s and early 1990s, will flesh out this conceptual framework and illustrate its application. The main alliance groups in the RISC industry are closely comparable in that they were motivated by common industry trends and competed head-to-head with one another. Each sought to promote its own version of RISC technology, but there was still substantial variation in each group's structure and history. For these reasons, the RISC industry in the late 1980s and early 1990s represents a unique laboratory for studying group-based competition.

The alliance groups of Mips, Sun, HP, IBM, and Motorola came out of the gate at different times between 1987 and 1991, although each aimed at the same finish line and ran on the same course. Each horse had different qualities and was ridden by a different jockey. The progress of this race—which is not over yet—reveals much about collective competition.

Strategy and Structure of the RISC Groups

At a fundamental level, the RISC groups were similar. Most members of each group were allied to the lead firm, either through licensing arrangements, joint development projects, or supply alliances. Often these members were also linked to each other. Furthermore, some members were more important than others, either because they were early allies or because they were responsible for major tasks in the alliance group. Finally, there were often classes of members in each group. (See Figure 9.)

The Mips group, as we have seen, had a special class of allies called the Semiconductor Partners. This subgroup was restricted to six partners that were licensed to make and sell general-purpose chips with the Mips design. Other semiconductor licensees received the rights to make special-purpose chips. Mips chose its semiconductor partners carefully, to ensure global coverage and access to first-rate production capabilities. The role of these partners was to produce and market the microprocessors that were at the heart of every Mips computer.

Another class of allies was charged with developing, making, and selling computer systems using the Mips chips. These partners were licensed to adapt the Mips software as needed, and often bought components from Mips itself. Many of these components, in turn, were produced by other partners. Mips thus served a coordinating function in the network—channeling parts, providing technical designs, and promoting its design with software vendors and users.

The pattern of relationships in the Mips network demonstrates how multiple alliances help to fill gaps in a firm's capabilities. The evidence also indicates that the different alliances in the network complement one another. But to what extent can we generalize this view of alliance networks? Is it unique to small firms, like Mips, faced with larger and more powerful competitors? The case of Hewlett-Packard suggests that even larger competitors sometimes need alliance networks, and that the logic of their network is no different from those of the small firms.

The precise motivations behind the creation of HP's alliance group differ somewhat from those of Mips. HP had more capabilities in-house, but still sought partners that complemented these capabilities. Mips depended more on its partners for basic functions. As a small start-up, Mips had no presence in the market, and it needed as many "sponsors," or partners, as it could get. HP had substantial market presence worldwide, and used its partnerships more selectively to address niches where it was weak.

In both cases, however, the firms in the network complemented one another; at least, they were selected with that intention. Mips and HP both sought partners who could work together, and both tried to design a network structure that enhanced complementarity. Neither Mips nor HP could achieve alone what each hoped to achieve in a group; nor could a single alliance, even a major one with a partner such as Hitachi or DEC, take either of them where they wanted to go.

This network effect, which enhanced the value of the bilateral alliances in a group, appears in the other RISC groups as well. IBM's group was even smaller than HP's, but it, too, was designed with complementarity in mind. Sun's group was different in the way it achieved complementarity among firms, relying less on joint planning and more on internal competition. But Sun, too, required an alliance group to achieve its aims.

There were also important differences among the RISC groups. Once all the major contenders in the RISC business adopted the network strategy, these differences—not the similarities—became important as sources of competitive advantage.

ELEMENTS OF GROUP DESIGN

At the core of each major RISC group was a microprocessor-design firm—Mips, Sun, HP, and IBM. The other firms in each group based their components, systems, and software on the technology designs of this "lead firm." (Other firms—like Intel and Intergraph—had their own RISC designs, but they were less important players.[6] Motorola was an early entrant to the RISC field, and developed its own group, but it soon dropped out of the race and joined IBM's group. DEC first was part of the Mips group, and then left to promote its own design.)

The extent to which each of these lead firms exercised power and leadership in its group, however, varied from case to case. Although I generally refer to each group by the name of its lead firm, other members may have had substantial influence.[7] For example, DEC played an important role in the Mips group early on, and Apple and Motorola became key participants in the IBM group.[8]

The characteristics of these alliance groups were partly driven by the characteristics of the lead firm. For example, because Mips and Sun had no semiconductor operations, they used a relatively large number of licensed suppliers. HP and IBM, in contrast, were large firms active in all aspects of the business and needed fewer firms in their groups. In other aspects, too, the Mips and Sun groups differed from those of IBM and HP.

The RISC evidence suggests that four structural dimensions affect a group's competitive advantage:[9]

1. Size

2. Composition

3. Degree of internal competition

4. Collective governance mechanisms

The first two dimensions—size and composition—relate to the capabilities assembled in the group. Groups of varying sizes and compositions have different sets of capabilities; in practice, the groups in the RISC field in the late 1980s and early 1990s tended to assemble a similar set of capabilities. This meant that some groups were composed of many, relatively small, niche players and others were composed of a few large, integrated players. Size and composition thus also indirectly affected the control structures of the groups.

The other two parameters of group design—internal competition and collective governance—were more directly related to the structure of control in the group. Some groups were marked by duplication and had multiple competing sources of specific capabilities; others had a strict division of labor, with few players in each role. Internal competition generally made it harder for the group to act as a unit, even though governance mechanisms attempted to set common rules. These mechanisms generally attempted to define common standards and goals to keep group members' strategies aligned. Rather than controlling the decisions of members outright, these mechanisms tried to reduce divergence in their interests.

COMPARISON WITH ALLIANCE DESIGN

Three of these four elements of group design correspond closely to the key aspects of any alliance, even simple bilateral partnerships. The first group element—number of partners—obviously does not apply to bilateral alliances; by definition, the latter are composed of only two partners. But the next three group elements each have a counterpart in alliance design, as follows:

Elements of group design	Elements of alliance design
Composition of group	Partner capabilities
Internal competition	Partner goals
Collective governance	Alliance structure

It is well known that the selection of a partner and the selection of an alliance structure are critical decisions in any bilateral partnership. Existing studies suggest that the best partner matches are those in which the firms have complementary capabilities and compatible goals. The best alliance structure is one that creates incentives for collaboration among the partners.[10]

By extension, groups with complementary partners—in which the composition of membership covers a range of different capabilities—might be expected to perform better than those in which the members duplicate each other's capabilities. Similarly, groups in which the members have compatible goals are likely to have less internal competition and, again, perform better. In addition, the collective governance mechanism in a group can help align members' interests and encourage effective collaboration.

The Effects of Group Size

Size is often an advantage in group-based competition, particularly when the rationale behind group formation is to gain market share or economies of scale and scope. Depending on the precise strategy of the group, different measures of size are important. I will therefore use several indicators in this section and in chapters to come.

A caveat is in order regarding the methods used. In comparing the sizes and overall capabilities of the RISC constellations, I begin by ignoring their structures. For example, I will consider the total size of a constellation's production capacity, regardless of whether that capacity is divided among two, three, or many more members. Later, in discussing the internal competition and collective governance of the groups, I will consider the separate effects of these structural differences. The first question to ask is what pool of capabilities each group had at its disposal; the second is how effective the group was at exploiting these joint capabilities.

In standards battles, the number of firms in a network and especially their combined share of the total market are critical. These numbers reflect the degree to which a standard has been accepted among potential sponsors.[11] Early in the RISC battle, for example, Sun persuaded a large number of firms to sign on to its technology. Because Sun was already dominant in technical workstations by the time it introduced its RISC chip, potential partners were eager to join its group. As a small company, Mips had a more challenging task in attracting partners; but after DEC, NEC, and other major firms joined its group, others followed. Still, the growth of the Mips network was more modest than that of Sun. In 1991, however, Mips tried to leapfrog Sun with its Advanced Computing Environment (ACE) initiative, as discussed in the case study preceding Chapter 4 and shown in Figure 13.

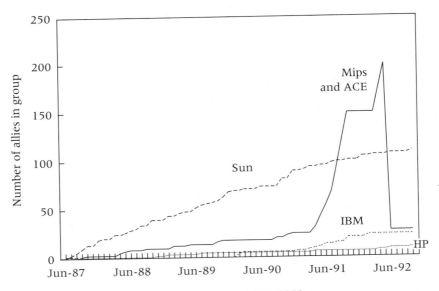

Figure 13 Growth of RISC alliance groups, 1987–1992.
(Sources: Survey of press reports—see Appendix B—and company interviews.)

Table 9   Market presence and production scale of RISC groups, c. 1992

	Mips	Sun	HP	IBM
Semiconductor Business				
RISC chips shipped (1992)				
Thousand units	331	295	64	67
Number of suppliers	7	5	1	1
Share of lead firm[a]	0%	0%	100%	100%
Total semiconductor production (1991)				
US$ (billions)	$14.5	$11.7	$5.0[b]	$10.0[b]
Number of suppliers	6	7	2	2
Share of lead firm[a]	0%	0%	10%[b]	60%[b]
Systems Business				
RISC workstation revenues (1992)				
US$ (billions)	$2.1	$3.0	$1.8	$1.5
Number of suppliers	7	5	2	1
Share of lead firm[a]	0%	92%	95%	100%
Total microcomputer revenues (1991)				
US$ (billions)	$5.5	$7.3	$2.2	$15.4
Number of suppliers	8	11	2	5
Share of lead firm[a]	0%	24%	46%	47%

Sources: RISC semiconductor and systems data from Dataquest; other data from Dataquest and Gartner Group. The table includes only the members of each group for which data were available; data on the most important members were available for all groups.

a. "Lead firm" refers to the firms in the column headings.

b. Estimated, as most of this production is captive and not reported.

MARKET PRESENCE AND PRODUCTION SCALE

The number of firms in a group is not the only way to measure group size. More direct measures of market share and of scale of production are useful in judging the competitive advantages of one group versus others. IBM and HP lagged behind Mips and Sun in the number of firms in their networks, for example, but the market presence and scale of the IBM and HP groups were substantial (see Table 9, which also presents other measures of group size).[12]

In the semiconductor portion of the business, the Mips and Sun groups produced more RISC chips in 1992 than did the IBM and HP groups; this advantage was in part a result of the late start by the latter two groups. Even so, Mips and Sun had more semiconductor partners, and the combined production of these partners was larger than that of the IBM and HP partners.

Total semiconductor production is also a relevant measure of size in this case, because investments in process technology, equipment, and human resources could often be shared between different types of semiconductor devices. For example, even though NEC produced only 110,000 RISC chips in 1992, it could draw on capabilities developed in its $6 billion semiconductor business.[13] The two small firms—Mips and Sun—lacking their own semiconductor production facilities, used alliances to "match" the capabilities of the two large firms, HP and IBM.

In the systems portion of the business, too, Mips and Sun used their alliances to approximate the scale of operations of the much-larger HP and IBM. Because of Sun's early dominance of the technical workstation business, the Sun group sold more RISC workstations in 1992 than did any of the other groups ($3 billion). Considering that Mips had no headstart in workstations, the $2.1 billion sales of its group are remarkable. The Mips sales figure is due to the strong collection of firms in this group, which included DEC and major Japanese and European firms. HP and IBM were not far behind Mips, but they relied mostly on their in-house capabilities.

If we take total microcomputer revenues as the measure of scale, we find that the IBM group surpassed all the others because it combined the systems business of IBM and Apple. An alliance between two, or a few, large firms can thus overwhelm groups of smaller firms in terms of scale of operations. Still, the number of firms in a group remains important, regardless of their combined scale. IBM recognized this when it began distributing technical information to all firms, large or small, that were interested in making personal computers based on the PowerPC RISC chip. "This is the clearest sign so far that IBM is intent on starting a new bandwagon," reported an industry journal.[14] The comment recognizes the value of momentum in standards battles and the role of sheer numbers of adopters.

The size of the group is also important in alliance groups motivated by globalization. The relevant measure of size in these situations is usually the volume of business in the activity that enjoys global economies of scale. Swissair's alliance network, for example, aimed to maximize bookings on trans-Atlantic and Euro-Asian flights and to increase scale in procurement and maintenance of airplanes. Overall size is less critical in networks driven by industry convergence, where the idea is to link complementary technologies or markets. Nevertheless, when each of the partners can exploit economies of scale in its own industry, a greater volume of joint business can help.

The Effects of Group Composition

Aside from size, the mix of members in a group is an important source of differentiation among groups. A good way to think about this is to consider the pooled capabilities of the group. Does the group contain the mix of firms that give it the capabilities needed for advantage? In sum, group size yields scale economies, and membership mix yields scope economies.

The mix of firms is critical in groups driven by industry convergence and by globalization, because group composition needs to reflect the new opportunities for combining technologies and markets. In fact, competing alliance groups typically consist of firms that give each group roughly the same set of capabilities and market position. This "matching" phenomenon is striking in today's RISC and multimedia groupings as well as in the automobile networks formed in the 1980s.[15] The alliance networks of Ford and GM both contained members with comparable skills and specialties—strong Japanese firms (Mazda with Ford, and Toyota with GM), Korean small-car makers (Kia and Daewoo), European luxury car makers (Jaguar and Saab), and European truck makers (Fiat and Volvo).

Group composition also matters in standards battles. The leading firms in RISC technology designed their groups explicitly to include all the capabilities they thought they needed. The differences in the mix of firms among these groups depend greatly on the capabilities of the RISC designer itself (see Figure 14).

Neither Mips nor Sun produced its own semiconductor chips; instead, each allied itself with a handful of producers. Aside from that, Mips focused more on systems manufacturers; and Sun, on OEM resellers and software producers. The difference in strategy between these two firms stemmed partly from the fact that Sun, unlike Mips, was already successful in making and selling its own workstation systems. Sun itself accounted for 92 percent of the sales of RISC systems in its group (see Table 9).

The Sun group was more like HP and IBM than Mips in terms of its share of the group systems business. All three firms were responsible

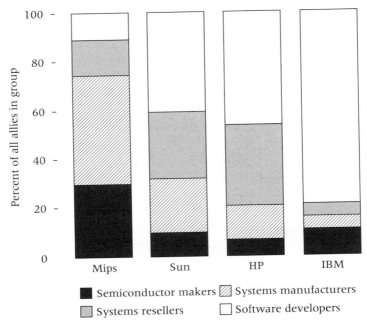

Figure 14 Composition of RISC alliance groups, 1992. Total number of members in each group: 27, Mips; 110, Sun; 11, HP; 23, IBM. The Mips total includes only allies of Mips prior to ACE.
(Sources: Survey of press reports—see Appendix B—and company interviews.)

for over 90 percent of the sales of RISC systems in their group, even though only IBM and HP dominated the production of the chips themselves (see Table 9). In effect, this means that they competed against their own systems partners. Mips was different: it chose from the beginning not to compete against its own OEM partners and resellers.

Three lessons about group composition emerge from this evidence. First, the competitive advantage of a group depends on whether it can exploit the economies of scope inherent in complex businesses. To do that, the group needs to contain members active in the various parts of the business, in different geographic markets, or in different market segments. In the RISC groups, this meant members from the semiconductor business, from the systems business, from software, and so on. Second, the precise mix of members also depends on the in-house capabilities of the lead firm, because alliances are only attractive in areas where this firm needs external help. Third, the diversity of members in a group will only work if the structure of the group encourages collaboration and limits conflict.

Internal Competition

The success of bilateral alliances often depends on managing the delicate balance between conflict and collaboration. Because the allies remain separate, some degree of conflict is usually inevitable, yet too much conflict reduces the gains from collaboration. Alliance groups exhibit parallel effects, but the role of competition is inherently more complex in networks of three or more firms.

Internal competition affects the behavior and performance of an alliance group in subtle ways. Japanese *keiretsu* are known to follow what one scholar has called the "exclusion rule," which states that there should not be duplication in the group.[16] Among the RISC groups, HP explicitly tried to enhance complementarity and to reduce conflicts within the group, but Sun encouraged competition. Mips, too, attempted to control competition among its semiconductor partners by limiting the total number to six and by choosing firms in different parts of the world. Furthermore, Mips encouraged standardization across its semiconductor partners, whereas Sun allowed each to develop its own chip.

COMPETITION AND GROUP PERFORMANCE

The degree of internal competition in a group is thus likely to have two opposing effects on performance. Internal rivalry is often beneficial to the group up to a certain point, as it may increase flexibility, drive innovation, and provide security of supply. But internal competition becomes counterproductive to the group when it fragments a part of the business so much that none of the members reach efficient scales or earn a sufficient return to reinvest in growth. Too much competition can be destructive, and just enough competition provides creative tension.[17]

The pattern of competition in the Sun group demonstrates these opposing effects. In 1987 Sun Microsystems entered the market for RISC-based workstations with the Sun-4, based on the company's proprietary SPARC architecture. Sun's first licensee was Solbourne Computers, a small U.S. firm controlled by Japan's Matsushita. By

1991 Solbourne had produced a SPARC "clone"[18] and was competing against Sun in the marketplace. Other major licensees were Unisys, AT&T, Xerox, Prime Computer, ICL, Philips, Fujitsu, Toshiba, and Matsushita itself. Many East Asian clone makers also adopted SPARC, including Tatung, Hyundai, and Twinhead. As of March 1991 a total of thirty vendors had announced SPARC-based systems.

By promoting clones, therefore, Sun was able to spread its architecture worldwide, thus attracting more users and software applications. Yet most of these clone makers ultimately failed, because they could not compete against Sun itself. They copied Sun machines and did not pay a license fee, so that they had lower development costs than Sun. At the same time, they also had lower volumes of production and no previous market presence. In addition, because Sun was used to operating on a slim margin, there was little room for the clones to enter the market with lower prices.[19] And when the clone makers tried to come into Sun's installed base, Sun blocked them:

> [Sun] has tried to set an industry microprocessor standard and let companies clone the technology, but so far there's only one winner: Sun. Despite Sun's posturing as an "open systems company," the company has made progress difficult for SPARC-compatible vendors. . . . Earlier this year, Sun issued an edict to its VARs, barring them from selling Sun clones. It also lowered its prices to undercut the least expensive SPARC clone machines. Sun's paranoia about the potential success of SPARC-compatible vendors is jeopardizing the very market Sun is trying to create.[20]

Sun's executives argued that companies adopting SPARC had to make "compatibles," not clones, of Sun's machines.[21] Compatible machines, they argued, added value to the technology developed by Sun; clones simply copied Sun's work. In other words, the products either had to be differentiated from Sun's in one way or another, or they had to use a different channel or market segment. These managers cited examples of companies that had been successful with SPARC-based systems compatible with Sun's: Toshiba made portable computers, Tadpole made laptop machines, Cray made supercomputers, ICL made minicomputers for the European market, and Amdahl made mainframes.

This model of complementary offerings also seemed to work in Japan, but for different reasons. Fujitsu, Toshiba, C-Itoh, Nippon Steel, and several other companies resold Sun systems in Japan; these systems were, for the most part, not differentiated from each other. In total, these companies sold about $400 million worth of SPARC machines in 1992; Sun had no direct sales in Japan. But these companies did not compete directly with each other in Japan, because each sold to its own traditional customers.[22]

In the systems business, therefore, Sun competed with its allies but tried to bring "order" into the group by encouraging partners to offer complementary products. The conflicts between Sun and its allies tended to reduce, not increase, the value of this network of alliances.

BARGAINING POWER OF MEMBERS

Internal competition often derives from conflicts between the lead firm and some of its allies, as it did in the Sun constellation. Although the lead firm may seek allies in its quest for scale and market share, it may be reluctant to give up too much control or influence to these allies. The role of the lead firm in group activities can thus influence the degree of internal competition in the alliance group.

For example, if the lead firm actively markets the product and also forms alliances for this same purpose, then there are likely to be disagreements among allies about which market channel to use. Of all the RISC groups, Sun's had the most internal competition by this measure, in part because of Sun's dominance of the workstation market. Sun also encouraged competition among its multiple allies when that enhanced its own power within the group.

Sun benefited from having many potential chip vendors in its world, even though it used only one for each generation. But competition among Sun's semiconductor suppliers tended to benefit only the lead firm, not the whole group. Sun's dominant position in the group gave it a firm-based advantage against other group members, regardless of whether the group as a whole benefited.

The Mips approach was different. The company did not have a sales force and committed itself *not* to compete with its allies.[23] It did manufacture systems, but sold them to allies or to special customers, such as software developers. Mips systems vendors benefited from this approach, but Mips itself remained dependent on them for the promotion of its product; the company never did develop a profitable systems business. The weak position of Mips in the systems business ultimately doomed the company, as we will see.

Collective Governance

The degree of internal competition affects another element of group-based advantage—the governance of the group. As defined here, an alliance group need not have a common governance mechanism, that is, an organization in which each member has decision rights. When group members are all allied with a central firm, that firm can govern the group without such a mechanism. But large groups, in particular, often benefit from using an organization to establish and maintain common goals and rules of behavior.

GROUP NORMS AND STANDARDS

Governance mechanisms play much the same role in alliance groups as they do in bilateral alliances. We have seen how contracts, jointly owned ventures, and other organizational arrangements help to align the interests of partners in bilateral alliances. This alignment improves the competitiveness of the allied firms. The objective in alliance groups is similar, even though the governance task itself is more demanding.

Many, though not all, alliance groups use formal mechanisms to align the interests of members and to help them make joint decisions. Generally, the less competition there is between members, the easier it is to govern the group, and the less need there is for formal mechanisms. Regardless of how difficult it is to manage the group, collective governance structures are likely to affect group behavior and performance.

The RISC groups came to recognize the importance of collective governance mechanisms by trial and error.[24] At first few had any formal way of managing their respective groups. One of the earliest such organizations was the 88Open consortium, formed in 1988 to support Motorola's 88000 RISC chip and future chips in its so-called 88K family. Many RISC organizations that followed took 88Open as a model. The history of this group shows, however, that collective governance alone does not guarantee success.

The rise and fall of a model organization. From the start, the intention of 88Open was to support use of the 88000 chip and thereby counter the "tidal wave" of support that appeared to be gathering around Sun's SPARC.[25] (At that time, Mips was still financially weak.) The initial push for 88Open came from early 88000 adopters, specifically Convergent, Tectronics, and Data General. Motorola supplied 50 percent of the funding for the group. 88Open was incorporated as a separate entity and had a staff that, at its height, reached thirty people.

88Open sought to re-create the environment that had made PCs popular. This meant revising the software to operate on the chip, which would attract users and thus create volume. To do this, 88Open worked to create a common standard to which all members would adhere.[26] As a result, the same applications could run on the different systems. 88Open was the first organization that attempted to create such a standard.

The group succeeded at this task. It then launched a testing and certification program for software and hardware. All products passing its tests would be certified as compatible with the standard. Software that ran on one certified machine, therefore, was guaranteed to run on others. Six hundred application programs and 70 hardware systems were certified in this way.

But the success of 88Open did not ensure the success of the 88000 chip. The chip came out in 1989, a bit behind schedule; the delay meant that competitors' chips equaled or exceeded it in performance.[27] Data General, Motorola's computer division, NCR, Unisys, Apple, and Omron were early adopters of the chip. But these same firms were also important users of the Intel x86 and Motorola 68K lines of CISC microprocessors; except for Data General and Motorola's computer division, they did not commit to the 88000.[28]

At the same time, Motorola's competitors raked in successes. Mips signed Compaq, Siemens, and Bull as allies. These firms had all been leaning toward adopting the 88000; now they were in the enemy camp. Apple stayed with the 88000, although it never sold a machine based on that chip. In 1990 Apple dropped the bombshell that sealed the fate of 88Open—Apple's alliance with IBM. Not long after that, the network of 88000 adopters began to fall apart: NCR and Unisys moved to Intel; Tectronics left the workstation business; Compaq first chose Mips and later went back to Intel.[29] As a result, 88Open was dismantled and by April 1994 it was largely out of business.

Proliferation of the model. Regardless of the ultimate failure of Motorola's strategy, the company's competitors copied its organizational model. Sun and its SPARC partners created SPARC International; Mips launched the ACE initiative;[30] HP formed the Precision RISC Organization (PRO); and IBM and its partners formed the PowerOpen Association (POA).[31] Each organization served as a forum for the exchange of information among members. Some also aimed to develop common technical standards or pursued public relations campaigns. The degree of autonomy and organizational procedures of these consortia varied; some were truly governed by their boards of directors, while others were more or less arms of the lead firm in the network.[32] All, however, aimed to enhance the ability of the network to act as a group.

LEADERSHIP IN GROUP DECISION MAKING

Such elaborate organizations are not essential in every field. They work in the computer industry because of the importance of hardware and software standards; without common standards, many potential benefits of cooperation are lost. In other industries, however, it is often enough for one firm or a small group of firms to manage the network centrally. Swissair, Delta, and Singapore Airlines, for example, have developed a tight working relationship at the center of their network; from there, each maintains its own partnerships with other allies. Automobile networks tend to be even more centralized, with products and technologies driven by the decisions of one lead firm.

Whatever the formal governance structure of a group, the collective has to have some way of making joint decisions and of coordinating the actions of members. Without leadership or an agreed-upon formula for taking joint decisions, a collection of firms cannot be expected to formulate and execute a consistent strategy. Instead, internal divisions and differences in perspectives among members will most likely pull the constellation in different directions. An analogy from American Wild West movies is apt: out in the barren desert, cowboys would tie their horses to each other at night, knowing that each horse would pull in a different direction and the group would go nowhere.[33] An alliance group without leadership and collective governance is usually no different.

The RISC constellations varied according to their source of leadership. Mips was too small and financially weak to exercise much influence on its giant partners; in the end, its own product development efforts suffered from this lack of central power. The ACE group, an outgrowth of the Mips constellation, was even more divided at the center; at different times, it seemed to be led by Mips, DEC, or Microsoft. Sun's dominance of the workstation industry, in contrast, meant that it effectively drove group decisions. IBM, Apple, and Motorola formed a close triad at the center of their group, with other members occupying a definite second tier in decision making. HP controlled most of its group's decisions; the Precision RISC Organization was not a stand-alone consortium, but was run by an HP executive.

These differences in structures of control could be expected to affect the relative advantages of the groups. To see how, consider two characteristics of complex businesses. First, these businesses are composed of several parts or segments, each of which requires specialized knowledge and capabilities. Second, these parts need to be integrated into a whole, which requires a definition and implementation of the "fit" between the parts. This balance between the need for integration and for specialization also characterizes the degree of centralization and decentralization in firms.[34]

In complex businesses where integration is more important than specialization, single firms or tight constellations—those with relatively more unified control—can thus be expected to have an organizational advantage over looser constellations. The reverse is likely to be true if integration is less important, but benefits from specialization and division of labor are high. Integration is likely to be important when the interfaces—or linkages—between components are ill defined and varying; in such situations, unified control may be better than dispersed control. When such interfaces are standardized, however, a loose constellation of specialty firms working more independently from each other may perform better than a single firm or tight constellation.[35] The following RISC evidence bears out these general conclusions.

Competitive Performance of Groups

Because of the differences in the designs of the RISC groups, each had varying degrees of success in building group-based competitive advantages. In the remainder of this chapter I shall use measures of technological performance and market share to evaluate the relative success of each group.

Technological performance and market share are imperfect and indirect measures; ideally, we would compare the long-run profitability of the sets of firms. But because the RISC business is still young, many of the players are still investing for the future, rather than reaping profits. Even these investments—and any profits—are impossible to measure, because the RISC activities in many of the firms are part of much larger businesses and are not reported separately. It is also not at all clear which firms—if any—will emerge as the eventual "winners." For some, success may not even require winning—a respectable showing or simply "qualifying" to play the game may be enough. By necessity, therefore, we will be drawing inferences from imperfect measures and from early trends and patterns.

TECHNOLOGICAL PERFORMANCE OF GROUPS

One way to measure the technological performance of a firm or constellation is by comparing the quality of its products with that of other competitors' products. Consider the performance of the best machines in each RISC group (see Figure 15). By technical measures, HP and IBM have performed the best, with Mips and Sun in the next tier. This result is perhaps to be expected, given the substantial resources of HP and IBM and their much greater experience in the industry. Further-

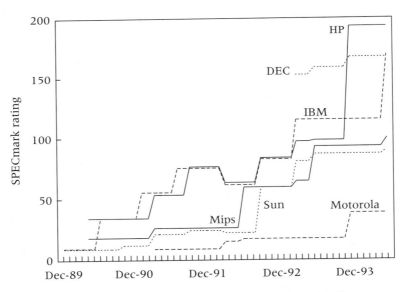

Figure 15 Technical performance of RISC systems, 1989–1994. Shown are the SPECmark ratings for the highest-performance system of each vendor, at its earliest appearance and until its performance is superseded by another machine. Before 1992, the SPEC89 system was used; after that, the SPEC92. The SPECmark rating is a measure of the speed with which a machine performs certain tasks.
(Source: Compiled from data published by SPEC, a nonpartisan testing organization.)

more, HP and IBM designers contend that there are still advantages to vertical integration, which was the traditional approach in computer design. In their view, vertically integrated companies can fine-tune their proprietary architectures to get better performance. DEC's Alpha chip, too, was the product of an integrated company and performed at high levels, although it did not appear on the market until 1993.

Because open-systems companies are typically not vertically integrated, they must cater to the often conflicting demands of allies and partners; as a result, they may sacrifice performance in design.[36] The lower technical performance of Mips and Sun might thus reflect a disadvantage of being a constellation.

The actions that Sun and Mips took to close the gap with IBM and HP seem to reflect this idea. Sun had traditionally left microprocessor development to its partners; it encouraged competition among these partners and did not promise in advance to use their components. This strategy reduced Sun's dependence on individual partners, but it may also have reduced potential benefits from combined R&D on components and systems. Partly in response to its performance lag, Sun decided in 1992 to work more closely with Texas Instruments (TI) in developing the third generation of its RISC chip. In 1994, moreover, Sun and Fujitsu developed a plan for the joint development of future chips. Through these moves, Sun sought to increase coordination in R&D and encourage greater commitment from its partners.

Mips also suffered from the looseness of its constellation and eventually moved to a tighter coupling among partners. The collapse of ACE, as we shall see in the next case study, was in part due to the dispersion of decision making in the constellation. The large number of partners and the weak position of Mips itself created multiple and opposing demands on the microprocessor developers. The R4000 chip around which ACE's plans revolved tried to be all things to all partners—as a result, its development was delayed and its ultimate performance was below par when it finally came out.[37]

The solution to this problem in the case of Mips appeared when Silicon Graphics (SGI) acquired the company. SGI was highly successful in developing and manufacturing computer systems built around the Mips chip. By bringing the Mips development team in-house, SGI was able to integrate systems development and chip development better than before. In 1993–1994 the Mips team—now housed in an

SGI subsidiary—working with engineers from SGI and Toshiba, developed the highest-performance Mips chip to date.

The evidence suggests a general lesson about constellation performance. The reason a single firm or a tightly coordinated constellation appears to do better than a loosely coordinated constellation revolves around the requirement of integration. RISC technology was certainly complex in the sense defined in this book—it consisted of separate elements of chip architecture, chip implementation and production, systems design, and software. A constellation could therefore benefit from combining separate capabilities from firms specializing in each field. But, in addition, performance could be improved by the close coordination and integration of the designs of these elements. This fact gave single firms the edge—provided they already possessed all the needed capabilities.

These conclusions apply to small constellations—pairs and triads—as well as to large groups. The case of Xerox and Canon shows how the conclusions can be extended. When the need for global integration of product development rose in the 1990s, Canon moved ahead of Xerox in innovation and market share. The response of Xerox and Fuji Xerox was to tighten their collaboration through more joint R&D projects, a new division of labor, and a new organization to align their interests better in the laser printer business.

MARKET SHARES OF GROUPS

Market share figures tell a different story about the race among RISC groups and lead to slightly different conclusions. Integration among partners is less important here, and the wide dispersion of decision making has greater benefits than in technical development. When partners target the same market, however, their rivalry can be expected to reduce group-based advantages.

One measure of market penetration is the share of total system revenues received by the vendors in each RISC group; this measure is plotted in Figure 16.[38] During most of the period 1988–1991, HP and Sun vied for market leadership; IBM and Mips were in the second tier. But by 1992 the Mips share had risen to close to that of Sun, and by 1994 Sun, Mips, and IBM were almost even.

The market strength of Mips and Sun—despite their technological lag—is evident in these numbers. Mips and Sun developed much more

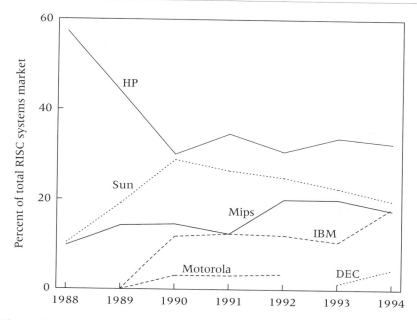

Figure 16 Market shares of RISC systems, 1988–1994. The shares are based on systems sold by all members of each RISC group. For example, the Mips shares include sales of Mips-based systems by Silicon Graphics, Siemens, Tandem, and other vendors.

(Sources: Compiled from data in *RISC Management*, 1988–1992, and *Inside the New Computer Industry*, 1993–1994. Data for Motorola and Intergraph were not available for 1993 and 1994, and data for DEC were not available before 1993.)

active and extensive networks than did HP and IBM, at least before 1993. Apple's adoption of the PowerPC chip boosted IBM's share in 1994. DEC's network was the most poorly developed as of 1994; even though the Alpha chip was among the most powerful in the industry, its market share lagged behind the others.

Both Mips and Sun realized that they had no chance of competing successfully against these giants unless they made themselves look like giants. Their collection of partners gave them that appearance. "Because of the NEC connection," explained Mips president Charles Boesenberg in 1991, "we are almost bigger than life in Japan."[39] The Mips alliances with Tandem, SGI, DEC, Siemens, and Bull had similar effects in other market segments. Mips received a further boost in the market when it launched the ACE initiative in 1991. Even after this initiative collapsed and Mips was acquired by SGI, the combined market share of the Mips allies hardly declined.

The general lesson is that in marketing, unlike in technical development, a large number of sponsors is an advantage.[40] The relative positions of HP and Sun, however, seem to contradict this conclusion. Sun's share fell continually between 1990 and 1994, while HP's share rose. Sun did have many more partners than HP, but many of these partners worked at cross-purposes to each other. In contrast, HP's network was carefully designed not to create internal competition—there was minimal overlap between the markets of different partners. In addition, of course, HP's products were superior to Sun's in performance (see Figure 15). In this match-up, therefore, a smaller and better-coordinated constellation outperformed a larger and more chaotic group.

This finding reinforces the findings in Chapter 2 regarding market competition between allies. In large groups as well as in simpler pairs and triads, competition in the market erodes collaboration and the potential advantages of the constellation.

PERFORMANCE OF LEADING FIRMS IN GROUPS

We have considered how the groups as a whole performed; but how did the firms within the groups fare? The evidence suggests that the small firms—Mips and Sun—were substantially aided by their alliance groups. Mips, for one, would not have survived beyond its infancy were it not for the alliance strategy and the support of Kubota, DEC, NEC, and other giants. Furthermore, its technology would not even be in contention today were it not for ACE and the Mips alliance with Microsoft. But the fact that Mips ultimately merged with one of its partners demonstrates that alliance groups are not all-powerful; at the heart of the group there must be a viable firm.

The advantages that Sun drew from its alliance group are more debatable. Sun continued to represent the bulk of the sales in its group, and it effectively killed the clone business. Its allies helped it penetrate Japan, and a flexible strategy involving multiple sources of components gave it bargaining power in semiconductors. Yet would a more orderly alliance group have yielded even greater advantages? This may have been another of Sun's goals in reorganizing its alliance group in 1994 and deepening its relationships with a few key partners.

The advantages of the group strategy for the large firms—HP and IBM—are less obvious, but real nevertheless. To some extent, both firms followed in the footsteps of Sun and Mips, which had allied themselves with large firms like DEC, Fujitsu, NEC, Toshiba, and Siemens. These companies were direct competitors of HP and IBM in Europe and Japan, if not in the United States. HP and IBM, therefore, could not afford to face the Sun and Mips groups alone, but had to find their own Japanese and European allies.

IBM's alliance strategy, in particular, was a coup. Its alliance with Apple and Motorola created an instant market and source of supply for the PowerPC. As a result, this group became the most serious threat in years to Intel dominance in personal computers. By the end of 1994, the industry was rife with talk about the possibility of a new PC standard.[41] Could IBM, by itself, have whipped up such excitement? Probably not.

It is revealing to compare this battle for market dominance with one that took place a decade earlier. In the early 1980s, IBM's line of personal computers unseated Apple, then the dominant microcomputer vendor. But in 1994 Intel was more entrenched in microprocessors than Apple had ever been in personal computers. By 1994, furthermore, IBM was weaker and had lost its aura of invincibility. More important, even in the early 1980s, IBM's strategy for its IBM-PC line had involved an alliance group—Intel supplied the chip, Microsoft the operating system, and an array of suppliers and clone makers helped proliferate the standard.

Given the greater odds against IBM in 1994 as compared with 1982, it is unlikely that the PowerPC could unseat Intel without the alliance group formed around IBM, Apple, and Motorola. In addition, the ground for the IBM assault had been prepared by a decade of activity in the RISC field. Rivalry among RISC groups had driven the development of the technology and pushed it into new markets. The strategies of the RISC players had evolved as each learned from the mistakes and successes of the others. ACE, in particular, raised the possibility that somebody's RISC might someday replace Intel's CISC. But ACE and Mips were not up to the challenge, for reasons discussed in Chapter 4.

These data demonstrate that what is best for the group is not always best for the central firm, and vice versa. For example, the Mips constellation survived and proved to be quite successful in the market; but Mips disappeared as an independent company. Sun, in contrast, was a profitable company, but it is questionable how much its partners gained from participation in the constellation. IBM seemed to strike a balance between these two aspects of performance—both Apple and IBM appeared to gain from the constellation, and Motorola was poised to do so as demand for the PowerPC increased.

This divergence between benefits to the group and to individual members is not unique. It often proves to be a source of conflict in simpler alliances as well. Xerox and Fuji Xerox, for example, disagreed over the transfer price of laser printer engines, even though they collaborated in making and marketing the product. In the language of negotiation, alliances create value through collaboration, and partners claim value through bargaining with each other over ownership shares, transfer prices, and so on.[42]

Because constellations are voluntary associations, no firm will stay in one for long if it does not derive private benefits from the group. But a firm may join a group solely on the expectation of such private benefits. It might expect that more firms will join soon, and that a larger constellation will yield benefits that can then be shared by all. Even then, the firm's own benefits will be a function of its bargaining power within the group.

These trade-offs between firm benefits, group benefits, and the bargaining power of group members help us interpret some of the choices that individual firms made in the RISC industry. Motorola, for example, had a better bargaining position in its own group, formed around the 88K chip, than it did in the PowerPC group. But the group benefits of the PowerPC constellation were likely to be larger than those of the 88Open constellation; Motorola thus switched from its own group in favor of a lesser role in a more powerful group.

Toshiba chose to do the reverse; it moved to a less powerful group but gained bargaining power in doing so. Even though it did not conclude an early licensing deal with Mips, Toshiba remained interested in the technology. Toshiba was an early vendor of Sun systems, but, like other Sun partners, it faced serious competition from Sun itself and from other partners. In the Mips constellation, Toshiba could expect a more privileged position. Thus even though the market share of the Sun group exceeded that of the Mips constellation, Toshiba moved to join Mips in 1991.[43]

The trade-offs between firm benefits and group benefits also help explain the rapid growth of some groups. In essence, firms would join a group even before they were assured of a net benefit, because they expected others to join too. When others joined, they reasoned, the group's overall competitive advantage would rise, and all would gain a share in the benefits. This process could create a bandwagon effect and lead to an acceleration in the growth of the group, as discussed in the next case study and Chapter 4.

Conclusion

Competition in the RISC industry in the late 1980s and early 1990s was driven by groups, not by firms. Lacking scale or other overriding competitive advantages, each RISC player chose to abandon the idea of competing as a single firm. By 1990, alliance groups had become the true units of competitive and economic power in this field.

Having formed their groups, the RISC firms discovered that mere numbers were no guarantee of success. As in simpler constellations, internal structures determined how the entities competed. As a consequence, each group had to find the best way to control the capabilities of its members—capabilities in semiconductor production, in systems design and manufacture, in software development, and in sales and service. How the groups mixed and matched these capabilities was critical. Aside from size, therefore, the composition of a group, the degree of internal competition, and the form of collective governance shaped their competitive behavior and performance. Because of the importance of integration in technical development, the loose constellations were at a disadvantage compared with tight constellations and with the large, single firms. Internal coordination was less important in marketing, although here too internal competition reduced group-based advantages.

The internal structure of a constellation also affected the fate of each individual group member. In some cases, members competed fiercely with each other. Sometimes one firm—often the lead firm in a group—could play off one ally against another. These internal processes influenced the bargaining power of one group member versus another, and so helped determine the private benefits that members drew from their groups.

Even as the RISC firms sought new competitive advantages through alliance groups, they encountered new challenges. The growth of their groups was often driven by a race to surpass other groups. Collective competition thus spread rapidly through this industry. As this happened, new risks and hidden costs emerged.

The ACE Bandwagon Runs Out of Steam

Until about 1990, the Mips group was an extensive and well-organized network of alliances. Its growth in the previous three years had been gradual and deliberate. The alliance strategy had saved the once-floundering Mips by furnishing resources, credibility, and market access. This strategy entered a new phase in late 1990, when the Advanced Computing Environment (ACE) initiative was launched.

The greatest potential for RISC sales lay in the personal computer segment of the industry, which was dominated by Intel's proprietary standard—85 percent of PCs were made with Intel chips. Going after the PC market, then, would mean competing against Intel; that is exactly what ACE intended to do. The growth of ACE was explosive and shook the industry. But ACE's grandiose plans ultimately failed. The rise and fall of ACE teaches important lessons about the dynamics of alliance groups.

The Origins of ACE

Late in 1990, Compaq Computer—the third-largest personal computer maker, behind IBM and Apple—announced that it was investigating the possibility of a new RISC-based, high-end PC line. It was rumored that Compaq had narrowed its choice to Mips or Sun as a supplier of the RISC chip for its new products. Working in Mips's favor was a previously announced alliance with software developer Microsoft Corporation. Microsoft had agreed to adapt its popular Windows operating environment to run on Mips's RISC architecture.

By February 1991 an alliance was forming around the Mips R4000 chip. Under development since 1989, the R4000 was expected to be available by late 1991. Led by Compaq, the alliance announced support for two hardware platforms—Mips's R4000 RISC chip and the Intel X86 microprocessors that dominated the PC market—as well as two operating systems, a "unified" version of Unix, based on a version from Santa Cruz Operations, a software company, and Windows New Technology (Windows NT) from Microsoft. In this way, alliance members hoped to create new hardware and software standards for desktop and laptop computers. They also hoped to capitalize on the huge installed base of Windows application programs, which would be recompiled to run on Windows NT even though they would not exploit its most advanced features.

When the ACE initiative was formally announced in April 1991, over twenty-one firms had already joined. Key members included DEC, Control Data, Silicon Graphics, Prime, Wang, and Pyramid Technology in the United States; Olivetti, Siemens-Nixdorf, and Bull/Zenith in Europe; and NEC, Sony, Sumitomo, and NKK in Japan. Robert Miller summed up the challenge for Mips: "At the end of the day, the winner—a relative term, anyway—will be the one who gets the customers' desktops converted. Our new mission is to provide as much enabling technology to the ACE members as possible."[1]

ACE membership continued to grow rapidly, topping sixty in July and approaching two hundred in October. Many of these new members were foreign clone makers and small software firms.[2] But in October Mips announced a new semiconductor partner: Toshiba. As it had done with its other semiconductor partners, Mips licensed Toshiba to make, sell, and develop Mips R3000 and R4000 chips and incorporate these into its systems. The signing of Toshiba was particularly noteworthy because that company had been one of the first licensees of SPARC, Sun's RISC technology.[3]

First Cracks in the Strategy

Even as ACE and the Mips architecture seemed to be gaining momentum in the second half of 1991, Mips's financial prospects began to look less promising. The company incurred a loss of $597,000 in the second quarter of 1991, which compared unfavorably with its $624,000 profit in the first quarter and $4 million profit in the second quarter of the previous year. The third quarter of 1991 was equally unkind to Mips. "Mips Computer has a beautiful future behind it," wrote *Business Week* in October;[4] the article reported an expected loss of $15 million for the quarter. By then investors had driven Mips stock down to $11 per share from its earlier level of $21 in March 1991.

Part of the blame for the loss lay with the disruptions in relations with resellers that followed Mips's decision to phase out high-end systems in favor of ACE-compliant desktop systems. Groupe Bull was among the systems vendors reportedly unhappy with this shift, as was Wang, which became a reseller of IBM workstations. It began to look as if Bull, too, might follow that route: in December the company was considering adopting either IBM's or HP's RISC chip to replace Mips's chip.

The ACE initiative, itself, also began to exhibit cracks. DEC was close to introducing its own RISC processor, the Alpha chip, and several ACE members forced the group to accept a second version of Unix, which was incompatible with the Santa Cruz version. This meant, effectively, that there would be no common ACE Unix standard. The work on a common Windows NT standard, however, continued.

At the same time, the early momentum behind ACE spurred competitors to action. IBM, Apple, and Motorola began working together, and Sun offered a version of its Solaris operating system for Intel-based computers, which Compaq was considering adopting. Meanwhile Intel, still the one to beat in the PC world, reported good progress on its Pentium chip.

Mips's third quarter 1991 results were even worse than *Business Week* had projected. Revenues fell 27 percent from the second quarter, and the company incurred a net loss of $37.3 million, which included a $25.5 million special charge for corporate restructuring. This restructuring, explained Mips executives, was needed to shift the company's activities to support the goals of ACE. In particular, Mips continued to contract its high-end systems business and increase work on low-end products targeted at the PC market.

The End of Mips Computer Systems and ACE

On March 12, 1992, Mips announced that it would merge with one of its biggest customers, Silicon Graphics, Inc. (SGI), a rapidly growing firm specializing in 3-D graphics workstations. Through stock swaps, SGI was to pay nearly $400 million for Mips. On May 5, after first-quarter results were available, the two parties announced an amended merger agreement, which lowered the sale value to near $200 million.[5]

Under the terms of the agreement, Mips would become a wholly owned subsidiary of SGI, with Robert Miller still at the helm. In June the merger was approved by stockholders of both companies.

The ACE group, which by now was a key element in Mips strategy, continued to crumble. Compaq left ACE in April of 1992, when the company's president and founder, Rod Canion, was replaced. Canion had been a strong supporter of both RISC and ACE, and his resignation signaled a renewed focus on the low-end PC business. Previously, Compaq had sold the 13 percent share it had in SGI and had terminated a joint venture with SGI that had planned to develop advanced Mips systems. Shortly after the Compaq decision to leave ACE, Santa Cruz Operations announced the suspension of its efforts to develop a Mips version of its Unix system.

Mips chairman Miller remained publicly optimistic, in part because other ACE members voted to continue. Olivetti began to ship R4000 systems compatible with ACE standards. Bill Gates, founder and CEO of Microsoft, also gave a positive assessment, saying that the SGI-Mips merger strengthened Mips and ACE. Other ACE members planned to buy stock in SGI to help complete the merger; these members included Control Data, Integrated Device Technology, NEC, Sumisho Electronics, Sumitomo, Tandem Computers, Tata Enterprises, and Toshiba. "The intention of these eight companies to invest in Silicon Graphics is a firm vote of confidence in the openness of the Mips RISC architecture, and it is an important endorsement of the Silicon Graphics/Mips merger," said Silicon Graphics CEO Ed McCracken.[6]

In addition, SGI began efforts to save the Mips architecture. It transferred production of Mips products to its own lines, closed all Mips manufacturing facilities, moved all employees to its own buildings, and dismissed 450 Mips employees. Sixty percent of Mips's fixed costs were thereby eliminated. Still, second-quarter results for Mips were not encouraging. Analysts estimated that, as a stand-alone firm, Mips would have posted an estimated $20 million operating loss, much more than the $597,000 loss of the previous year.

Because 80 percent of Mips's sales came from its top seven customers, SGI and Mips executives discussed their plans in detail with each partner. Even so, doubts remained about the commitment of key Mips allies. DEC, an early Mips supporter, prepared to introduce the Alpha chip, which it said would be ready later in the year. Olivetti, another Mips ally and ACE member, announced in July that it would introduce systems based on the Alpha chip. The agreement between DEC and Olivetti also called for DEC to take an equity position in the Italian computer maker. Another Mips ally in Europe, France's Groupe Bull, decided to adopt an alternative RISC processor. After intense competition between HP and IBM for Bull's business, the French government pressed Bull to accept IBM when the American firm agreed to invest several hundred million dollars in the ailing French company.

By the time the merger between Mips and SGI was complete, therefore, Compaq, Santa Cruz, DEC, Olivetti, and Bull had all left the Mips group. ACE was dead. There was no official statement, in part because ACE had never been a legal entity. Still, the Mips group, as a constellation of firms, continued to exist. And the group did achieve three of its main goals—to create a unified Unix operating system, to create a Windows NT version for Mips, and to develop a common hardware architecture.

SGI Reorganizes the Mips Group

Mips Technologies Incorporated (MTI), now a subsidiary of SGI, created the Open Design Center to continue the strategy initiated by ACE. Engineers from different companies worked there on Mips-based Windows NT programs. The center also tried to get PC companies to adopt Mips chips, as ACE had done. To reduce the barriers to entry for makers of Mips PCs, MTI attempted to use the infrastructure that already existed in the PC industry. For example, MTI designed and provided full board layouts for Mips PCs. Often these boards were designed to fit into the slots of existing PCs that used Intel chips. This strategy meant that makers of Intel PCs could adopt the Mips chip at little additional cost.

At the same time that MTI was promoting the adoption of its chip, the company raised the price of its technology licenses. Before the merger, Mips had sold an architecture license for about $1 million; after the merger, MTI set the price closer to $30 million. This change in pricing recognized that Mips's financial decline was in part due to its dependence on technology sales. Having identified this dependence and the problems it had created for Mips, MTI hoped to earn a higher return on its R&D. This action was also likely to deter new technology alliances.

SGI planned to shift the strategy of MTI toward higher-performance systems. It would continue to support the common hardware platform developed by ACE, to compete in the high-volume market against

IBM, HP, and Sun. But SGI would also use its new control over the Mips architecture to push into 3-D graphics and multimedia applications, which were SGI's strengths.

SGI and MTI maintained most of the existing alliances of Mips, although some partnerships were ended and others were restructured. The Mips allies in the systems business were generally less eager than the semiconductor partners to remain tied to MTI. One reason was that SGI was a formidable systems vendor, whereas Mips had never succeeded in that business. Thus the Mips systems allies suddenly encountered potential conflicts with their technology supplier.

The situation facing the Semiconductor Partners was different.[7] Except for DEC, the others remained with Mips and the relationships with several were expanded. NEC and Toshiba began to work together on a high-end version of the Mips chip as well as on a version for multiprocessor machines. NEC and Toshiba also developed still other versions for specific uses. Through this strategy, MTI attempted to create greater differentiation between the offerings of the partners than had existed previously. In effect, the group set out to develop four different versions of the chip, each to serve a different product segment.[8]

This new chip development plan differed radically from the earlier Mips strategy. Previously, Mips had committed to developing one chip (the R4000) to serve all ACE members. This led, by one account, to "creeping featurism." Even after the definition of the chip's functions had been agreed upon, various ACE customers continued to demand different features. DEC, for example, wanted features for both its uniprocessor workstations and its multiprocessor systems; Tandem wanted features for two kinds of fault-tolerant systems; many other partners, especially ACE members, wanted a low-cost desktop chip.[9]

In the end, the R4000 chip could not fulfill all these demands: it sacrificed high-end graphics performance for functions needed by PC vendors; and it was a large chip, which made it expensive to produce. Furthermore, it was introduced at least six months behind schedule. This delay, in turn, was a major reason behind the collapse of Mips and ACE.

ACE had come and gone in the span of a few years. Apart from the changes it wrought in the computer industry, this episode posed central questions about the dynamics of constellations. Why did the group grow so rapidly? Why did it collapse so suddenly? Was it a fad? If so, are we in danger of falling prey to similar fads again?

The Spread of Collective Competition

The rise and fall of ACE was not an isolated event. Rather, it reflected the general tendency of collective competition to spread in waves. The rise of ACE encouraged other groups, notably those of HP and IBM, to form and expand. These groups also grew in spurts, though none exploded on the scene the way ACE did. Perhaps because of that, none reached limits to growth as rapidly as ACE did, either.

Competition between large groups of firms represents the culmination of collective competition. Once alliance groups appear on the scene, they are often contagious and cause collective competition to spread throughout an industry. As a result, the competitive environment can be transformed rapidly and thoroughly.

Collective competition can spread in two ways. First, more single firms might join other single firms to form new constellations. Second, existing constellations may grow by adding new members. We will examine both of these processes.

The Dynamics of Alliance Waves

In many businesses, alliances have spread in waves. A period of increasing alliance formation has typically been followed by a slowdown. In the computer hardware industry, for example, the formation of both international and domestic alliances increased dramatically in the first half of the 1980s and declined in the second half (see Figure 17). A new wave of alliance formation seemed to start in the early 1990s.

At the level of individual firms, too, the rate of alliance formation has risen and fallen in waves. During the 1980s and early 1990s, IBM

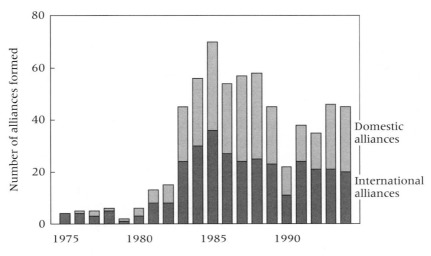

Figure 17 The spread of alliances in the computer industry, 1975–1994.
(Source: Survey of press reports; see Appendix B.)

experienced three such waves, with peaks in 1984, 1988, and 1991 (see Figure 18). In each wave, IBM's rate of alliance formation rose from under five per year to over ten or fifteen per year. At DEC, which was second to IBM in terms of total number of alliances in our sample, the rate of alliance formation peaked once in 1988 and appeared to be headed upward again in the early 1990s. Olivetti and Fujitsu—the non-American firms with the largest number of alliances—also experienced bursts of alliance formation, which peaked in about 1985.

Similar patterns of alliance formation can be seen in other industries and firms. In the early 1990s, there were waves of alliance formation in the telecommunications, airline, health-care, and commercial real estate industries, to name a few disparate examples. Biotechnology alliances were most popular in the mid-1980s. Earlier, the late 1970s and early 1980s saw alliance waves in the automobile, aircraft, and chemicals industries. Historical data on the foreign operations of large U.S. manufacturing firms indicate an increase in the use of joint ventures in the late 1950s, followed by a sharp decline in the 1960s.[1]

These observations raise two related questions. First, why do firms in an industry seem to increase their use of alliances at about the same time? This clustering of alliance strategies, of course, is what causes the rate of alliance formation to rise for the industry as a whole. Second,

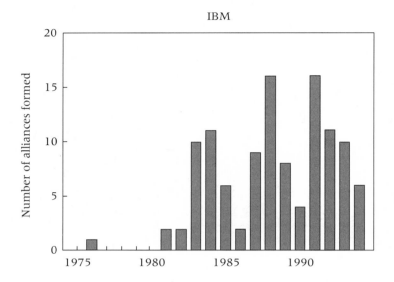

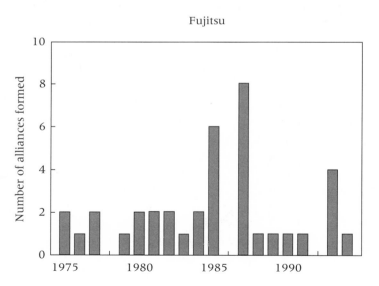

Figure 18 Alliance formation by top computer firms, 1975–1994. Note that vertical scales differ.

(Sources: Survey of press reports—see Appendix B—and company interviews.)

DEC

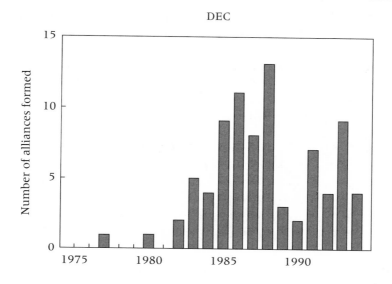

Olivetti

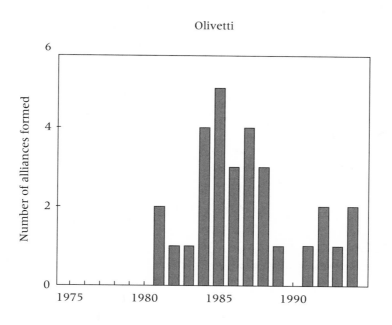

why does the rise in alliance formation come to a halt and even decline after a few years? Because the rises in alliance formation among firms in an industry are typically correlated, the declines are too. As a result, we see the popularity of alliances wax and wane in the industry.

For some analysts, the answer to these questions is that alliances are a fad—a temporary, popular fashion without economic rationale.[2] Managers have been known to follow fads in other instances. A diversification fad occurred in the 1960s, a portfolio planning fad in the 1970s, and merger-and-acquisition fads have swept through at several points, most recently in the late 1980s. This explanation has a ring of truth.

But there is more method to the madness. The temporary nature of the popularity of a strategy does not make the strategy irrational. Nor does a decline in alliance formation prove that an earlier rise was a mistake. Similarly, competitors often have good economic reasons to imitate one another's moves. The alliance "fad" too has an underlying economic logic.

To understand this logic, we must examine two sets of forces: those that drive and those that limit the formation of alliances. Table 10 classifies these forces and identifies whether they originate inside or outside a firm's network of alliances.

The clustering of alliance formation among firms might be explainable by the existence of drivers that are common to all the competitors in an industry, such as general trends in demand and technology. Several such environmental factors were identified in Chapter 1. Here we will focus on those drivers that are inherent to collective competition itself and that are not imposed on an industry from the outside.

Table 10   Determinants of the spread of alliances in an industry

	Drivers of alliance formation	Limits to alliance formation
External to each constellation	*Rivalry* First-mover advantages Oligopolistic imitation Partner preemption	*Crowding Out* Strategic gridlock
Internal to each constellation	*Synergy* Specialization	*Coordination Costs* Demands on management Costs of rationalization Dependence

Chief among these is rivalry among constellations, which causes them to react to one another in ways that accelerate the formation of alliances. Another driver inherent in the process of collective competition is synergy among the alliances of a firm, which causes one alliance to breed another.

Similarly, the decline in alliance formation in a firm can be in part explained by limits that arise only after a firm's network of alliances has grown to a certain size. Some of these come about as competing constellations crowd out one another's alliance opportunities. But many limits are internal to the firm's network—they depend on the rising costs of controlling a large and complex group.

Pressures for Alliance Formation

Oligopolistic competition between groups generally encourages the groups to expand. Among the most important pressures for growth are (1) battles to gain first-mover advantages of scale, scope, and standards; (2) imitation of rival groups to reduce risk; and (3) efforts to preempt rivals from linking up with attractive partners.[3]

THE PURSUIT OF FIRST-MOVER ADVANTAGES

In their pursuit of first-mover advantages, constellations are no different from single firms in an oligopolistic environment. When an industry has high economies of scale, high customer switching costs, or steep experience curves, competitors of both types can be expected to try to establish early footholds and a dominant market share. Acting singly or in collectives, the firms that move early can then gain some advantage over those that move later.

When firms use collaboration as part of such a strategy, however, they can often shorten the time needed to establish a lead position; or, if they are latecomers, they can erode the position of the lead firm. For example, for a firm to expand its market share, it may need to invest in promotional strategies that take time to yield fruit. Unless the firm is large to begin with, it may not have sufficient capital to invest aggressively. Sometimes it will have to win market share from other firms. Alliances can overcome these hurdles to market share expansion. A constellation can be used to combine the markets of several small competitors, without each one's having to invest in new marketing programs and without needing to win share from each other. Alliances may thus quicken the race for first-mover advantages.

Evidence from the RISC industry illustrates the ways in which the growth of constellations can be motivated by the pursuit of first-mover advantages. The underlying purpose of each group was to establish a customer base committed to its architecture. In the late 1980s, RISC was used mostly in technical workstations. Apollo Computers had established an early lead in this industry before the introduction of RISC; Hewlett-Packard and Sun Microsystems were in second and third place.

From its founding in 1983, Sun mounted an aggressive campaign against Apollo, using a cluster of alliances and financial partners, including powerful AT&T. This strategy began to chip away at Apollo's position and ultimately forced it close to bankruptcy. Hewlett-Packard then acquired Apollo in 1986,[4] but the combined HP-Apollo operations continued to lose market share against Sun, which by this time had developed a powerful line of workstations and a large group of supply and marketing alliances.[5] At this stage RISC technology was on the horizon, but was not yet being used extensively in workstations.

After Mips introduced its RISC technology, HP and Sun followed quickly, because the new technology promised to increase the power of workstations. Sun already had a large constellation of allies, which for the most part stayed with Sun as the company made the transition to RISC. This constellation and its established market share in workstations represented a substantial first-mover advantage for Sun. Both HP/Apollo and Mips entered into alliances intended to erode Sun's advantage, but to little avail—HP/Apollo's market share in RISC systems fell until 1990, and Mips made only minor headway into Sun's turf (see Figure 16).

The Mips constellation did help that company survive; without the alliances with DEC, Siemens, NEC, and Kubota, Mips would have gone bankrupt. Even though these alliances did not seriously challenge the leader in engineering workstations, they kept Mips in the game for the next round—the battle for commercial users.

Early on Mips had recognized that it needed to tap into markets in which Sun was not already dominant. Mips thus emphasized workstations for commercial applications, not engineering applications, which were Sun's strength. At the time, personal computers built with Intel or Motorola CISC chips were used in commercial applications. Over time, therefore, the Mips strategy became one of introducing RISC to the personal computer market. But Intel proved to be an even tougher opponent than Sun was.

The rapid expansion of the Mips constellation in 1991–1992 was driven by the pursuit of first-mover advantages in RISC personal computers. The ACE initiative brought together PC giants like Compaq and Microsoft and aimed to develop a common architecture that could challenge Intel. The ACE constellation exploded in size, and for the first time, adherents of Mips outnumbered those of Sun (see Figure 13).

The growth of ACE shook the industry. The Mips constellation appeared to challenge Intel's dominance of the microprocessor industry as no other firm had been able to do before. The Mips strategy aimed to erode Intel's advantage as well as to establish a first-mover advantage among the competing RISC architectures. This strategy ultimately failed, in part because of the limits to growth the constellation encountered.

IMITATION OF RIVALS

The growth of the Mips constellation also set in motion other processes that encouraged the spread of alliances through the industry. Every other RISC vendor began to copy the Mips strategy. Rivals in a loose oligopoly, whether they are single firms or constellations, often imitate one another's strategic moves.[6] A competitor is likely to follow the alliance moves of a rival to reduce the risk of falling behind.

The reasoning behind oligopolistic imitation in alliance formation is as follows. Assume that constellations A and B are rivals and that A expands its group by adding new members. If B decides not to follow and A's new strategy generates advantages, then B falls behind. Of course, if A's strategy fails, B has a chance of moving ahead. But if B follows by expanding its own group, then the two rivals are likely to stay close competitors, regardless of how the strategy turns out. When competitors are averse to risk, they are likely to choose the follow-the-leader strategy, which lowers their chances of either moving ahead or—more important—falling behind their rivals.

Managers of firms are often assumed to be risk averse, because they may lose their jobs if they fail. Managers in constellations are probably no different. Indeed, because constellations involve mutual commitments among members, it may well be more difficult for them to get all members behind a risky strategy than to seek to conserve the conditions under which the alliances were formed. Constellations, in

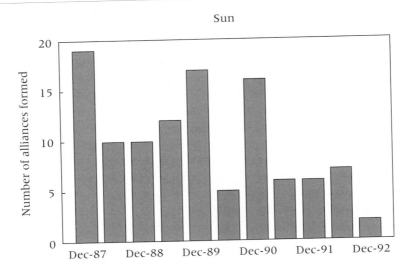

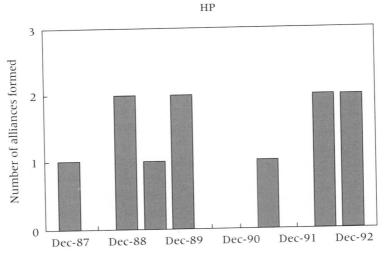

Figure 19 Biannual addition of members to RISC groups, 1987–1992. Note that vertical scales differ. Each bar represents the number of alliances formed in the preceding six months.
(Source: Survey of press reports; see Appendix B.)

Mips

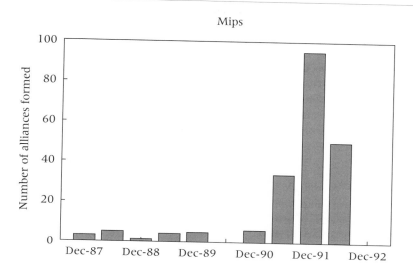

IBM

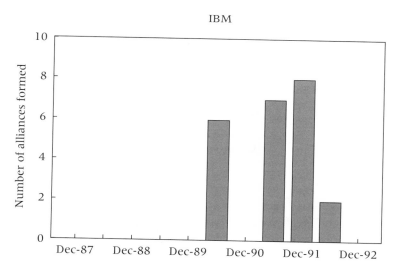

other words, may be strategically more conservative than firms, and so will tend to imitate one another's moves.

The behavior of the RISC competitors after the rise of ACE demonstrates how alliances spread through imitation. Sun already had a large constellation, and did not change its behavior to match that of Mips. But IBM and HP did, as the data in Figure 19 suggest. Both HP and IBM expanded their use of alliances in 1991–1992, just when ACE was growing rapidly. HP and IBM also established new organizations to govern their RISC constellations at about this time. And both began to target the personal computer industry, as ACE was doing.

IBM had earlier tried and failed to promote its RISC architecture without the aid of any allies. In 1990 it surprised the industry by forming the PowerPC constellation, with Apple and Motorola at the core. Multiple motivations lay behind these alliances; the threat of ACE's growth was one. The rise of ACE had dealt a major blow to Motorola's own efforts to promote its 88K RISC architecture. Several companies that had been leaning toward adopting the 88000 chip joined ACE instead, leaving Motorola without large partners. Apple, meanwhile, though it had been a loyal Motorola customer before, did not relish the prospect of being the only major user of the 88000 chip. It conducted an exhaustive evaluation of all the RISC technologies available, and settled on IBM's.[7]

The IBM group then grew to become the successor of ACE in challenging Intel. Like ACE, the PowerPC group attempted to establish common standards for the use of IBM's chip in personal computers, although it did not develop a common hardware architecture right away. An agreement between Apple and IBM on such an architecture came in 1994; even then, there was no common software architecture like that which ACE had tried to develop. Still, the PowerPC constellation grew rapidly, in part by attracting members that broke off from other constellations. Bull and Wang, for example, were among the first to leave ACE and join IBM. Olivetti, which had left ACE for DEC's Alpha, switched to IBM's group in 1994.

Rivalry among ACE, IBM, and HP thus led them to pursue similar strategies—in this case, to form similar types of alliance groups. Because of this pattern, the composition of the constellations in terms of the mix and sizes of members were closely matched, as we saw in Chapter 3. The pace and character of alliance formation in this industry, therefore, were driven in part by imitation among competitors.

PREEMPTIVE ALLIANCE STRATEGIES

Under certain conditions, rivals may take imitation strategies one step further—they may attempt to preempt rather than just follow each other. A competitor is more likely to try to preempt a rival if it thinks that by moving first it can secure a choice position or, conversely, that by always following a leader it will end up with less favorable choices. In many strategic games, it may not matter much who moves first—a follower may even be able to learn from the mistakes of a leader. But in alliance formation, there are often substantial advantages to moving first and, therefore, to preemptive strikes.

The advantages of moving first in alliance formation derive from the set of opportunities for collaboration that exist at any point in time. The opportunities for collaboration are limited by the number of potential partners, which usually have varying capabilities. The first firm to form an alliance has the greatest choice among these partners and is more likely to end up with the most attractive partner.

The extent of this type of first-mover advantage depends on how much less attractive the second-most desirable partner is and on how many potential partners are left after the first alliance is formed. In fields with only a few attractive partners, we can expect more preemptive alliance formation than in fields where there are many potential partners of roughly equal capabilities. In addition, in the early stages of the spread of alliances through an industry, the incentives for preemptive moves may be less than in later stages, when the threat of partner scarcity looms larger. Paradoxically, this effect may accelerate the spread of alliances even as the choice of partners dries up.

A firm's incentive to form alliances preemptively also depends on its expectations about its rivals' moves. The more likely it appears that a rival will form an alliance, the greater the incentive to preempt. This tendency, too, can accelerate the spread of alliances: the formation of alliances breeds the expectation of further alliances, which leads to preemptive alliances by firms that would otherwise remain single.

Examples of such preemptive strategies are hard to find in the public record, perhaps because of their predatory flavor. But they do occur. Motorola effectively blocked a 1989 licensing arrangement between Mips and Toshiba by intervening to delay conclusion of the contract even after a letter of intent had been signed. Motorola, which had an ongoing joint venture with Toshiba, suggested that it needed help in commercializing its own RISC chip, the 88000. As it turned out, Motorola and Toshiba never worked together on the 88000. But when the Toshiba-Mips deal stalled, NEC jumped at the chance to form an alliance with Mips.[8] Toshiba finally joined the Mips group in 1991.

Sometimes a firm uses a portfolio of otherwise minor alliances to preempt rivals. In the 1980s, IBM Europe noticed that in several cases, agents' or dealers' business with IBM significantly decreased after they were taken over or received equity investments from IBM competitors. IBM therefore embarked on a defensive strategy to protect its access to its agent channels. From 1987 to 1990, the number of IBM's equity alliances in Europe jumped from 6 to 150, of which some 100 were for this type of channel protection. In these alliances, which typically involved IBM's purchasing a 10 percent ownership in the agent, IBM remained a passive investor without board representation. Many of these defensive alliances were in Italy and France, where national computer companies (Olivetti and Bull) threatened IBM's position in microcomputers. With small preemptive investments, IBM was able to defend its market position by blocking the moves of the competitors.[9]

Preemptive alliances can also lead to severe rivalry over partnerships. Instead of competing over resources or markets, rivals may compete over partners. HP and IBM, for example, both tried to form a RISC alliance with Bull after Bull became dissatisfied with the direction in which ACE was headed. This rivalry in effect bid up the "price" of the partnership to such an extent that HP did not think it worthwhile. IBM ended up investing over $200 million in Bull, more than HP was willing to offer.[10] This episode suggests that a partner that is highly sought after can skew the terms of an alliance in its favor.

SPECIALIZATION

The three "external" processes discussed so far—the pursuit of first-mover advantages, imitation, and preemption—help drive the spread of alliances in an industry. The rationale behind alliance formation in these processes differs from the basic reasons for collaboration discussed in Chapter 1, which revolved around the exploitation of synergy—the idea that firms with complementary capabilities could gain from collaboration. Synergy is therefore an "internal" process driving the spread of alliances. One form of synergy, in particular, encourages the formation of large groups—the opportunity to specialize.

Adam Smith was the first to analyze the economic benefits of the division of labor. In a system of specialized laborers, he argued, each can do what it is best at, each will become more adept at the assigned task, specialized machinery can be used, and there will be fewer bottlenecks or idle assets in production. In a famous chapter title he declared that "the division of labor is limited by the extent of the market."[11] The greater the volume of production of a good, the more opportunities there will be for dividing the production process into specialties.

The same principle applies to specialization within a constellation. The larger the constellation, the more opportunities there will be for allocating tasks to specialists within the group. A finer division of labor increases the members' opportunity to focus on what they do best. Specialization thus creates internal incentives for the growth of constellations. The RISC constellation of Hewlett-Packard provides an illustration.

Compared with Mips and Sun, HP formed fewer alliances in the RISC field; it relied more heavily on in-house efforts. This difference is to be expected, given HP's excellent internal capabilities in virtually all the areas needed to compete. Furthermore, HP's network was anchored by a broad alliance with Hitachi, another firm with a full range of internal capabilities. As a result, the members in the Hewlett-Packard RISC constellation were chosen to fill specific niches in which each had a comparative advantage.

Hitachi, for example, focused on developing low-cost, low-performance, general-purpose RISC chips as well as embedded RISC chips designed for use in appliances and machinery; these were both areas in which HP was not active. Samsung, another Hewlett-Packard RISC partner, also had a specific role to play in the constellation. According to Lewis E. Platt, executive vice president of HP computer products at the time, Samsung was "to provide low-cost, high-volume manufacturing, advanced semiconductor technology, and fast time-to-market."[12]

With its Hitachi and Samsung alliances, HP was not so much filling the gaps in its capabilities, as Mips did, as extending the scope of its operations in a flexible fashion. These partners, one at the high end and one at the low end of the market, were delegated to pursue quite different goals. Using alliances, HP could pursue these different strategies without losing its own focus.

The philosophy behind the rest of HP's alliance strategy was to select a principal supplier for each class of its RISC chip.[13] HP wanted each partner in the group to make a unique contribution, with little overlap or duplication. The members of HP's alliance group thus played distinctive roles in different parts of the RISC value chain (see Table 11).

Table 11   Members of Hewlett-Packard's RISC network, with their roles, 1993

Member	Role
Chip Development, Production, and Sales	
HP[a]	Desktop and high-performance; no embedded chips
Hitachi[a]	Desktop, high-performance (for own use) and low-cost, including embedded chips; possible second source for HP
Oki[a]	Embedded chips only
Samsung	Workstations and embedded chips
Winbond[a]	Desktop and embedded chips
Systems Development, Production, and Sales	
HP[b]	Workstations, servers, minicomputers
Convex[b]	Massively parallel processors
Hitachi[b]	Workstations, servers, supercomputers
MELCO	Industrial control systems
Oki	Embedded telecommunications systems
Samsung	Workstations
Sequoia	Fault-tolerant computers
Stratus	Fault-tolerant computers

Operating System Software Development and Sales (each firm develops the software for its own systems)
HP
Convex[c]
Hitachi[c]
MELCO[c]
Oki[c]
Samsung[c]
Sequoia
Stratus

Source: Interviews at Hewlett-Packard, August 1993.

a. These firms coordinate their planning so that the contributions of each to the group are unique.

b. HP and Convex work jointly on standards, as do HP and Hitachi.

c. HP has also licensed its Unix operating system software to these firms, in an effort to increase compatibility.

Hidden Limits to Alliance Formation

The external and internal drivers of alliance formation operate with little resistance during the expansionary phase of an alliance wave. As alliances spread and constellations expand, however, new limits appear that were hidden before. In the contractionary phase of the wave, these limits to growth halt the formation of new alliances. In some cases, they may also lead to the dissolution of existing alliances.

Most of the limits to alliance formation are internal to the constellation, but one is external. Growth may slow owing to an "overcrowding" of the field—a scarcity of unattached partners for new alliances. This external limit, almost by definition, is reached only after alliances have spread throughout the industry. The external forces, therefore, do not stop an alliance wave until it has run its course. Will internal constraints on alliance formation limit the wave earlier?

The internal limits to the growth of a group revolve around the marginal costs and benefits of adding new members. In the early stages of a group's growth, the addition of members tends to support specialization and division of labor. As the size of a group increases, the added benefit of a new member diminishes because of increased duplication. At the same time, the added costs of collaboration increase: (1) greater organizational effort is needed to control a larger group; (2) internal conflicts rise; and (3) individual members suffer a loss of control. Therefore, there are diminishing returns to group size. Put differently, as the group grows, the network effects of new members decline to zero.

But, like the external constraints, these internal limits also often fail to stop constellation growth until well after the point of diminished returns. The internal costs are difficult to measure and predict, particularly because few firms have much experience as yet in managing large constellations. The costs are hidden in the beginning, and only emerge after they have accumulated for some time.

The growth of an alliance group was nowhere as rapid as in the case of Mips. In this group, as a result, the limits arose early and with a vengeance, leading ultimately to the fall of ACE. First, Mips could not attract certain partners that were already tied to other competitors—an external limit that I call "strategic gridlock." Second, Mips managers were burdened by the time and effort required to manage their large and complex group. Third, the costs of rationalizing the group increased with growth, in part because of the different goals of the partners. Fourth, and finally, the dependence of Mips on its growing number of partners ultimately doomed the company. The evidence from other RISC groupings confirms the roles played by these limits to alliance formation.

THICKENING STRATEGIC GRIDLOCK

The external limits to the spread of alliances revolve around the options for forming new partnerships that are available to the group; these options are used up as alliances proliferate.[14] The simplest case of this type of constraint occurs when the pool of eligible partners diminishes because of the boom in alliance formation itself.

Paradoxically, the environments most conducive to alliance formation are also those where strategic gridlock is most likely to be encountered. First, non–arm's length transactions between firms are most likely to occur when there are few possible suppliers and buyers.[15] Because the buyers and suppliers are then highly interdependent—one's success depends critically on the actions of the other—they will try to manage their product exchange through vertical integration or alliances. When there are many possible partners for a transaction, there is little need to link closely with one of them through an alliance. Second, the logic of building an effective alliance group often requires including members that bring to the group specific capabilities that are not readily or widely available.[16] Consequently, as different firms build competing groups, the partners with desirable capabilities gradually become unavailable.

The race to build alliance groups in the RISC field illustrates this pattern. For example, in its efforts to sign up a major Japanese semiconductor partner, Mips found its options limited because of the alliances that Sun and Motorola had with, respectively, Fujitsu and Toshiba. One firm's alliance strategy thus limited the options available to a competitor.

This pattern, of course, hurts latecomers more than early movers. HP's options were even more limited than were those of Mips, as it followed Sun and Mips in building a RISC group; still, Hitachi was available. By the time DEC began to look for partners for its Alpha chip, it could only find Mitsubishi, a second-tier semiconductor producer. IBM's early efforts at finding a Japanese partner faced the same fate;

only late in 1994 did Toshiba and Hitachi sign up as major allies in the IBM group, and even then, they continued to hedge their bets by maintaining their existing alliances with Mips and HP, respectively.[17]

INCREASING DEMANDS ON MANAGEMENT

A scarcity of management capacity is frequently emphasized by practitioners in alliance groups. Negotiating each agreement requires great effort, and major alliances require the continual, direct, and personal involvement of top management. These demands on management increase with the size of the group and the complexity of member interactions. Mips CEO Robert Miller commented on his company's core group of alliances: "The key ingredient to our Semiconductor Partnership program is perseverance. Keeping five companies on the same strategic path can be difficult; it takes diplomacy, time, and energy at the senior level. [Mips president] Chuck Boesenberg and I spend a lot of our time resolving issues to keep us all in the same line."[18] The British economist Edith Penrose argued many years ago that demands on management also limit the size and complexity of a single firm. In her view, the finite size and capabilities of the top management team limit the amount of new activity a firm can take on.[19] These limits to growth also apply to an alliance group, and are perhaps accentuated by the often personal bases for interfirm partnerships.

Few firms are experienced in managing large numbers of alliances. It appears, however, that the most experienced firms in this field are able to mitigate the management constraint. The constraint appears binding only in the short term, that is, within a given company structure. Expansion of the top management team and delegation of alliance activities to lower levels of management may loosen the constraint. In this way, the experienced firms follow the same general principles as lie behind the development of divisional structures to deal with product-line and geographic expansion.[20]

IBM and, to a lesser extent, Olivetti have been trying to deal with alliance management constraints by distributing the burden among a number of executives. They partition the task of alliance management and delegate individual parts to different middle-level executives. In each case, alliances are classified by their structure (for example, equity investments, relations with original equipment manufacturers [OEMs], joint ventures, acquisitions) and each group is managed by a different executive. Still, top management remains deeply involved in the most important relationships. At Olivetti, one executive is responsible for all alliances. At IBM, different members of the top management team act as "champions" or advocates for bilateral alliances. Xerox, too, has assigned a senior vice president to oversee all alliance activities.

Collective governance structures of alliance groups can also alleviate the management burden on individual companies. 88Open, for example, took over many of the group governance tasks that otherwise might have fallen on Motorola. The Precision RISC Organization did the same for HP; the PowerOpen Association did so for IBM; and SPARC International functioned similarly for Sun.

The structure of SPARC International (SI) is a variant on this theme. SI grew out of the SPARC Vendors' Council, which consisted of four SPARC semiconductor suppliers. When the organization was formed in 1989, four systems vendors were added.[21] As a result, SI began by acting as a common forum for shared strategy among these firms. Later, two separate camps developed within the SI organization. The first camp consisted of Sun and its main suppliers (Texas Instruments and LSI Logic); the second was composed of Fujitsu and its allies (ICL, Amdahl, Ross, and HaL). Each camp had its own operating systems and products. SI developed a technical standard to bridge these two operating systems.[22] This example suggests that the formation of subgroups, or clusters, within constellations may be another way in which firms can distribute the burden of managing large groups. In this case, Fujitsu managed the relationships among the firms in its cluster, and Sun managed the links within its cluster.[23]

The management constraint on growth in alliance groups thus acts as a signal to reorganize the group; it is not a rigid limit. It remains to be seen whether or not firms indeed find ways to manage the flood of new alliances, especially as some of their partnerships begin to fail. Should delegation prove difficult or impossible, management capacity may become a more stubborn constraint.

RISING COSTS OF COORDINATION

The role of coordination costs as a constraint on alliance formation surfaced in the earliest studies of international joint ventures.[24] Coordination costs expressed themselves in these studies as a problem of geographic rationalization—the coordination of a firm's global activities to achieve higher total profits. As a general matter, multinational firms aim to maximize global profits, while local partners aim to maximize local profits. Because these two objectives are not always congruent—for example, a global firm might want to incur costs locally to reap added benefits globally—the interests of the partners are often at odds. Local alliances and joint ventures may thus effectively block the global firm from rationalizing its operations worldwide.

This argument is not limited to joint ventures between multinationals and local partners. Conflicts of interest can occur whenever the objectives of partners differ. This type of conflict is common when an alliance is part of the group of operations of one of the partners, but represents a self-contained venture for the other partner.[25] Whatever the root causes, such a conflict of interest will add to the coordination costs of the group.

Even constellations consisting of only two partners can encounter this constraint. For example, Bull found it difficult to rationalize its global operations because NEC owned a minority share of Bull's U.S. subsidiary. As a solution, the partners changed NEC's investment into an ownership share in the parent company. In another example, Philips bought out the minority partners in its North American subsidiary in an effort to gain greater control over these operations. This buyout occurred soon after North American Philips refused to adopt the Dutch company's proprietary VCR format early in the VCR standards battle, and instead opted for the VHS format of JVC. In both cases, the firms managed the problem by modifying the structure of their alliance or by eliminating the alliance.

Mips faced a more insidious version of the same problem when it was pulled in different directions by its many partners. As we have seen, one of the strengths of the Mips group was the diversity of its membership; together these firms helped Mips penetrate markets as varied as personal computers, graphics workstations, and fault-tolerant computers. But this diversity also led to conflicting demands on the designers of the R4000, and helped delay completion of this chip. That delay contributed greatly to the collapse of ACE.

These coordination problems are often difficult to recognize and manage. The problems do not surface in all alliances, simply because not all alliances involve serious trade-offs between partner interests. In some situations the need to rationalize operations on a worldwide basis may not exist. Xerox, for example, argues that in its copier joint ventures this problem is minimized because many economies of scale and scope are regional, not global. Consequently, it can have one joint venture in Europe (Rank Xerox) and one in Japan (Fuji Xerox), each covering mostly the regional market.

Moreover, even when there are reasons for coordination across alliances, this constraint may be manageable, sometimes by creating another alliance. In the low-end printer business, Xerox recognized that economies of scale in production and R&D would favor a unified approach to the Japanese and U.S. markets. For this reason, it created Xerox International Partners to align the interests of its Japanese joint venture with those of its wholly owned operations in the United States.[26]

The new relationships between the Mips Semiconductor Partners illustrate how the Mips group managed coordination across alliances. After the merger with SGI, Mips encouraged each partner to specialize. By definition, that strategy would lessen overlaps and conflicts among them. In addition, the partners launched joint projects among themselves. Collaboration among partners is likely to help them coordinate and rationalize their roles in the group.

This type of collaboration did not arise in the Mips network until the group had grown substantially and the limits to growth had already taken their toll. Why this delay? One reason is that problems of group rationalization are not easily recognized early in the growth of a group. At that stage, the reasons for alliance formation overwhelm the arguments against it. The benefits of adding new alliances to a group may be greater than the costs of managing any conflicting goals between partners. Yet these two opposing pressures may not be wholly independent of each other. In fact, as a firm's alliance network grows, the pressures for rationalization are likely to increase. To see why, we must consider the opportunity costs of *not* rationalizing a group.

There is usually a greater potential for conflict among partners in a large group than in a small one.[27] But this also means that there are greater potential benefits to rationalization. Rationalization of a group's activities tends to reduce conflicts among members and increase group-based advantages, as we saw in Chapter 3. The benefits of rationalization thus increase as the group grows. Stated differently, the opportunity cost of not rationalizing a group grows with size.

Gradually, this opportunity cost will come to outweigh the benefits from creating new alliances. Every new alliance adds something to the group but also generates greater potential for intragroup conflict. At some point it will no longer pay to add new members, unless the group is rationalized. The difficulty of achieving this, therefore, tends to limit the growth of the group. If members find ways around this constraint, the group can, of course, continue to grow without losing effectiveness. Otherwise there will be diminishing returns to adding new members.[28]

RISING DEPENDENCE

An altogether different category of limits to the growth of constellations revolves around the effect that a large number of alliances can have on a firm's performance. The extensive use of alliances leads to two problems: loss of control and loss of appropriability. These are additional reasons why an expanding group faces diminishing returns after a certain point.[29]

Loss of control. Central to any alliance is a sharing of control. The trade-off in joint ventures between the acquisition of capabilities and the loss of control identified by scholars some time ago holds equally well today for alliances of different forms.[30] Even minority partners in a joint venture influence the decisions of the joint venture and thereby affect the degree of control of the majority partner; often, minority partners have veto rights on crucial decisions. Licensors frequently allow others to use their technology in ways that may not be specified precisely in advance, and they usually have little control over the marketing of the end product.

The more alliances a firm has, therefore, the more influence its partners will have on its destiny and overall performance. Firms that pursue business strategies centering around alliances—such as IBM in PCs, and Mips and Sun in RISC—run the risk of losing effective control over the performance of these businesses.

This loss of control manifests itself in various ways. One problem is that alliance groups may reduce the range of instruments available to the firm in implementing its business strategy. For example, a firm selling exclusively through OEM alliances usually lacks the ability to promote sales with advertising or direct sales forces. The firm can then affect sales only through its pricing of intermediate goods and through indirect promotion. But these actions may not have any effect if the OEM partners do not market the product aggressively. Furthermore, the firm will have little influence on other aspects of marketing strategy, such as product positioning and geographic coverage. It can try to chart a marketing course for the product through its choice of alliance partners, but this method is a slow and loose way to implement strategy.

Mips encountered problems with dependence on external suppliers. Its R6000 chip, which was of a different type than earlier chips, had been licensed only to Bipolar Technologies, a small U.S. firm. Problems with supply cost, reliability, and quantities resulted in substantial delays in making the product commercially available. Even though the chip was announced in the fourth quarter of 1989, it was not shipped in large volume until 1991. This delay, in turn, affected sales of R6000-based systems.

An alliance group may also reduce a firm's control over how its technology is used. This problem can usually be managed if it is recognized at the beginning and if adequate oversight mechanisms are built into the alliance contracts. The examples of Sun and Mips are again instructive. Sun licensed the SPARC instruction set without attempting to control the physical format in which these computer codes were actually represented on a SPARC chip. As a result, SPARC chips produced by different licensees used different physical designs and were incompatible at the hardware level. Mips, in contrast, licensed its instruction set together with its own physical chip design, and even certified the chips produced by its licensees with a trademark stamp. These chips were fully compatible and interchangeable at the hardware level. The Mips strategy gave the company greater control over the ways in which its technology would be used.

Firms also risk losing control over their destiny because the growth of their alliance network can shift the center of gravity of the group. Initially, the loss of control is limited to bilateral alliances—a risk of technology leakage here, a loose marketing approach there. But particularly for small firms building large groups, the network may begin to assume a life of its own. Mips began by constructing its group consciously and carefully, and initially had great success with this strategy. As its partners came to include giants such as Compaq, Microsoft, DEC, NEC, and Siemens, however, it became unclear who was in control. Particularly after ACE was formed, the strategy seemed to be both succeeding and spinning out of control at the same time. From then on, Mips's future depended on ACE, and ACE, in turn, depended on collaboration among a handful of big players. In the end, a series of defections by Compaq, DEC, and others doomed both ACE and Mips.

Limited appropriability. Besides forcing a sharing of control, alliances inevitably imply a sharing of returns. In equity joint ventures, profits are usually shared according to ownership percentages. Nonequity alliances also imply a sharing of profits, although the distribution among partners is less clear. License contracts, for example, are notoriously poor at maximizing the return to the technology provider, owing to high transaction costs. As a result, firms that rely heavily on licensing can expect to earn lower returns than comparable firms that are able to use their technology in their own operations.[31]

This appropriability problem is exacerbated when alliances are motivated by a race to diffuse their technology in a standards battle. The objective of technology diffusion squarely contradicts the objective of profit maximization—the fastest way to diffuse technology is to give it out freely. In reality, few firms go to this extreme, if only because they need to recoup the costs of technology development and transfer. Still, firms that pursue alliance strategies with the objective of diffusing technology may suffer sluggish profitability. This problem may help explain Mips's poor profitability, which contrasted sharply with the rapid growth of its constellation.

When a firm expands its alliance group to promote its technology, it must cleverly negotiate a dangerous path. On the one hand, a large group usually helps spread a firm's technology more quickly and widely. On the other hand, if the firm does not appropriate enough of the returns on its efforts, then it will lack the cash needed to invest in further R&D, causing it to fall behind competing technologies.

The latter happened to Mips. Without sufficient profits to invest, Mips could not maintain product leadership. At the same time, its rivals HP, IBM, and Intel redoubled their investments and R&D efforts. The Mips R4000 chip arrived too late to counter this onslaught. The growth of an alliance group in a competitive standards game thus may represent either a virtuous or a vicious circle, depending on how growth is managed and, possibly, contained.[32]

All the limits to growth discussed here conspired to end the explosive growth of the Mips group. Other constellations may face these limits one at a time, find solutions to each dilemma, and so be spared this fate. These findings carry implications for other firms, however, and for the pattern of competition among groups.

Conclusion

This analysis begs the question of whether the high-technology alliance boom of the late 1980s and early 1990s will come to an end. Certain limits to alliance booms, as we have seen, result from overcrowding of the alliance field. When this happens, it is likely to affect all firms in an industry or geographic segment, whether or not they have been directly involved in creating the previous alliances. In addition, a distinctive feature of the alliance boom of the 1980s and 1990s is the involvement of leading firms from all countries. As a result, a few firms in each segment are responsible for much of the new activity. When the constellations of these firms reach their internal limits, the aggregate trend, too, may well peak.

But nothing in this book predicts *when* this retrenchment might occur. It is possible—even likely—that retrenchment from alliances in one field will occur while other fields experience an increase in collaboration. In the RISC field, for example, many more alliances were formed in the second half of the 1980s than in the first half of the 1990s. Yet the latter period saw a new boom in the formation of alliances in the multimedia field. Although alliance activity in different fields may be "bunched" in time, the overall pace of collaboration in the economy will show less variability.

The phenomenon of interfirm collaboration, in other words, is here to stay. In industry after industry, the alliance revolution is likely to transform the way firms compete. Strong external pressures for alliance formation will often mean that the rise of one constellation will lead to another. Internal limits to growth might give managers pause, but these limits are unlikely to halt the alliance bandwagon until it has progressed far. In this chapter, we saw these processes at work in the RISC industry. In the next case study we see how collective competition engulfed another industry—the field of personal digital assistants. The result, again, has been a transformation of the structure and dynamics of competition.

The Thickening Web of Multimedia Alliances

Personal digital assistants (PDAs) burst onto the market in the early 1990s.[1] These hand-held electronic gadgets were one of the first install-ments in the emerging business for multimedia products. They were intended to be part cellular phone, part notebook computer, part electronic calendar, part information organizer, and part computer game. An AT&T commercial showed their promise: sitting on the beach in the Caribbean, a relaxed businessman received a fax from one office, sent a reply to another, and then returned to his favorite electronic entertainment.

The product concept was not the only thing that was novel—so was the new industry's structure. From the start, the business of develop-ing, making, and selling PDAs was conducted through a thick web of alliances. Collective competition did not spread gradually as it did in computers; it arrived full-blown with the first PDAs. As a result, the organization and dynamics of the industry revolved around the pat-terns of alliance formation and the competitive behavior of constella-tions. Alliances were no longer just the result of environmental forces—they *were* the environment.

The Context of PDA Alliances

Alliances were so pervasive in PDAs for three reasons. First, the field was born from the convergence of at least four industries—computer hardware, computer software, telecommunications, and consumer electronics. Major companies in each of these areas participated in the PDA business, but each had a different vision of the new product. Even though there were giants among them, these companies also were limited in their ability to enter the PDA market. Depending on its industry of origin, each firm was strong in one aspect of the PDA emerging business, but lacked other needed capabilities. IBM, Apple, and HP approached the PDA business from their experience in computer hardware; Microsoft and Lotus, from computer software; AT&T, BellSouth, and Motorola, from telecommunications; and Sharp, Casio, Tandy, and Amstrad, from consumer electronics. Consistent with our framework from Chapter 1, constellations arose to combine these dissimilar capabilities.

Second, alliance formation in PDAs was driven by the great uncertainty regarding several aspects of the business, including customer demand and product and process technologies. This uncertainty was a function of the immaturity of the field, but also of the fact that the product was to represent a merging of capabilities from different existing industries. Uncertainty and convergence compounded each other, so that, although would-be PDA producers knew that they had to combine technology and components from different industries, they did not know the precise "mix" of ingredients needed for a successful product. As a consequence, they used alliances to experiment with different mixes.

Third, most of the players thought that the timing of the introduction of their product to the market was critical. An early introduction, they believed, would boost their recognition and image; more important, it might help them set technical standards that would sustain their market position as the industry matured. Conversely, a latecomer was likely to have to follow design standards set by the first-movers, and might even have to pay royalties for technologies that had become widespread. Many firms saw alliances as a way to get a product to market quickly.

These incentives for alliance formation led to the thick web of linkages shown in Figure 20. From this chart, it looks as if every firm is connected to every other firm. In reality, however, there were distinct groups, organized around leading firms, as shown in Figure 21. (A few firms participated in several groups at once, as will be discussed later.)

From the start, therefore, the competition in the PDA field was not among individual firms, but among groups of allied firms. All the PDAs studied here were developed in a collaboration between two or more firms. The number of alliances in each of the competing groups varied

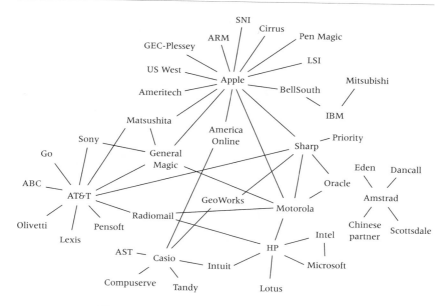

Figure 20 The web of alliances in PDAs, 1994.
(Sources: Industry press reports and company interviews.)

from over twenty in Apple's group to four in Amstrad's. But in every group, each member contributed specific capabilities and fulfilled specific functions in the cycle of product development and launch. As a result, the design of each group and the effectiveness of collaboration among group members helped shape the product offerings and the competitive advantage of the groups.

The Growth and Composition of PDA Groups

Although there were differences in the degree to which the PDA companies relied on alliances, the uses to which they put their alliances tended to be similar. As in other fields, firms in PDAs used alliances for three purposes: (1) to learn or develop new technologies; (2) to gain access to components and services; and (3) to position themselves in the market.[2]

Not only did the PDA firms use each of these types of alliances, but they did so systematically during the process of developing and launching their products. As a result, the growth of the alliance groups followed the pattern depicted in Figure 22.

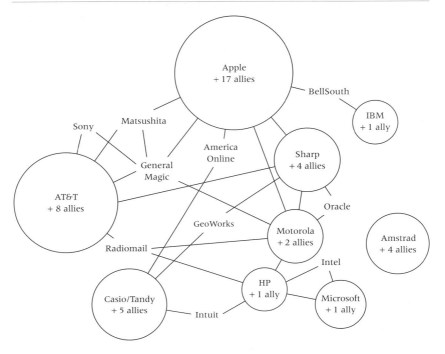

Figure 21   Alliance groups in PDAs, 1994. The total number of alliances here is greater than in Figure 20, because several minor alliances are included. (Source: revised from Benjamin Gomes-Casseres and Dorothy Leonard-Barton, "Alliance Clusters in Multimedia: Safety Net or Entanglement?" paper presented at the Colliding Worlds Colloquium, October 1994, Harvard Business School.)

Each of the PDA entrants began with one or two learning alliances; on average, these were formed one or two years before the product was launched. Learning alliances helped shape the basic design of the product and accounted for most of the new technology developed. In the last year or so before the introduction of the product, the companies lined up suppliers for critical components and services. On average, each of the groups examined here contained about five such supply alliances by the time the product was being sold. Finally, just before product introduction, and for some time after that, the companies lined up partners to help them penetrate markets, sell abroad, and spread their standards. The groups varied greatly in the use of this last class of alliances, with Apple having the most and HP having none.

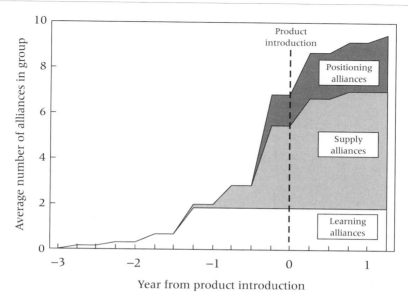

Figure 22   Growth and composition of PDA alliance groups. Shown are the averages of the data for the groups of Apple, EO, HP, Amstrad, and Sharp. (Source: Benjamin Gomes-Casseres and Dorothy Leonard-Barton, "Alliance Clusters in Multimedia: Safety Net or Entanglement?" paper presented at the Colliding Worlds Colloquium, October 1994, Harvard Business School, p. 42a.)

The systematic distribution of alliances over the PDA development cycle stemmed from a complex relationship between product development and collaboration. At some times during the cycle, the alliances were the outcome of preceding product design decisions; at other times, the design decisions were the outcome of earlier alliance choices. Alliances, in other words, were both causes and effects of the product development process.

LEARNING ALLIANCES

It is easy to see how product design choices lead to alliances when the firm lacks the capability to implement a chosen design. Because all PDAs combined technologies and markets from different industries, all new entrants needed alliances to fill gaps in their capabilities.

It is less obvious how alliances influence product designs; the data provide some evidence of this type of effect. Six PDAs studied in depth were each developed by a pair or triad of companies—the early learning alliances in the product development cycle. In each case, the specific skills and visions of this small set of allies shaped product design decisions. Apple relied primarily on its internal software capabilities. But its hardware alliances with ARM and Sharp helped shape the Newton; this PDA used ARM's chip and Sharp's miniaturization hardware. Similarly, EO combined Go's operating system, telecommunications technology and a microprocessor from AT&T, and the vision and miniaturization expertise of the Active Book Company. The Hewlett-Packard LX series embodied at its core the technologies of HP and Lotus, the pair of companies that linked up early in a learning alliance. Amstrad and Eden's PenPad, Casio and Tandy's Zoomer, and IBM and BellSouth's Simon were each developed by pairs of allied firms.

The companies in the initial pair or triad developing each product always came from different industries. But the precise combination of industries varied—Apple and Sharp combined computers and consumer electronics, HP and Lotus combined computer hardware and software, IBM and BellSouth combined computer hardware and telecommunications, and so on. This variation affected the design of the initial PDA products: the Newton was stronger in computing than the EO and the Simon, the 95LX was strong in calculating functions, and the PenPad and Zoomer were designed from the start to be mass-market products. The variation in PDA products on the market in 1994, therefore, stemmed not only from variety among the entering firms but also from variety among the combinations of early allies.

SUPPLY ALLIANCES

The starting points of the PDA groups thus differed from each other. Over time, however, the groups came to look more and more alike, as each expanded to encompass a similar pool of capabilities. This growing similarity in the combined capabilities of the groups was achieved through the use of supply alliances after the initial designs of the products had been established.

The new wave of supply alliances complemented the internal capabilities of the initial set of companies that designed the product. While HP and Lotus had software, hardware design, and manufacturing capabilities in-house, for example, they went to Intel for chips, to Motorola for communications technology, to Microsoft (and later to Intuit) for more software, and to Radiomail for communications services. Each of the other groups had a similar mix of capabilities, embedded either in the original designers or in their allies. All groups had to have software capabilities, manufacturing, and chips; most also had communication and information services as part of the pool. The rival constellations thus appeared to have matched one another's alliances, even though there was great uncertainty regarding which capabilities would be critical to success.

Other PDA alliances were less readily explained as imitative moves and reflected other strategies. Some companies allied themselves with several competing partners. Sharp licensed Apple's Newton operating system as well as GeoWorks's GEO; AT&T supported both Go's operating system and General Magic's Magic Cap; and Apple allied itself with three telecommunication services providers. In each case, these companies were creating a portfolio of options through these overlapping alliances. The fear, it appears, was of being left without an alliance with a firm that would later prove to be the source of a key service or component.

POSITIONING ALLIANCES

The alliance groups in PDAs differed substantially in one respect—the number of marketing or positioning alliances in the group. EO, PenPad, Zoomer, and Sharp each had one such alliance, but Apple had eleven. This points partly to a difference among the firms in ambition and competitive strategy. From the beginning, Apple attempted to make certain components of the Newton into an industry standard, from which it hoped to earn royalties. It also signed on six licensees and four distribution partners in vertical or foreign markets. None of the other firms attempted such a strategy.[3]

One reason Apple stood alone in promoting its technology through alliances lay in the design and alliance choices it had made early on. Apple aimed for a radically new technology and did most of the work internally. Other firms shared the responsibility for developing their PDAs and were more conservative in technology choices. As a result, compared with the other firms, Apple had technologies that could be of greater value when licensed and promoted.

Lotus and Hewlett-Packard represent another approach to collaborative design. Lotus originally thought that it could license the design for a PDA with a built-in spreadsheet and collect royalties, much as Apple aimed to do with the Newton. But in the joint development of the product, HP had funded Lotus's work on the LX and had also paid a handsome royalty for the use of Lotus software. For Lotus to promote the technology as an industry standard would have required breaking the relationship with HP, as HP wanted to keep the technology proprietary. Lotus's dependence on the profitable HP business—and HP's own lack of control over all the pieces of the technology—barred this constellation from pursuing a standards-promotion strategy.

The importance of standards, as well as the high degree of uncertainty in the industry, lies behind many of the links between alliance groups shown in Figure 21. The alliance groups in PDAs were particularly "blurry" at their boundaries, unlike, for example, the groups in the RISC field. The companies that tended to span the boundaries between alliance groups (that is, that belonged to more than one group) tended to be those offering a broad service—such as BellSouth, America Online, and Radiomail—or those with the potential for becoming a standard in PDAs—such as General Magic, GeoWorks, or Intel.

Even this brief sketch indicates how deeply collaboration shaped business rivalry in the emerging PDA industry. No firm competed on its own in this market, and all products were an amalgam of ingredients from allied producers. Alliances were the norm here—as they were in the RISC field—and collaboration became part of the very fabric of competition. This, again, is an extreme case, but it holds lessons for other industries characterized by collective competition. The implications of the alliance revolution for the structure and dynamics of competition are explored in Chapter 5.

Alliances and the Organization
of Industry

When collective competition spreads widely in an industry—as it has in RISC, PDAs, and other high-technology fields—the whole climate of business changes. Competition is restructured and transformed; in the process, rivalry often intensifies, as it did in the industries studied here. This chapter returns to the question posed in the Introduction: the puzzle of how collaboration may enhance—not reduce—competition.

The answer to this puzzle stems from the basic rationale for alliances. As we have seen, firms use alliances to combine capabilities, thus creating a competitive entity that is stronger than the members would be by themselves. Dominant firms seldom do this, but second-tier firms often form alliances to catch up with the leaders. At the same time, the firms that form alliances tend to mimic one another and create units of competition that are more or less evenly matched. All these conditions—stronger competitors, narrower competitive gaps, and less differentiation among players—tend to intensify rivalry in a business.

This does not mean that alliances never suppress rivalry. A key condition for an effective constellation is precisely the suppression of internal competition. Every constellation suppresses rivalry among its members; in that sense, the traditional view of competition and cooperation is correct. The suppression of internal rivalry, however, often translates into fiercer external competition, as constellations marshal the combined resources of their members to compete against other constellations. It is therefore important to recognize the multiple levels in collective competition: alliances always suppress rivalry at one level and often intensify it at another, higher level.

The broad evidence in this book supports this view of how alliances reshape business rivalry. To be sure, alliances may have another effect; they may contribute to the formation of industrywide cartels and to a general reduction in competitive rivalry. But the systematic and anecdotal evidence suggests that these outcomes are exceedingly rare. The mechanisms through which alliances can enhance rivalry are diverse, powerful, and widely applicable.

How Alliances Reshape Industries

The new units of competition created by the alliance revolution are subject to continual reshaping—expansion, contraction, and reorganization. The capabilities and market shares of these competitors change accordingly, rising when new firms are added to the group and falling when there are defections. The organization of an industry consisting only of single firms is likely to be more stable.[1] The potential for rapid shifts in the positions of competitors compounds the uncertainty of business in high-technology industries.

The role of alliances in changing industry dynamics is apparent both in emerging industries and in mature industries undergoing a process of restructuring. In PDAs, for example, a number of rivals were able to launch new products quickly, because each used alliances to provide key inputs it lacked. And because the alliances accelerated the rate at which new products were introduced, they also increased the rate at which earlier product generations became obsolete. This pattern of accelerated product introductions destabilized the rival alliance groups, as firms dissolved old alliances and formed new ones in a process of continual market experimentation.

In mature industries in the process of restructuring, too, alliances allow firms to change position rapidly. The experience of the global chemical industry illustrates this process. When the industry was faced with excess capacity worldwide in the early 1980s, leading companies began to form alliances and mergers. In Europe and Japan this collaboration was in part sanctioned and encouraged by governments, but in the United States the companies acted on their own. Within a few years, they had managed to reduce excess capacity and rationalize production.[2]

Alliances, therefore, reorganize the way capabilities are controlled in an industry. In the process, they reshape rivalry in the industry in two crucial ways. First, they affect the structure of competition—the conditions that influence the degree and pattern of rivalry among incumbent firms. Second, they affect the dynamics of competition—the processes that enable new entry and that determine the pace of change in the industry.

Before considering the effects of alliances on the structure or dynamics of competition, however, a word about methods. The analysis will proceed in two steps. First, we will examine the evidence on the impact of alliances in selected industries. As is often the case when studying economic change, counterfactual analysis must be used here. The actual structure of an industry will be compared with a best guess at what the industry would have looked like were it not transformed by collective competition. This approach will therefore require assumptions and conjectures about what might have been.

The chief source of evidence in this chapter will be the RISC workstation industry; a second source is the PDA industry. We will compare the actual organization of the RISC industry in the early 1990s with what it might have been in the absence of collective competition. The counterfactual case thus assumes that the main firms in the industry—Intel, IBM, Sun, Mips, HP, Motorola—and other minor players did *not* form constellations to promote their technology.

In the absence of any alliances, we will assume, the main competitors in the industry would have been these single firms. In reality, of course, the competitors in the industry were constellations of firms. We will explore whether rivalry among these actual constellations was different from what it might have been among the imagined single firms.

In the second step of the analysis, we will ask whether the differences suggested by this comparison are inherent in the use of constellations, or whether the industry is an exceptional case. Here we will draw on the conceptual arguments developed earlier and look at evidence from other industries. As it turns out, the very logic and dynamics of alliances suggest that the conclusions from our sample are widely applicable.

The Structure of Competition

The intensity of rivalry in a business depends to a great extent on the number and the nature of existing competitors. Most industrial economists and business strategists would agree that rivalry will be most intense when:

· The number of competitors is high;

· The competitors are equally matched in their capabilities;

· The competitors' products are similar (low differentiation);

· The competitors are diverse in their strategies and goals;

· The competitors draw on different national advantages;

· Exit barriers are high; and

· The stakes of the battle are perceived to be high.[3]

The spread of collective competition affects each of these industry conditions. In the industries studied here, the overwhelming impact of these changes has been to increase rivalry: the numbers of competitors increased, the competitors became more evenly matched, product differentiation decreased, and so on. By these measures, collaboration brought with it fiercer competition.

THE NUMBER AND SIZE OF COMPETITORS

All the main competitors in the RISC workstation business entered the field in the second half of the 1980s. Although IBM engineers invented the RISC concept in the late 1970s, the company did not pursue it commercially until after Mips had introduced the first commercial RISC chip in 1985.[4] Sun, HP, Intel, Motorola, and Intergraph[5] all introduced their own RISC architectures in the late 1980s. But DEC did not do so until 1992, having relied on Mips technology up to that point.

Two sets of capabilities were required for commercializing these technologies. The first set were capabilities involved in designing and manufacturing microprocessors; the second were those involved in designing, manufacturing, and selling microcomputer systems embodying the RISC chip.

The leading RISC firms varied by their in-house mastery of the requisite capabilities. Those that lacked sufficient internal capabilities sought allies that could supply the needed inputs. In order to judge the impact of these alliances on the structure of the industry, therefore, we need to compare the capabilities of the lead firms with and without their allies.

Figure 23 shows the size distribution of the competitors in the RISC industry in 1991, measured by the value of their production of all kinds of semiconductors (left-hand panels) and their sales of microcomputer systems (right-hand panels). These measures are proxies for the overall capabilities and assets of the competitors in these two segments of the RISC business. The top panels of Figure 23 indicate the capabilities of the lead firms without their allies; the bottom panels indicate the total capabilities of the members of the actual constellations. In other words, the "competitors" in the top panels are always single firms. In the bottom panel, most of the competitors are constellations; only Intel competed as a single firm.

An important caveat is in order here, similar to one issued in Chapter 3. The fact that we are adding the capabilities of members of a constellation to get a measure of the total pool of capabilities of the group does not mean that the group used this pool effectively. Depending on the structure of a constellation, it may be more or less successful in exploiting the scale offered by the group. Differences among these structures, of course, are essential elements in collective competition. Still, the sum of capabilities of members indicates the potential pool available to well-organized constellations.

These graphs suggest that, in both semiconductors and systems, the number of competitors was at least as high for the constellations (bottom panels) as it would have been if the lead firms had remained without allies (top panels). In the semiconductor end of the business, there would have been four competitors if the lead firms did not form alliances; in fact, there were five competitors. In the systems business, the number of competitors remained the same. Collaboration, therefore, did not reduce the number of competitors in the RISC business.

The effect of collaboration on the size distribution of the competitors is perhaps more important than the sheer number of players. The degree of rivalry in a business depends on how many firms there are of roughly equal capabilities. Visual inspection of Figure 23 suggests that the competitors would have been less evenly matched if the lead firms did not form alliances (top panels) than they in fact were (bottom panels). A few ratios confirm this impression.

Without alliances, the largest firm measured by semiconductor production would have been IBM, which was 50 percent larger than the

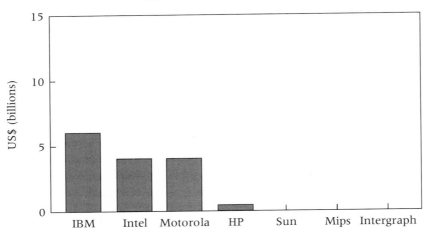

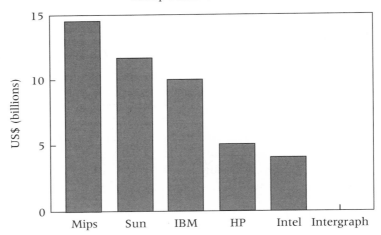

Figure 23 Production scale of RISC competitors with and without allies, 1991. The panels show the total value of production of semiconductors and microcomputer systems. In the top panels, the figures are for the lead firms noted, without any of their alliances. In the bottom panels, the figures are for the sum of the members in each alliance group. In the bottom panels, Motorola is included in the IBM group, and PC-compatible vendors that use Intel chips are not considered Intel "allies" because the Intel chips could be secured through arm's length transactions. Production is measured by value of sales; semiconductor production includes estimates of captive sales; systems production includes sales to OEM customers.
(Sources: Industry press and company annual reports.)

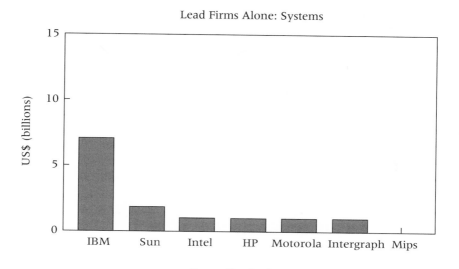

Lead Firms Alone: Systems

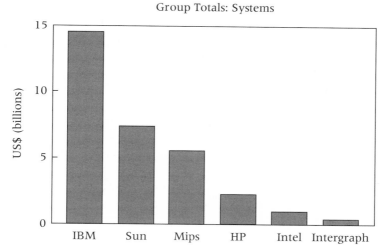

Group Totals: Systems

next largest firm, Intel. When the production of allies is counted, the Mips group was the largest, but by a lesser margin—it was 24 percent larger than the next largest group, Sun's. If systems sales are used as the measure of size, IBM would again have been the number one firm without alliances, being almost four times as large as the number two firm. The systems sales of the IBM *group* were also the largest among the constellations, but its sales were only twice as large as those of the second largest group.[6]

In the RISC industry, therefore, collaboration seems to have increased the number of competitors and generated more equally matched competitors. Can we expect such a result in other industries too, or was this industry an exception?

The analysis in the preceding chapters suggests that the spread of alliances can be expected to have a similar effect in other industries. To see why, we must again consider the typical motivations for forming alliances. Assume that the market shares or production capacities of the firms in an industry are distributed from high to low. Assume also that there are increasing returns to scale. The firms at the top of the size distribution are then likely to be the dominant, or at least the leading firms, and those at the bottom are likely to be the lagging firms. Which type of firm is more likely to form alliances, and how will these alliances change the distribution?

We have seen that dominant firms tend to shun alliances. They have little need of external aid to expand their capabilities. This means that the largest firms in an industry are unlikely to get any larger or more dominant by using alliances. IBM, for example, formed its RISC alliances only after the Mips, Sun, and HP constellations had grown to substantial size.

The small firms, in contrast, will be forced from the beginning to increase their scale, perhaps through collaboration with other small or medium-sized firms. Mips and Sun—the smallest firms in the RISC field—were the first to create constellations. Using alliances, lagging firms are able to close the size gap between themselves and the leaders.

Lagging firms also use alliances to catch up with leaders in other ways, as we have seen. When first-mover advantages and learning economies are important, laggards can narrow the gap with leaders by using alliances to acquire technology and gain experience. Again, the leaders will have a lower incentive to seek alliances than the laggards, because they already have the necessary capabilities and experience.

The distribution of firms by size and experience can thus be expected to become more even, but at the same time we may well see a reduction in the number of competitors. If three small firms coalesce into one constellation, for example, there will be two competitors fewer than before.

In the RISC industry, the number of competitors did not fall, because the firms sought scale economies by forming alliances with new entrants, not with incumbents. In particular, the Japanese semiconductor firms that were included in the RISC constellations had not been a presence in the RISC industry. Still, the alliance between IBM and Motorola was between incumbents, as was the alliance between Sun and Intergraph.

Even when there were alliances between incumbents, however, the resulting constellations did not become dominant. Motorola's position in RISC was weak before it joined IBM; and, although the PowerPC group promised to become powerful, the alliance between IBM and Motorola did not automatically make it so. Intergraph was also weak by the time it allied with Sun; no dominant constellation was created by this move.

Because alliances encourage new entry as well as consolidation among incumbents, the number of competitors may either rise or fall with the spread of alliances. But because weak firms join together more eagerly than do dominant firms, the new competitors will be more evenly matched than the old. Together, these effects suggest that alliances are often likely to increase rivalry.

THE DIVERSITY OF COMPETITORS

The tendency of alliances to narrow the gaps between firms also makes itself felt along competitive dimensions other than size. The spread of collective competition tends to reduce the differences among the product offerings of competitors.

Differences in scope. When economies of scope are important in an industry, narrow-scope firms will tend to form alliances that enable the constellation to match players with broader scope. In the RISC industry, the clearest example of this effect is found in the way alliances transformed the "vertical scope" of the competitors. There were several parts to the RISC business, as noted, including the development, manufacture, and sale of both microprocessors and systems. Some of the competitors were primarily semiconductor vendors (Motorola and Intel), some were vertically integrated firms (IBM and HP), and at least one (Sun) was purely a systems vendor.

Without alliances, there would have been great differences in the vertical scope of the competitors, as shown in the top panel of Figure 24. The constellations of allied firms, however, were much more evenly matched in this regard, as the bottom panel indicates. Alliances thus narrow this gap too—they lower the differences among the product portfolios of competitors.

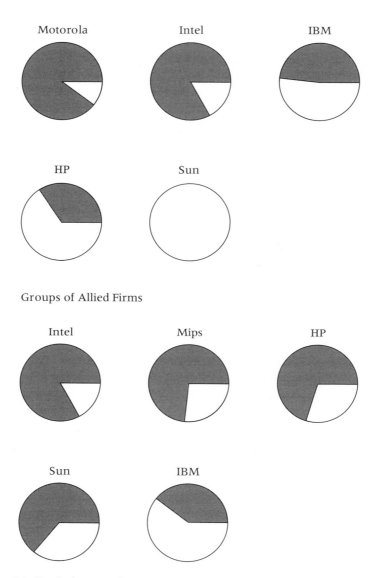

Figure 24 Vertical scope of RISC competitors with and without their alliances (by value of production), 1991. The black segments indicate shares of semiconductors in total production; the white, shares of systems. See Figure 23 and surrounding text for further details on methods.
(Sources: Industry press and company annual reports.)

This pattern in the RISC industry is likely to reflect a more general phenomenon. Firms seek allies with complementary capabilities. The firms that cannot exploit economies of scope internally will seek to do so through alliances. Consider other examples of this pattern:

- The PDA field required complementary capabilities from the computer, telecommunications, and consumer electronics fields. As a result, most of the constellations that developed the first PDAs in the early 1990s contained firms from each of these fields.

- The globalization of the airline industry in the 1990s required that competitors serviced American, European, and Asian markets. As a result, the constellations that emerged included firms from each region. The global alliance among Swissair, Delta Airlines, and Singapore Airlines is an example.

- The role of scope economies has been growing in the automobile industry as well. After the oil crises of the 1970s, U.S. firms found it valuable to sell small, fuel-efficient cars in addition to their traditional offerings. GM and Ford each formed alliances with Asian firms to acquire these cars. In the 1990s, these firms saw benefits in offering European-style luxury models, and each formed alliances for this purpose.

In all these cases, the alliances transformed the competitors in the industry, making their product portfolios more alike. This decreasing differentiation among competitors tended to intensify rivalry in the industry.

Differences in strategies. Even in collective competition, however, there remain important differences among competitors. The size and structure of the constellations are likely to differ, as we have seen. Furthermore, the leading firms in the constellations may differ substantially from one another. As a result, the goals and strategies of the constellations are likely to vary more than in the case of closely matched single firms. Here, diversity among competitors—not similarity—sharpens competitive battles.

What could be more different, for example, than the large, sprawling constellation formed around tiny Mips and the small, tight-knit constellation formed around IBM, Apple, and Motorola? From the beginning, Mips was different from its competitors in that it had no CISC business to defend; this accounts partly for its aggressiveness in pushing RISC products. Only traditional players like IBM, HP, Motorola, and Intel would have been able to compete in the RISC field without using alliances—and all had important CISC businesses to protect. From this perspective, Mips and, to a lesser extent, Sun were the "outsiders" that upset the balance that might have existed among the traditional incumbents.

The constellations in the PDA field were similarly diverse in their leadership and goals. In this case, the differences revolved around their vision of the PDA product. The groups led by telecommunications firms typically saw PDAs as sophisticated cellular phones and stressed communication features in their designs; the groups led by computer firms saw PDAs as extensions of portable computers and stressed data processing and data entry. These product trajectories seemed to converge over time, as one camp added features of the other. But the diversity of approaches and goals made for particularly intense competition.

Differences in nationalities. The spread of alliances often has one more important effect on the nature of competitors in an industry: it often enables the competitors to draw on capabilities rooted in different nations.

All the leading RISC firms were based in the United States, but their constellations typically included members from Europe and Asia (see Table 12). If the firms were to compete without alliances, they could only have drawn on U.S.-based capabilities or on capabilities in those countries where they had subsidiaries. For IBM and HP, this would not have been much of a handicap, as both had extensive foreign investments. But Mips and Sun were much more dependent on their U.S. locations, and would have had to invest abroad to gain access to foreign capabilities. It is not surprising that these two firms were eager to form foreign alliances—these ties gave them a way to match the multinational configuration of IBM and HP.

The alliances of Sun and Mips, and to a lesser extent those of IBM and HP, thus facilitated the globalization of the industry. Because of the multinational scope of the RISC constellations, their competitive advantages could come from multiple sources across the globe. As a result, competition among the constellations is likely to have been more intense than if the players were confined to a U.S. base of operations.

Table 12   Nationalities of main allies in RISC groups, 1992

United States	Asian	European
	Mips Group	
Mips Computer Systems	Daewoo	Bull[b]
DEC	Kubota	Nixdorf
LSI Logic	NEC	Olivetti
Prime	Sony	Siemens
SGI	Toshiba[a]	
	Sun Group	
Sun Microsystems	C-Itoh	ICL
AT&T	Fujitsu	Philips
Cypress	Goldstar	
LSI Logic	Matsushita	
Tandon	Nippon Steel	
Texas Instruments	Toshiba[a]	
UNISYS		
	HP Group	
Hewlett-Packard	Hitachi	Winbond
Convex	MELCO	
Sequoia	Oki	
Stratus	Samsung	
	IBM Group	
IBM		Bull[b]
Apple		CSF-Thomson
Motorola		
Sears		
Wang		

Source: Interviews.

a. Toshiba's semiconductor division was allied with Mips; the systems division was allied with Sun.

b. Bull left the Mips group in mid-1992 and joined the IBM group.

This pattern is likely to hold in other industries too. Alliances diversify the national origins of competitors in an industry, because firms often seek foreign allies to enter foreign markets or to gain access to foreign factors of production. Indeed, antitrust regulation and the greater likelihood of overlapping businesses among domestic firms may make international alliances more attractive than domestic ones. The spread of alliances therefore often leads to more competitors with global scope.

EXIT BARRIERS

Alliances shape not only the distribution and type of competitors in an industry but also their perception of the urgency of the competitive battle. In particular, alliances increase barriers to exit for constellations. Barriers to exit are the costs a competitor would incur if it were to leave an industry. High exit barriers keep firms in an industry that would otherwise have left; these firms are likely to fight more fiercely than others, because their alternatives are so grim.[7] Constellations may "stay and fight" in situations where single firms would have exited.

This claim appears to contradict our earlier findings about the instability of constellations. If alliance relationships are so fluid and prone to breaking at the slightest pressure, why would they increase barriers to exit? The answer is that while the barriers to exit for the individual members of a constellation may not be high, those for a constellation as a whole usually are, especially if the constellation is composed of many members.

The high exit barriers facing large constellations stem from the fact that the groups are webs of interlocking alliances. If there are only two members in the constellation, there is only one alliance to break, and the survival of the constellation will be just as weak as this one alliance. Such a pair, therefore, effectively exits a business when one or both firms decide to exit. With three members, however, there are often three alliances in the web; with four members, there may well be six alliances; with five members, there may be ten alliances, and so on. Furthermore, in large constellations, every member will develop an allegiance to the group as a whole, and the group may be governed collectively. Breaking one alliance in a group does not eliminate the group as a whole—members can exit the group, but the group survives.

The evidence from the RISC industry supports this contention. Even though competition has been fierce, only two competitors have exited the industry; both were RISC firms with few alliances. Motorola and Fairchild were among the first firms to announce a commercial RISC microprocessor in the late 1980s. For different reasons, both chips failed to gain momentum and allegiance from a substantial group of users. Fairchild sold its "Clipper" technology to Intergraph, which maintained the technology for a few years and then ultimately switched to Sun's SPARC chip. Motorola abandoned its own 88K chip when it joined IBM in developing the PowerPC chip. When Intergraph abandoned Clipper, there were no major allies to keep the technology alive. When Motorola stopped work on the 88K, a small group of allies—including Data General, which had built a substantial business on the 88K—maintained the 88Open Association for a while, but ultimately abandoned that effort as well.

The history of the Mips constellation is replete with examples of loose alliances that broke up under competitive pressure. But through it all, the Mips constellation survived—even after Mips itself was gone.

DEC, Bull, and Olivetti were important and early Mips allies, but one after the other they left the group in 1992. The scores of firms that joined the ACE initiative in 1991 left just as quickly as they had signed up. Exit barriers for these members of the constellation were not high.

Those members that had made substantial and dedicated investments in Mips technology, however, faced higher exit barriers. Silicon Graphics was one such firm. It had built a whole line of successful workstations on the Mips chip and expected to differentiate itself from other workstation vendors through continued development of this technology. When Mips began to flounder in 1992, SGI acquired the company.

This acquisition could have been the end of the Mips constellation, but it was not. Even though SGI had little interest in the low end of the Mips market, it found that some existing Mips allies—including NEC and Toshiba—remained committed to that business. These allies had signed contracts with Mips guaranteeing them access to future technologies. Such contractual promises had been one way that Mips had assured its allies that it was committed to long-term relationships. Now these promises helped ensure that the constellation would survive. Even in 1995, therefore, the Mips group remained a significant player in the RISC market.

Alliances thus generate competitors that in many ways have greater staying power than individual firms. This too makes the competitive battle among sets of allied firms more intense than it would be for single firms.

The Dynamics of Competition

Alliances reshape not only the structure but also the dynamics of competition. Most industries are continually changing as new firms enter the field, new products and technologies are introduced, and competitors jockey for position and advantage. The pace and direction of these changes are greatly influenced by alliances.

The dynamics of competition are in part influenced by the extent of barriers to entry—factors that make it costly or difficult for a new player to enter the industry. Similar factors may also constrain the ability of an existing firm to reposition itself in an industry, say, by moving to compete in a different market segment; these factors are then called barriers to mobility.[8] Costs that typically represent barriers to entry and mobility are scale and scope requirements, access to distribution channels, and any large advantages of incumbents, including first-mover advantages and control over unique resources and proprietary technologies. Alliances affect each of these barriers.

The dynamics of competition are also influenced by the pace of innovation. New products and technologies can upset the existing structure of an industry and the relationships between competitors. There is a long and unresolved debate in economics regarding the conditions that encourage innovation.[9] I will not address that broad question here, but will focus on the narrower question of how alliances affect the pace of innovation in an industry.

THE PARADOX OF "BARRIERS TO COLLABORATION"

Alliances have paradoxical effects on barriers to entry. The option of collaborating, taken by itself, tends to reduce entry barriers—it facilitates entry by helping firms expand their capabilities or share the capabilities of incumbents. But once the practice of collaboration spreads widely in an industry, the web of alliances raises new barriers—it blocks entry by foreclosing further opportunities for sharing capabilities.

The two-stage process whereby alliances first lower and then raise barriers to entry leads to intense competition over partnerships in the first stage. Firms considering entry will feel pressure to do so quickly, lest their options for partnerships be foreclosed by other entrants. At the same time, if these firms manage to "lock up" attractive partners, they will be on the other side of that table—they will be able to profit by foreclosing further entry.

Alliances may thus enhance rivalry by generating a special kind of competition. This competition revolves around what I call "barriers to collaboration"—the costs of forming and maintaining alliances. Firms entering the first stage will later seek to raise barriers to collaboration for those that follow them. These barriers serve as proxies for barriers to entry: they deter entry by deterring collaboration.

Although the prospect of rising barriers to collaboration may enhance rivalry, the barriers themselves limit the growth in the number of competitors in the second stage. Like traditional barriers to entry, barriers to collaboration lead to an industry structure in which a few incumbents compete with each other while being protected from new entry. This protection from unlimited entry can generate profits and raise the competitive stakes for the incumbents. High stakes, in turn, may become further drivers for intensified competition, especially when they are paired with the high exit barriers common in collective competition.

Access to markets and capabilities. The most direct way in which alliances can affect barriers to entry is by first facilitating and then blocking access to markets and capabilities. An alliance that grants a firm privileged access to another's market or capability typically involves some degree of commitment and dedicated investments among the partners. These investments generate the costs of switching partners—another form of barrier to collaboration.

We have already seen how a small firm like Mips could enter the RISC industry by using allies to supplement its own meager resources. Even though Mips was the first to introduce a commercial RISC microprocessor, it did not acquire substantial first-mover advantages. Large firms in related industries could easily refashion their existing channels and assets to produce RISC chips, if they chose to do so. IBM, HP, and even Sun had substantial advantages by virtue of their incumbency in the CISC field. In this context, the Mips alliances with DEC, Siemens, NEC, and others facilitated its entry by giving it access to the market channels and production capabilities of other CISC incumbents.

At the same time, these moves by Mips raised new barriers to mobility for the CISC incumbents—the costs of entering the RISC field increased when Mips created a global alliance network. In order for IBM, HP, and Sun to move into the RISC field, they, too, would need to form alliances with regionally based Japanese and European firms and with American firms that could offer either special technologies or markets. As each did this, they created multinational constellations.

By the early 1990s, these constellations had grown so much that there were few viable partners left unattached. At that point, the web of alliances became a serious barrier to entry to newcomers—in particular, to DEC. This web of alliances reflected commitments among users, suppliers, and buyers; changing an alliance partner typically involved a cost of switching. The Alpha chip introduced by DEC in 1993 won accolades for its raw power and technical sophistication, but it gained market share slowly because most large users—other than DEC itself—were already committed to other RISC chips. Alliances here deterred entry.

The comparison between Mips and DEC is an excellent illustration of the paradoxical effects of alliances on barriers to entry. Mips used alliances to enter the industry; DEC was blocked from entry by alliances. The difference between the two was timing: Mips entered in the stage when barriers to collaboration were still low, and DEC entered in the later stage when these barriers had risen.

Scale and scope requirements. Barriers to entry rose in the RISC field not only because partners were locked up but also because the formation of large constellations raised the requirements of scale and scope in the industry. The data used earlier in the analysis of the number and size of competitors are pertinent here. Figure 23 indicates the increase in scale requirements and Figure 24 gives one measure of the increase in scope requirements.

Without its alliances, the largest RISC firm based on the value of its annual semiconductor production was IBM at $6 billion; the median for these firms—again without alliances—was $4 billion (calculated from Figure 23, top left graph). If we include alliances and measure the total annual semiconductor production of the RISC groups, the largest constellation was that of Mips ($14.5 billion) and the median was $10 billion (Figure 23, bottom left graph). Measuring scale by the size of the systems businesses of the firms and constellations gives a similar result; the median there was $1 billion for firms alone and $4 billion for the constellations (Figure 23, top and bottom right graphs).

These rough estimates suggest that the scale of operations of the RISC constellations was larger than the scale of the lead firms competing as single entities would have been. This does not mean that the larger scale was absolutely required for effective competition, of course; we have no data on the degree of penalty imposed by small size. Furthermore, the constellations surely could not draw on their total pool of capabilities as effectively as would a single firm. Yet it is likely that a constellation with a larger overall pool of capabilities would have an advantage over one relying on a narrower base.

A similar argument applies to scope requirements—the need for competitors to make and sell a variety of products. The measure of scope used in Figure 24 was the degree to which a competitor was involved in both semiconductors and systems businesses. The groups of allies were fairly evenly active in both fields; if competing by themselves, the lead firms would have been more specialized, either on semiconductors (for example, Motorola) or on systems (for example, Sun).

As alliances spread in this industry, therefore, they first facilitated entry and then raised scale and scope requirements, two traditional barriers to entry. Ultimately, this made entry by single firms less likely and, at the same time, foreclosed further opportunities for entry through alliances.

THE PACE OF INNOVATION

Because collaboration facilitates learning and technology transfer, firms often use alliances to shorten the development time of their new products. As a result, technology races can lead to alliance races in which rivals vie for partnerships that might give them an edge in innovation. This strategy, too, is contagious—alliances can spread among rivals and ultimately quicken the pace of innovation.

A good example of this process is the role that development alliances played in the PDA industry. Virtually every competitor in that industry used alliances to design, make, and sell its product. Some of the lead firms could have undertaken these tasks internally, but that would have taken longer. Instead they rushed to market with products assembled from the existing technologies of their partners.

When HP and Lotus collaborated on the 95LX, for example, each contributed tried-and-true technologies and skills. Lotus had the dominant spreadsheet on the market and a great deal of experience with DOS-based software. HP was the market leader in high-end calculators and had a burgeoning business in small computers. Furthermore, these partners used Microsoft's well-established MS-DOS operating system and Intel's standard 8086 microprocessor. These allies still had to collaborate intensively to make all these pieces of the puzzle fit together, but they were not inventing major new pieces. The product was developed and launched in about sixteen months, which executives at HP and Lotus considered a short time-to-market.

At the other extreme, firms that aimed to introduce a radically new technology frequently relied more on internal development efforts. Apple is the best example of this model. Most of the features of the Newton MessagePad were new to the market, and Apple's previous experience was only loosely related to the work behind the Newton. Even though Apple and Sharp collaborated in the design of the product, most of the new technologies came from inside Apple. The development of the first MessagePad took longer than that of the 95LX. Apple first invested in ARM—the supplier of the Newton's central processing unit—in November 1990, almost three years before the Newton was launched. By then Apple had already begun internal research on PDA technology.

In the PDA industry, the use of alliances in product development coincided with great market uncertainty and experimentation. A parade of new products burst on the market in 1993, but the excitement died down just as rapidly. By late 1994 only a trickle of new products was still making it to the market, and the rush was gone. Although the early alliances enabled firms to move rapidly, they did not guarantee success.

Still, the evidence suggests that when alliances speed up product design and launch, they also accelerate the rate of experimentation in the industry and shorten product life cycles. Other scholars have also noted that alliances can increase innovation. Suppliers that were dependent on a large buyer, for example, were found to be more willing to innovate than independent suppliers, provided that they knew what innovations the buyer wanted.[10] The Japanese *keiretsu* structure has been found to aid innovation by providing linkages between users and producers, and by supporting new ventures with resources of established firms.[11] In various economic models, as well, joint ventures and joint R&D projects increase the rate and diffusion of innovation in an industry.[12]

As the pace of innovation in an industry increases, however, existing alliances may become unstable; in the PDA industry, for example, firms dropped and added partners to pursue new experiments. Collaboration allows firms greater flexibility in responding to market feedback. Ironically, alliances make the environment less "patient" and forgiving of failure by speeding up the race. But they themselves are likely to be the first casualty of the greater rivalry between experiments. AT&T's Eo, for example, was one of the first products to be withdrawn from the market after poor sales. AT&T then chose to liquidate its PDA business because it could not obtain sufficient commitment from its partners to maintain the constellation.

The experimental nature of the PDA constellations made them inherently less stable than the RISC and other alliances we have examined. This instability meant that the industry's structure was subject to continual change, as constellations appeared and disappeared. Capabilities could be rapidly assembled and disassembled in pursuit of new experiments. Collaboration in this industry thus did not stabilize and moderate competition, as cartels and collusive arrangements typically do. Instead, collective competition helped make the industry even more chaotic.

Competition and Collusion through Alliances

The evidence and analysis in this book thus strongly suggest that alliances have enhanced business rivalry in the cases and industries examined. Other empirical studies have come to conclusions that support this contention. Studies of the aluminum and semiconductor industries found that joint ventures or alliances facilitated entry; another study found that the composition of business groups in France promoted rivalry rather than collusion; and yet another found no evidence of anticompetitive effects in a large cross-section of industries.[13]

But these results run counter to the mainstream economic view that cooperation among firms reduces competition, a view supported by a well-established literature.[14] How can these two views of cooperation be reconciled with each other?

One way to reconcile them is by recognizing that the degree of competition in a market depends on many variables other than cooperation among firms. High-technology business, in particular, is continually buffeted by a stream of new innovations and by the rise of new entrepreneurial firms. Furthermore, the global integration of markets has brought competitors from different nations face to face and has increased the sheer size of the relevant market. As a result, what might have been a collusive arrangement in a narrower market is now part of a much wider arena with more players. Alliances, one might argue, are just one aspect of this dynamic world—by themselves they are unlikely to reduce rivalry.

It is, of course, true that competition is affected by a multitude of variables. But this way of reconciling our findings with the traditional view skirts the issue. It does not explain the effect of alliances, saying merely that the effect is immaterial.

Another way to reconcile the two views is to say that because alliances often promote innovation and learning, they intensify dynamic competition, even if they suppress competition in a static sense. In other words, they may help firms race for new technologies and vie for new customers, albeit at the cost of collusion and higher prices in today's markets. Indeed, the alliances studied here often aimed to develop new products and markets, and so definitely enhanced dynamic competition. This argument, therefore, is also borne out by the evidence, and it is supported by a wider literature.[15]

The third way to reconcile our findings with the traditional view is by recognizing the possibility that cooperation on one level might enhance rivalry on another level. This is the mark of collective competition. It is conceivable, of course, that cooperation among firms might also create a constellation that dominates an industry or engages in collusion with other firms and constellations. Yet we have seen few instances of alliances that were created for collusive and anticompetitive purposes. Why is that? The answer to this question helps reconcile our findings with the traditional economic view of interfirm cooperation.

PURPOSES OF CONSTELLATIONS

Our definition of an alliance certainly does not limit it to purposes that enhance competition; it is defined only by a structure—an incomplete contract between separate firms involving shared control. In theory, therefore, an alliance could aim to exploit the joint market power of its members. That is, after all, what one would expect in the traditional view.

All constellations suppress competition between their partners. There may be two motives for doing so, each giving rise to a distinct class of constellations.

First, a constellation may suppress internal competition to facilitate learning or to exploit synergies in complementary capabilities. In the end, costs of production may be lowered and the collusion among partners may benefit the firms as well as their buyers. I call these "synergistic constellations."

Second, a constellation may suppress competition in order to exploit the additional market power generated by cooperation. In the extreme case, the partners would not aim to learn from each other, combine their complementary capabilities, or try to best their competitors—they would simply coordinate output, prices, and marketing to maximize their joint power over buyers. I call these "anticompetitive constellations."

The puzzle to be addressed is why we see so few anticompetitive compared with synergistic constellations. Why do we not see more constellations created in the pursuit of dominance? Some are, in fact, created for that purpose. But they often do not last beyond the point of achieving their goal.

The well-known alliance of IBM, Microsoft, and Intel to create a PC architecture in the early 1980s is an example of this pattern. Apple dominated the market before IBM's entry, but the IBM PC constellation quickly gained market share and grew to dominate the standards in the industry. The alliance itself, however, did not last, as IBM first broke with Microsoft and later distanced itself from Intel. Microsoft and Intel maintained a close working relationship, but Microsoft's involvement in ACE and its encouragement of alternatives to Intel chips signified an attempt to reduce its dependence on the Intel. Although this constellation achieved a measure of industry dominance, the group itself was not sustainable; instead, key members of the group broke off to exploit their market power separately.[16]

Another example of cooperation to pursue dominance, with a slightly different outcome, is the constellation created by JVC to promote its VHS videocassette standard. Here again, another firm—Sony—had dominated the market when JVC entered. And again the new constellation—which included the giants Matsushita and RCA—ultimately won the standards battle.[17] In this case, however, the VHS constellation included so many licensees that none gathered much market power from participation in the group. Internal competition in the constellation limited the gains that individual members could garner from their collective "dominance" of the industry.[18] Again, industry dominance by an alliance group proved unsustainable. Why?

To determine why a constellation's dominance might not last, we may consider how a merger of firms—as opposed to an alliance—might approach the task of sustaining dominance. Economists have recognized that mergers too can have either synergistic or anticompetitive effects.[19] Both organizational forms combine the capabilities of two or more firms and create structures for joint decision making. But mergers create a structure for unified control; alliances create one for shared control. This difference between mergers and alliances is crucial in understanding the uses of each organizational form.

The shared control in alliances makes it difficult for them to deal with internal conflict. Conflicts of interest between partners tend to break alliances, as we have seen. A merger may also encounter conflict between the previously separate parties, but it can use central authority to resolve these conflicts and enforce cooperation. A merger is thus less likely to fall apart over the type of conflict that can destroy a constellation. This "comparative advantage" of mergers over alliances increases as the level of conflict between the parties increases.

Even though there have been no studies comparing the degree of conflict between parties in mergers and alliances, there is some evidence to support this argument. One study found that overlapping geographic markets between partners led to poor performance in alliances, but success in mergers. Another found that the most successful mergers were those with the greatest amount of overlap in business lines and markets.[20] Overlapping markets and businesses are classic sources of conflict and internal competition in alliances. It appears that mergers were much better at dealing with these conditions than alliances; for them, the overlaps were opportunities for rationalizing operations.

The notion of different degrees of conflict in the relations between parties is formalized by economists in a series of "games" with different payoffs to cooperation.

The famous Prisoner's Dilemma represents a case of extreme conflict between players. In this game, each player gets the highest payoff when he refuses to cooperate and the other player cooperates. In addition, each gets the lowest payoff if he cooperates and the other player does not. Without the assurance that the other will cooperate, therefore, the players will each follow their private interests and refuse to cooperate.

At the other end of the scale are games with less conflict; in one type of game, for example, each player always benefits from cooperating, whether or not the other player follows suit. In other games, the payoff of mutual cooperation is higher than that of unilateral cooperation, but each player still has a greater incentive not to cooperate. Finally, there are games in which cooperation simply does not pay.[21]

Students of international politics have long recognized that under some conditions it is natural for nations to cooperate, in others it is futile to think of cooperation, and in still others it is difficult but worthwhile to try to achieve cooperation.[22] Students of alliances have recently begun to recognize that interfirm relations, too, can have different degrees of conflict.[23]

Loose alliances are a poor way to implement cooperation involving payoff structures with high degrees of conflict. Reputation, lengthy time horizons, third-party relations, and other mechanisms will help solidify such an alliance, but the structure will be prone to breaking under the pressure of internal competition.

MEETING THE CHALLENGES OF COOPERATION

The two purposes of cooperation already identified—synergy and collusion—generate different degrees of conflict among the parties. In particular, cooperation for the purposes of synergy is likely to have lower degrees of conflict than cooperation for anticompetitive purposes.

Anticompetitive cooperation. To see why there are different payoff structures associated with these two purposes, it is useful to examine two classic cases. First, consider a case of anticompetitive cooperation—a cartel formed to raise prices to buyers. The Organization of Petroleum Exporting Countries (OPEC) is a recent and well-known example. OPEC could achieve its aims without exploiting any synergy among its members. The members did not transfer technology to each other, rationalize operations, or lower their costs through cooperation; they simply agreed to limit output and raise prices.

The payoff structure facing each member of this cartel, however, created a Prisoner's Dilemma.[24] By joining together to restrict output, the OPEC countries raised the world price of oil. But this increased price also benefited non-OPEC producers, such as Mexico, which did not have to follow the cartel's restrictions on output. By the same token, each OPEC member had an incentive to underprice its partners—secretly, if at all possible—because doing so would increase its sales at the expense of the others without seriously lowering the cartel's price umbrella. Yet if they each did that, the cartel would lose effectiveness. That is, of course, what eventually happened.

The essence of the OPEC game—as well as of most other cartels—was that each party could benefit from the cooperative effort without actually cooperating, a phenomenon economists call "free riding." But if all members choose to free ride, no benefits are generated. As one review concluded: "A cartel therefore contains the seeds of its own destruction."[25]

Mergers are better at squelching free riding than alliances, and so can implement monopoly pricing better than a cartel.[26] If the OPEC members were one state—or if all their oil resources were owned by only one of them—they would have been able to sustain the high oil prices of the late 1970s much longer. Non-OPEC nations could still undercut them, of course, but the temptation to match these outsiders could have been squelched through a central authority. In short, mergers may be better at collusion than alliances.[27]

Synergistic cooperation. The choices facing firms cooperating for synergistic purposes are likely to involve less internal conflict. Consider this second case: a set of firms cooperating to develop a technology that they will share. Any of the RISC groups is a good example. The dilemma facing the members of such a group is different from that facing the OPEC members. The RISC partners also aimed to create benefits from joint action, but these benefits would accrue only to members of the group, not to nonmembers. If the group developed a cheaper, faster microprocessor or software, only the members of this group would benefit.

The temptation to leave such a group is thus much lower than for members of a price cartel. In general, if one needs to contribute to a group in order to receive group benefits, the private incentive for members to defect will be less. The key assumption here is that the technology developed through collaboration will not be disseminated freely to nonmembers.

This combination of factors yields a simple result. When alliances are used for anticompetitive goals, they are not likely to be up to the task—they may not survive long, or they may simply be ineffective. When they are used for synergistic goals, they will be more effective and last longer. Knowing this, firms will tend to use mergers in anticompetitive strategies and reserve alliances for synergistic strategies. This is the final reason we observe more alliances that enhance competition than alliances that suppress competition.

Conclusion

The alliance revolution transforms not only the players in an industry but the organization of industry itself. Collaboration can systematically change the profile of competitors in an industry. We have seen how it increased the size and number of competitors and made them more evenly matched; it strengthened each competitor even while drawing in partners from disparate backgrounds.

Alliances also typically change the dynamics of competition. Early in the spread of collective competition, our alliances encouraged new entry. But later they raised barriers to entry by tying up sources of technology and access to markets and by raising scale and scope requirements. They also tended to raise the costs of exit, forcing more competitors to stay in the game. Finally, they usually increased the pace of innovation and shortened the life cycle of products.

The net result of these changes was intensified business rivalry. This finding does not rule out the possibility that alliances might be used for anticompetitive purposes, that is, to suppress rivalry and generate monopoly power. But our analysis suggests that mergers have a comparative advantage over alliances when it comes to collusion. Alliances are ill suited for this purpose—they are too fragile and quickly fall apart under the pressures of internal conflict.

This study of alliances thus helps us to resolve the puzzle of why competition persists in the face of cooperation. The answer, it turns out, does not come out of conventional approaches to economics and business strategy. As a result, many conventional arguments may need to be modified to account for the new realities explored in the preceding chapters. The broader implications of these findings are discussed next.

Rethinking Alliances and Rivalry

Our understanding of economic organization is always one step behind the reality. When Adam Smith explained the magic of the division of labor, workshops already used the system. John Maynard Keynes developed his ideas of macroeconomic policy by observing what governments were in fact doing during the Great Depression. In the last few decades, economists and business historians have discovered the role of scale and scope economies in production by studying organizations that began exploiting such economies in the late nineteenth century.

It is proper that reality should guide theory. But this means that we are sometimes faced with economic trends that do not fit neatly in the received wisdom. The alliance revolution is such a trend. The use of alliances has been increasing, although different observers may quibble about definitions and exact numbers. Most business leaders have not yet mastered the management of these organizations, although some are more experienced than others. And, as in other instances, our theoretical understanding lags behind the facts.

The conventional wisdom has treated alliances as an anomaly, but this view is changing. An illustration of this change is the evolution in the thinking of Oliver Williamson, one of the leading scholars on the theory of the firm. His 1975 book painted a stark contrast between markets and hierarchies. He later explained: "I was earlier of the view that transactions in the middle were very difficult to organize and hence unstable." By 1985 he had begun to believe otherwise: "I am now persuaded that transactions in the middle range are much more common." He urged greater study of these middle-range transactions, "to illuminate an understanding of complex organizations."[1] Still, even in that book, as well as in leading textbooks on the economics of organization, business alliances receive scant treatment.[2]

This book has sketched the reality of the alliance revolution and provided a conceptual approach for understanding the phenomenon. I have purposely focused on companies and industries in which this revolution has progressed far—that is, where alliances are common and penetrate every aspect of business. Examining the extreme cases has made it easier to recognize the radical changes wrought by the rise of collective competition.

But the focus on extreme cases means that the conclusions here do not apply equally to every business. The arguments in this book are likely to apply best in complex businesses undergoing rapid change. But there are likely to be cross-industry differences in the way collective competition operates, just as there are differences in patterns of oligopolistic competition. The preceding study of the PDA industry has already suggested that the uncertainty inherent in emerging markets generates a new role for constellations—they are used in market experimentation. The PDA constellations also seem to be more unstable than the RISC constellations, as their fates depend on the outcomes of these experiments.[3]

My conclusions are likely to apply most directly to situations where collective competition dominates an industry, as it has the RISC and PDA fields. Whether or not collective competition dominates in a given business is an empirical matter. One has to look carefully at the competitors in the industry and examine how products are developed, manufactured, and sold. Are alliances important in many parts of the value chain? Is the web of relationships in the industry dense and intricate? Are there few firms left that still compete as single entities, relying mostly on internal capabilities and on arm's length contracts with outsiders? Have constellations changed the terms of competition, such as the scale and scope required for success?

Notwithstanding this book's focus on high-technology businesses, we can expect collective competition to emerge in a wide variety of environments. Other manufacturing sectors have seen a proliferation of alliances in recent decades, as have service sectors. In many cases, the spread of alliances has created rival constellations like those we have examined; often, these constellations contain a large number of members (see Table 13).

Table 13   Selected businesses with collective competition, c. 1994

Business or industry	Selected rival constellations
Hardware and software for interactive TV	• Motorola, Scientific Atlanta, Kaleida • Time Warner, Silicon Graphics • Intel, Microsoft, General Instruments • HP, TV Answer
Video CDs	• Sony and Philips • Toshiba, Time Warner, Matsushita, others
Global telecommunications	• AT&T Worldpartners (includes 12 partners) • British Telecom and MCI • Sprint, Deutsche Telekom, France Telecom
Automobiles and trucks	• GM, Toyota, Isuzu, Suzuki, Volvo • Ford, Mazda, Kia, Nissan, Fiat, VW • Chrysler, Mitsubishi, Daimler-Benz
Biotechnology research	• Genentech network • Centocor network
Pharmaceutical marketing (U.S.)	• Merck and Medco (merger) • SmithKline and DPS (merger) • Eli Lilly and PCS (merger) • Pfizer and Value Health • Pfizer, Rhone Poulenc, Caremark, others
Global airline services	• Delta, Swissair, Singapore Airlines, SAS • KLM and Northwest • British Airways and USAir

Even in those businesses not dominated by collective competition, the framework developed here should be valuable. This book's underlying theme applies practically everywhere in modern business: competition and collaboration have become intimately intertwined.

We began with a focus on collaboration and ended with an analysis of competition. In early chapters we saw why and how firms collaborate; in later ones we learned how this collaboration became an integral part of competition. In the process, we have seen that the alliance revolution alters business rivalry in two basic ways. The first is a change in the firm as an economic unit. Alliances create new units of competition that supersede firms, and on which firms depend for their competitive advantage. The second is a change in the market as an economic environment. The proliferation of alliances generates new

Table 13   (continued)

Business or industry	Selected rival constellations
Global commercial real estate services	• Colliers International (44 companies) • International Commercial (23 companies) • Oncore International (36 companies) • New America Network (150 companies) • Cushman & Wakefield (52 affiliates) • CB Commercial (70 affiliates) • Grubb & Ellis (6 affiliates)

Sources: For interactive television, see "The Living Room War," *Business Week,* June 7, 1993, p. 100. For video CDs, see Jeffrey Trachtenberg, "Sony Alliance with Philips Faces Threat," *Wall Street Journal,* January 23, 1995, pp. A3, A5. For global telecommunications, see "Alliance Networks, Untangled," *Alliance Analyst,* February 3, 1995, pp. 1–5. For automobiles and trucks, see Nitin Nohria and Carlos Garcia-Pont, "Global Strategic Linkages and Industry Structure," *Strategic Management Review* (Summer 1991): 105–124. For biotechnology, see John Freeman and Stephen R. Barley, "The Strategic Analysis of Interorganizational Relations in Biotechnology," in *The Strategic Management of Technological Innovation,* ed. R. Loveridge and M. Pitt (New York: John Wiley, 1990), chap. 6. Pharmaceuticals data based on various press reports; for example, "Eli Lilly Agrees to Restrictions on Buying PCS," *Wall Street Journal,* October 26, 1994, p. A3. For airlines, see John Goodman, "Battle for the Skies: British Airways' Bid for USAir," Harvard Business School Case no. 9-793-059 (rev. 8/93) and "Swissair's Alliances," in David B. Yoffie and Benjamin Gomes-Casseres, *International Trade and Competition: Cases and Notes in Strategy and Management* (New York: McGraw-Hill, 1994). For commercial real estate, see Richard Kindleberger, "Global Reach," *Boston Sunday Globe,* December 4, 1994, pp. A1, A4.

patterns of competition, in which collaboration inside economic units affects their market behavior.

Analyzing Collective Competition

When firms use alliances in competitive battle, the nature of that battle changes. Collective competition exhibits distinctive patterns that do not always fit the mold of existing theory, and thus some of our economic tenets about competition need to be modified or extended to take account of the role of interfirm collaboration. Six central findings of this book have implications for the received wisdom and suggest avenues for further research.

THE SHAPE OF COMPETITORS

The first finding is that *the constellations of allied firms represent new units of competition.* Xerox and Fuji Xerox together competed against Canon, and

Mips and its partners formed a unit—albeit a loose one—that competed against the groups of IBM, HP, and Sun. The alliances among member firms in these constellations are linking and enabling mechanisms—they facilitate joint decision making between the separate firms. But for analytical and practical purposes, it is often useful to focus not on the firms or the alliances but on the totality of the capabilities and resources gathered under the umbrella of the constellation.

To the traditional units of analysis in business economics—such as the firm, the business unit, the market, and the transaction—we should thus add another: sets of allied firms. Admittedly, firms remain the basic unit of accounting in financial markets. But firms are no longer the only—or even the best—way to understand competition; we must alternately think in terms of both units of analysis, the firm and the constellation.[4] Because of the recent proliferation of alliances, constellations are becoming increasingly important, so that more of our thinking must take place at that level.

The second finding follows closely on the first: *The advantage of a constellation compared with a single firm depends on which structure best controls the capabilities required for success in a specific context.* When this context changes over time, the advantages of a given structure will rise or fall. For example, the Xerox constellation succeeded in the 1970s and early 1980s by giving Fuji Xerox a great degree of autonomy; this freedom allowed Fuji Xerox to innovate locally, which eventually helped Xerox fight back the assault from Japanese competitors. But when technology changed and Canon's growth raised the value of global scale, the autonomy of Fuji Xerox had to give way to closer collaboration and integration with Xerox. The changing context of this constellation thus required changes in the way the partners' capabilities were controlled.

At the risk of oversimplifying, it can be said that single firms have the advantage of more unified control, while constellations benefit from more flexible capabilities.[5] We already know that the single firm trades off such unified control against a certain rigidity in its capabilities and a degree of determinism in its evolution. This book has argued that constellations need not be bound by such inertia and "path dependence." Constellations can learn faster, as well as strike out in new directions, by adding and dropping partners as needed. But the constellation achieves this flexibility at the cost of split control and some loss of coordination.

Because of these trade-offs, *the specific design of a constellation helps determine its competitive advantage*. That is the third finding. Group-based advantages stem from the capabilities of all the firms in the group and from how the group is structured. In the RISC industry, every group tried to include some members that were strong in semiconductor production and others that were leaders in systems and in software. Furthermore, the most effective groups created an organizational structure that promoted collaboration between these members, rather than intragroup competition. Constellations with substantial internal friction—whether they were the large RISC groups or the simpler U.S.-Japan alliances—usually performed less well than others.

The importance of constellation design suggests that modern competitors cannot be treated as black boxes if we are fully to understand their behavior in the market. The black-box approach to firms, while still common, is fortunately beginning to fade in economics, as scholars examine the implications of internal control mechanisms on the external behavior of firms. The findings here complement these studies by emphasizing that the control mechanisms among *a set of firms* can affect their joint competitiveness. And because each member claims a share of the benefits of the group, every firm's performance will depend on the design of the group.

These three findings relate to the ways in which the rise of constellations modifies the shape of competitors. These ideas constitute the beginnings of a theory of constellations, which needs to be formalized and tested further.

PATTERNS OF COMPETITION

The final three findings are consequences of the changing shape of competitors just discussed. These conclusions have more to do with the market as a whole, and they suggest how the alliance revolution changes the competitive environment in an industry. Alliances are born of the competitive environment; but, as they spread, they also *become* the environment.

Finding number four is that *rivalry among a few competitors drives the spread of collaboration*. In both the RISC and the PDA industries, leading firms adopted alliance strategies partly in reaction to one another, and constellations often grew rapidly in what appeared to be races to attract new partners. More generally, whenever alliances are thought to yield substantial value in a competitive battle, rivals can be expected to compete for the most attractive partners. To reduce risk, close rivals might then imitate one another's alliance moves, and some will even try to preempt others from forming valuable alliances.

Collective competition thus exhibits the type of reactive strategies that are common in other forms of oligopolistic markets. But instead of competing over resources and markets—as oligopolistic firms frequently do—the constellations we studied often competed over partners. These partners were a proxy, so to speak, for resources and markets. Partnerships may play this role in other industries too, particularly where potential partners have control over key capabilities or privileged access to markets. These dynamics provide a logic behind what has appeared to some to be an alliance "fad."

We also saw the other side of this so-called fad: *There are limits to the size of an effective constellation and to the spread of alliances in an industry.* This is the fifth finding; taken together with the preceding one, it implies that constellations can grow past a point of diminishing returns. Some of the RISC groups subsidized their own expansion to pursue scale advantages. This expansion itself generated a bandwagon effect, as additional partners were attracted to the growing constellations. In the Mips constellation, however, rapid growth also brought increasing costs of internal coordination, which ultimately limited the group's effectiveness and helped precipitate its collapse.

These limits to the use of alliances have much in common with the limits to the growth and diversification of firms. Alliances can be viewed as a substitute for the internal growth of a firm, because they leverage the resources of a firm in expanding into new activities.[6] Such leveraged expansion, however, is not without cost. Many companies will face limits to the number of alliances that they can manage effectively. Furthermore, even though the available data suggest that alliances have been spreading through and across industries, there are likely to be limits to this trend in any given field.

Notwithstanding these limits to growth, *the spread of collective competition transforms the structure and dynamics of an industry and often intensifies rivalry.* This sixth finding is the consequence of the combination of changes that alliances bring with them. In the case of the RISC industry, collective competition seems to have intensified competition as measured by several indicators. Weaker firms gained strength through alliances, so that the competing constellations were more evenly matched than they would have been in the absence of alliances. At the same time, the constellations tended both to facilitate entry and to increase barriers to exit. In the PDA field we observed another competition-enhancing effect. Because constellations could assemble capabilities rapidly, the pace of new product introductions increased and product life cycles were shortened.[7]

This last finding may have important implications for both economic theory and public policy. Traditionally, economists and antitrust authorities have often assumed that interfirm collaboration suppresses competition. The questions they have usually asked in evaluating a merger or alliance, for example, have been whether the potential reduction in competition was serious and whether there were any compensating benefits.[8] The evidence in this book suggests that, first, alliances may be quite different from mergers in terms of their anticompetitive potential. Alliances are fragile organizations and tend to fall apart under the internal conflicts that are typical of anticompetitive collusion. Second, alliances may enhance competition by narrowing the gaps between leaders and second-tier competitors.

Taken together, these findings imply that alliances are more than just a tool of competitive strategy or an anomaly at the boundary of the firm, as previous studies have suggested. When alliances proliferate in an industry, as they have in the cases studied and in many others, they alter the shape of competitors and the pattern of rivalry. In this way, collaboration is woven into the very fabric of competition.

Managing Alliance Strategies

The intimate connection between cooperation and competition suggests that our practical approach to business strategy needs to change. The nature of collaboration within a constellation, as we have seen, helps determine the group's competitive advantage. Two implications for strategy follow. First, by *exploiting barriers to collaboration,* firms may interfere with a rival's alliances and so place the rival at a disadvantage. Second, firms that *build and manage their constellations* more effectively than others may have an edge in the marketplace.

EXPLOITING BARRIERS TO COLLABORATION

In the traditional approach to competitive strategy, the notion of barriers to entry or to mobility is central. By raising these barriers, incumbent firms can keep potential competitors at bay and exploit market power. When rivals can gain advantage through collaboration, however, another type of barrier can be used: barriers to collaboration. Anything that makes it costly to form and manage an alliance successfully constitutes a barrier to collaboration.

Like barriers to entry, barriers to collaboration are not absolute prohibitions to potential competitors—but they make life more difficult and more costly for them. And, like their traditional counterparts, barriers to collaboration are not always amenable to change through the actions of incumbents. But there are at least three strategies that a constellation can use to raise barriers to collaboration for a rival constellation. These strategies address the three elements of the framework introduced at the beginning of this book: capabilities, control, and context.

Military strategists have known for ages how important barriers to collaboration can be. For Sun Tzu, the famous Chinese military strategist, one of the first moves in war was: "Disrupt his alliances." His commentator Tu Yu added: "Do not allow your enemies to get together." And, with a slightly different twist, Wang Hsi elaborated: "Look into the matter of his alliances and cause them to be severed and dissolved."[9] This age-old wisdom suggests three offensive strategies that firms can use to raise the costs or reduce the effectiveness of a rival's alliances.

The first strategy is, as Sun Tzu said, *disrupting a rival's existing alliances*. For example, a firm might form a new alliance with a member of a rival group or even with common third parties. Competition along one leg of a triad tends to disrupt collaboration in the other legs, so that luring a rival's ally into collaboration with the enemy is likely to cause frictions in the rival alliance. IBM's overtures to lure Bull out of the Mips constellation had this effect, although IBM likely had other motivations too.

The strategy of disrupting a rival alliance thus aims to affect the structure of control in the alliance by creating disagreements and conflicts of interest. As a possible defense against this strategy, the rival may seek ways to improve control—for example, by a merger or by a restructuring of the alliance.

The second offensive use of barriers to collaboration involves *preempting a rival's potential alliances*. "Do not allow them to get together," to paraphrase Tu Yu. Knowing that its rival will need access to a given capability, a constellation may try to corner the market for that capability by forming alliances with the most attractive partners. Firms can do the same through acquisitions or alliances. For preemption to work, however, this move must credibly tie up the partner.[10] Loose alliances and mere discussions about collaboration with another firm do not preempt a rival alliance from forming. Alliances secured by equity investment or other substantial commitments, however, might effectively keep a rival at bay. IBM did this with its distribution alliances in Europe, and Motorola did it in preempting Toshiba from joining Mips.

This type of move limits the pool of capabilities on which a rival can draw. There is little a rival can do defensively once the pool has been limited in this way. But one defense is an earlier offense—to try to preempt the preemption. A firm may enter into a number of "duplicate" alliances even before it is clear which partner is best. Through such an options-like approach, the firm avoids being foreclosed by rivals pursuing preemptive strategies. Sharp, for example, had several competing alliances in the PDA field, each of which used a different operating system. Through this strategy, Sharp could avoid being shut out of future constellations that might coalesce around one of these systems.

The third way to reduce the effectiveness of a rival's alliances is by shifting the context of competition in such a way as to *place strain on the alliances of the rival*. "Cause them to be severed," in Wang Hsi's words. A constellation competing with a single firm may have an advantage when competition revolves around more complex, loosely integrated products and services. Single firms—which have the advantage of unified control—may thus try to redefine the industry context to make a narrow business focus and tight integration more important. If successful, such a redefinition would generate frictions in rival constellations.

Canon's rapid product development and scale-intensive manufacturing had precisely this effect on the Xerox group. It increased the value of global coordination of R&D and manufacturing—areas in which frictions between Xerox and Fuji Xerox could easily arise. The Xerox group's defense was to improve its structure of control—Xerox tightened its relationship with Fuji Xerox by creating a new joint venture. Xerox could just as well have tried to defend by shifting the competitive context to favor its own structure. The Xerox move toward becoming an integrated document-processing company—with capabilities in copying, computers, and software—may well play to that strength.

The idea of using barriers to collaboration has some antecedents in the literature. Some economists have examined how contracts with customers or suppliers can raise barriers to entry[11] or raise rivals' costs.[12] In another stream of related work, scholars have examined the strategies and tactics of firms seeking to establish a dominant standard.[13] My concept of barriers to collaboration suggests a generalization of these models. It applies to alliances with customers, suppliers, sources of technology, and any other owner of a capability that is potentially valuable in competition. We have also seen that there are several ways to raise and overcome barriers to collaboration—all of these are part of the new strategic arsenal.

But we still have little actual experience with these strategies. By necessity, managers will be experimenting when they follow these suggestions. Management scholars can help them learn about the practical implementation of these strategies by documenting and comparing cases in which firms have tried to use them. Because these strategies have a predatory flavor to them—as do many other competitive strategies—they are not likely to be "advertised" by firms. It will therefore take in-depth research to gather the necessary data and careful analysis to come to useful conclusions.

BUILDING AND MANAGING A CONSTELLATION

A constellation is only as good as its design and its management. In order to wield its weapons effectively, a constellation must also be able to defend itself from attack. In other words, it must organize itself internally to maximize the benefits of collaboration and minimize conflicts among members. Sun Tzu's words are again relevant: "He whose ranks are united in purpose will be victorious."[14] Even though this book has not focused on the practical management of alliances, the evidence suggests ways in which managers can improve their chances of success in collective competition. Five lessons for alliance management can be distilled from the analysis.

The first lesson is that managers need to *develop comprehensive alliance strategies, and not expect magic from high-profile "strategic alliances."*[15] An effective alliance strategy has several components. As one element, the firm's alliances need to be integrated into a broader business strategy. Xerox, for example, used its alliance with Fuji Xerox to transfer technology into its core operations; Mips used alliances to generate the volume it needed to attract software vendors and to benefit from scale economies in production. The partners in an alliance also need to invest in a long-term relationship, not in short-term deals. It is often helpful to build a whole web of relationships and joint projects, as collaboration on one project helps promote collaboration on another. When companies lose sight of the whole relationship—as Honeywell appeared to have done—their alliance and business suffer. Finally, many of the firms studied did not have one "strategic" alliance, but a collection of relationships that *together* created an effective alliance strategy. But such a portfolio of alliances needs to be internally consistent and purposeful. Constellations such as Sun's, for example, contained internal competition and duplication that reduced the effectiveness of the portfolio of partners.

The second general lesson for managers is that *the balance between competition and collaboration is delicate and needs to be managed constantly.* Allies can turn into serious rivals, particularly when partners develop joint products and share information extensively. Honeywell learned this lesson the hard way; Xerox appeared to have heeded it from the start of its relationship with Fuji Photo. The evidence suggests that market competition can seriously threaten the success of technological collaboration; precompetitive alliances are thus not likely to succeed. Conversely, alliances in which the future promises even greater benefits from collaboration have a better chance of success. The accumulation or destruction of relationship capital can often shift the balance between cooperation and rivalry. In Honeywell's case, early successes in collaboration generated trust between the partners and confidence in the future; but Honeywell's sudden change in strategy threatened to destroy the relationship.

Even so, our third lesson is that *alliance instability should be not feared, but embraced.* Indeed, managers should be wary of alliances that are too stable, a condition that may indicate stagnation or, worse, mounting pressure for change. Effective alliances evolve continually to keep up with changes in the environment and in the partners' capabilities and goals. In particular, a rival's use of alliances itself creates pressures for new alliances or for modifications to one's constellation. Furthermore, the terms of an alliance may need to change to allow the partners to pursue new opportunities, as Xerox and Fuji Xerox did in low-volume printers. At the same time, a recognition of the inherent instability of alliances also means that alliance dissolutions

may indicate success in achieving goals, rather than a failure in collaboration.

The fourth lesson flies in the face of the marriage analogy often used
to describe alliances; it is that *polygamy is often better than monogamy.* In
complex businesses, a firm's needs are unlikely to be met by a single
partner, as the RISC and PDA firms found. Still, using multiple partners
never implies indiscriminate collaboration. To continue the analogy:
Avoid promiscuity. Groups of alliances were thus effective strategies for
RISC and PDA companies, as long as the constellations were structured
to minimize the costs of multiple alliances. Large group size and internal conflict tended to increase the costs of managing such a group. A
large number of partners often made it more difficult to integrate
operations and to unify the group behind a strategic goal. Mips and the
ACE partners learned these lessons in spades. More generally, there is
a limit to the number of alliances that any one firm can manage
effectively. This means that the capacity to manage alliances is a scarce
resource in any firm.

In using multiple partners, firms must also heed a fifth lesson: *They
must position themselves strategically among as well as within constellations.*
Two different sets of factors affect the value that a firm can receive from
a constellation. One set influences the group's collective benefits, and
the other influences the firm's power to claim a share of these benefits.
Managers must be concerned not only with their own firm's profits but
also with those of their group of allies.[16] As in simpler, bilateral alliances, it is critical to choose one's partner and the structure of the
alliance carefully. In the case of alliance groups, this choice is more
complex. It involves weighing both the potential of the group for
generating collective advantages and the role that one's firm is likely
to play in the group.

Taken together, these lessons emphasize that alliances are inherently
neither good nor bad for a firm—it depends on how they are managed.
Constellations have potential advantages over single firms in given
contexts; but it remains the task of management to realize these advantages. I have focused on the economic logic behind the design and
behavior of constellations. There already exists a body of thought on
the implementation and practical management of alliances. Much of
this work focuses on how to manage bilateral alliances; the findings
here should encourage a broadening of this agenda to include management of alliance groups as well. In addition, the existing work tends to

focus on processes of collaboration; this work can be usefully extended to address more explicitly how collaboration influences processes of competition.

The Locus of Economic Power

The alliance revolution not only affects economic theory and management practice; it also modifies our world view. Collaboration is now increasingly accepted by managers as a way of doing business, and scholars have begun to explain the existence and behavior of alliances. Still, even further work in these directions will represent only incremental changes in thinking. A more radical analysis of collaboration strikes deeply at our conventional view of the firm and of competition. Collaboration between firms upsets this view because it dethrones the firm as the prime source of economic power.[17]

Firms, of course, have never been the sole source of economic power in society. Governments also wield economic power, and so do individuals possessing scarce capabilities. Furthermore, firms have always been interdependent, which means that most have not been free to chart their own course without regard for the actions of other firms. But, all in all, in most market economies, firms have ruled supreme.

Constellations are a different—and growing—source of economic power. They derive power from their constituent firms. But they wield this power in a different fashion than single firms would. They compete differently, they grow and decline according to unique patterns, and they create and erode advantages in new ways.

Where does economic power lie in this new environment? Like information in a computer network, it lies widely distributed and concentrated at the same time. Some power still lies with firms, and even with key individuals within the firm; other power lies at a higher level of aggregation, with pairs of firms or groups of allies. Put differently, the way economic rents are distributed in society now depends on competition among alliance groups and on the relative power of the firms inside these groups. Alliances, in this world, are the power brokers among firms.

This is not the first time that the distribution of economic power in society appears to be changing. In late nineteenth-century America, the rise of trusts and conglomerates transformed the economic landscape. Later, in the interwar years, cartels among giant firms redistributed and regulated power globally. These cartels were destroyed after World War II, but then the modern multinational corporation spread its wings.

Over two decades ago, as the controversy surrounding the power of the multinational corporation was heating up, one seminal study began as follows: "Suddenly, it seems, the sovereign states are feeling naked. Concepts such as national sovereignty and national economic strength appear curiously drained of meaning."[18] In reality, the author showed, multinational corporations were not the single-minded powerhouses feared by sovereign states.[19] Still, they represented a new source of economic efficiency and power.

Today, single firms are feeling naked, as the locus of economic power shifts toward constellations. The reality of alliances is complex, but their implications for every facet of economic competition are profound. No firm can afford to ignore the uses of alliances in competitive strategy. And all firms—whether they themselves use alliances or not—will face a new competitive environment, in which the players take on more varied shapes and in which the pattern of rivalry itself is transformed.

If we are to understand these economic changes, we must change the way we think about competition and collaboration. The two are not mutually exclusive, but neither can they be blended and mixed to produce a "softer" form of rivalry. Rather, collaboration between firms yields a new type of competition between sets of firms. These constellations are new players on the economic scene; we must broaden our conception of the firm to include these and perhaps other types of competitors. Externally, constellations often compete fiercely with one another. But their competitive power grows out of internal processes—the dynamics of collaboration among their member firms. That is the essence of collective competition, the new shape of business rivalry.

Appendixes · Notes · Index

Interviews

Each person interviewed for this book and related projects was spoken with at least once between 1989 and 1994; many were interviewed more than once. Most interviews were in person, a few were by telephone. The positions shown are those that the interviewees held at the time of the interview.

U.S.-Japan Joint Ventures

AMDAHL AND FUJITSU

At Amdahl: John C. Lewis, Chairman and CEO.

At Fujitsu: Masanobu Katoh, Liaison Representative; Kazuto Kojima, General Manager, Corporate Strategy; Michio Naruto, Managing Director and Vice General Manager, International Operations.

HEWLETT-PACKARD AND YOKOGAWA-HEWLETT-PACKARD

At Hewlett-Packard: Alan D. Bickell, Senior Vice President and Managing Director, Geographic Operations.

At Yokogawa-Hewlett-Packard: Shu Asai, Senior Director, Finance and Administration; Kyo Nakatsukasa, Director, General Manager; Kenzo Sasaoka, Chairman; Toshiteru Suwa, Senior Managing Director.

HONEYWELL AND YAMATAKE-HONEYWELL

At Honeywell: Ray Alvarez, Vice President and General Manager, Micro Switch Division; Michael R. Bonsignore, President, International; Joe Chenoweth, Senior Vice President, International; Matthew Gilfix, Director, Strategy and Business Development; Edward Hurd, President, Industrial Control Business; Loring W. Knoblauch, Vice President for Business Development, International; Richard Reed, Associate General Counsel, International; Jean-Pierre Rosso, President, Home and Building Control Business; Edson Spencer, former Chairman and CEO; Hiroshi Yamashita, Vice President, Japan.

At Yamatake-Honeywell: Ichiro Ido, President; Haruo Okinobu, Chairman and CEO.

IBM AND TOSHIBA

At IBM Japan: Masaaki Kawamitsu, Venture Management; Yoshikatsu Nishida, Director of Business Development.

At Toshiba: Hirohito Kobayashi, Senior Manager, Electron Tube & Device Group; Kozo Wada, General Manager, International Agreements Negotiations.

XEROX AND FUJI XEROX

At Xerox Corporation: Paul A. Allaire, Chairman and CEO; Ronald Campbell, Senior Vice President, Strategy; William Glavin, President, Babson College (formerly with Xerox); Wayland R. Hicks, Executive Vice President, Marketing and Customer Operations; S. Jefferson Kennard, Director for Fuji Xerox Relations; David T. Kearns, Chairman of the Board; Roger Levien, Vice President for Strategy; William C. Lowe, Executive Vice President; Rafik O. Loutfy, Manager, Research Planning, Corporate Research Group; Julius L. Marcus, Senior Vice President, Strategic Relations; C. Peter McColough, Member of the Board (former Chairman); Mark Myers, Vice President for Technology; Dan Murray, Manager, Research Planning, Corporate Research Group; Joseph O'Brien, Manager, Fuji Xerox Relations; Norman E. Rickard, Vice President for Quality; William J. Spencer, Vice President for Technology.

At Fuji Xerox: Toshio Arima, Director for Strategy; Katsumi Harashima, Manager, Corporate Technology Planning; Yokichi Itoh, Managing Director, General Manager, Corporate Research Labs; Ken-Ichi Karakida, Manager, Corporate Research Labs; Hideki Kaihatsu, Managing Director, Chief Staff Officer; Yotaro Kobayashi, President and CEO; Osamu Matsuo, Manager, General Service Business Office; Robert W. Meredith, Xerox Resident, Executive Director; Yoichi

Ogawa, Senior Managing Director; Yasuhiro Ohnishi, Managing Director; Masamoto Sakamoto, Director, Tokyo Marketing Business Unit; Nubuo Shono, Counselor; Matazo Terada, Associate Director, Office Research Institute; R. Tommy Tomita, Staff Manager, Corporate Planning.

RISC Groups

HEWLETT-PACKARD GROUP

James R. Bell, President and CEO, Precision RISC Organization; Gary Eichorn, General Manager, Workstations Business Unit, Hewlett-Packard; Larry Gray, SPEC Director, Hewlett-Packard; Hisashi Horikoshi, Director and Division Manager, Product Planning, Computer Group, Hitachi; Yurio Kojima, Assistant Manager, Overseas Planning, Computer Group, Hitachi; David Logan, Manager, CSG/Systems Technology Division, Hewlett-Packard; Peter Rosenbladt, Director, Group R&D and Strategic Alliances, Computer Systems Organization, Hewlett-Packard; Carl Snyder, Group General Manager, Systems Technology Group, Hewlett-Packard.

IBM GROUP

Robert A. Lauridsen, Vice President, Corporate Development and Strategic Investments, Apple Computers; Domenic J. LaCava, President, Power Open Association; Randall S. Livingston, Vice President and CFO, Taligent; Thomas E. Mace, President, Power Open Association.

MIPS GROUP

Didier Benchimol, President Directeur General, Mips Computer Systems (France); Charles Boesenberg, President, Mips Computer Systems; David Corbin, Director of Marketing, Mips Technologies; Joseph E. DiNucci, Vice President, Entry Systems Group, Mips Computer Systems; Susumu Kohyama, General Manager, LSI Division II, Toshiba; Kenji Kani, Vice President, Semiconductor Group, NEC; David Ludvigson, Chief Financial Officer, Mips Computer Systems; Keiji Matsumoto, Senior Manager, Microcomputer Division, NEC; Robert Miller, Chairman and CEO, Mips Computer Systems; Tom Oswold, Vice President, Finance, Silicon Graphics; Charles Perrell, International, Mips Computer Systems; Andy Pinkard, Technology Products Group, Mips Computer Systems (UK); Hideaki Sato, Japan Sales Office, Mips

Technologies; Klaus O. Schmidt, General Manager, Mips Computer Systems (W. Germany); Chester J. Silvestri, Vice President and General Manager, Technology Products Group, Mips Computer Systems; Skip Stritter, Chief Scientist, Mips Computer Systems.

MOTOROLA GROUP

Thomas E. Mace, President, 88Open Association.

SUN GROUP

Phil Huelson, President and COO, Sparc International; Derek Meyer, Director, Sparc Marketing, Sun Microsystems; Bill Raduchel, senior management, Sun Microsystems; Chet Silvestri, Vice President, Sales, Sparc Technology Business, Sun Microsystems.

Other Computer Industry

At Digital Equipment Corporation: Henry Crouse, Vice President, Strategic Relations; Howard E. Fineman, Strategic Relations; Michael Horner, Engineering Strategy Manager, International (Europe); Eric P. Sublet, Manager, Strategic Development, International (Europe).

At Hitachi: Soji Endo, Division Manager, Computer, Telecom and Office Systems Group; Toshiaki Katayama, Manager, Computer Division.

At IBM: Yardley Lazovsky, Business Development Consultant; Nick Perry, Strategy and Business Development (Europe); Peter L. Schavoir, Director, Strategy and Business Development; Fausto Talenti, Group Director, Strategy and Business Development (Europe).

At Matsushita Electric: Norio Gomi, General Manager, Legal Affairs; Mitsure Osugi, Manager, Research and Analysis Group; Gary Rieschel, Pana-Sequent Inc.; Naoki Sakagami, Senior Coordinator, Legal.

At MITI: Takeshi Furutani, Machinery and Information Industries Bureau; Nozomi Sagara, Machinery and Information Industries Bureau; Taigo Nishikawa, Machinery and Information Industries Bureau.

At NEC: Eiji Hayashi, General Manager, Engineering Coordination Division; Noboru Ishii, Assistant Manager, EDP Planning Office.

At Olivetti: Umberto Bussolati Dell'Orto, Vice President, Corporate Development; Roberto Maglione, EEC Liaison Office; Carlo Pagella, Manager, Product and Market Strategy; Elserino Piol, Amministratore Delegato; Roberto Vidra, Director, Product and Market Strategy.

At Philips: Ir. W. A. Ledeboer, Manager, European Affairs Coordination; A. E. Pannenborg, President Commissaris.

At Siemens-Nixdorf: Rudolf Bodo, Director; Niels Eskelson, Technical Cooperation; Rolf Kunkel, Director, Corporate Strategy and Development.

At Toshiba: Isamu Kuru, General Manager, Corporate Planning Division; Ken-Ichi Mori, Deputy General Manager, Corporate Planning Division.

Other: Andrew Allison, Editor, *Inside the New Computer Industry;* Randall F. Brophy, Gartner Group; Stan Bruederle, Dataquest; Toshi T. Doi, Senior General Manager, Super Micro Systems, Sony Corporation; James J. Gierson, Vice President, Business Development, Honeywell; Hermann Hauser, Co-Chairman and CTO, EO, Ltd.; David E. Mentley, Display Industry Research; K. Hugh MacDonald, Manager, External Projects, ICL; Nagayoshi Nakano, Dataquest (Japan); Ken Nakao, General Manager, Silicon Valley Office, Kubota Corporation; Leon Navickas, Lotus Development Corporation; Takanari Sasaki, Japan External Trade Organization; George Scalise, President and CEO, Maxtor Corporation; Satoshi Uchiyama, Dataquest (Japan); Leslie L. Vadasz, Senior Vice President, Intel; Timothy Williams, Hewlett-Packard Corporation.

Data and Methods for Alliance Survey

The aggregate data used in this book on alliances in the computer hardware industry were collected in two phases. In the first phase, I surveyed press reports with the help of Chris Allen, Dimos Arhodidis, Donna Hill, Neil Jones, and Paul Mang. Using the Predicast PTS PROMT on-line database, we searched for articles within the computers and auxiliary equipment (3573) industry classification in the period 1973 to November 1989, using twelve key words: alliance, acquisition, collaboration, consortium, cooperative, equity investment, joint development, joint production, joint R&D, joint venture, licensing, and sourcing.

Drawing on an analysis of the coverage that news sources give to alliance activity in the United States, Europe, and Asia, we searched ten publications: *Computer Weekly, Computer World, Electronic Engineering Times, Electronic News, Electronics, Information Week, The Financial Times, The Japan Economic Journal, MIS Week,* and *The Wall Street Journal.*

Because we were interested in data on how the world's leading computer firms used alliances, we searched for articles that reported on one or more of twenty-four of the largest computer firms worldwide:

American firms		Japanese firms	European firms
IBM	AT&T	Fujitsu	Siemens
DEC	Compaq	NEC	Olivetti
Unisys	Amdah	Hitachi	Bull
HP	Tandy	Toshiba	Nixdorf
NCR	Sun	Matsushita	Philips
Apple		Mitsubishi	ICL
			Ericsson

(To take account of mergers and name changes, we conducted a search on firms' earlier names as well.) Note that we looked not only for alliances *among* these twenty-four firms, but for any alliance involving at least one of these firms as a partner. As it turned out, the majority of the alliances included partners outside this group.

This search yielded more than two thousand titles with abstracts. We reviewed and coded the abstracts or, when necessary, the original articles. Our classification system recorded such items as partner names, date, structure, activities, motivations, and contributions. Because the search was not limited to "international" alliances, the coding system also distinguished these from purely domestic alliances. The coding process also separated the formation of new alliances from changes in existing alliances; only the former are used in this book. Finally, we discarded complete mergers and other nonalliance activities captured by the key words. In this phase, we recorded 449 alliances.

The second phase of the survey updated the database through December 1994. For that, I used ITSA, a commercial database developed by James Sharp from Itsunami, a California firm that monitors alliances in the information technology industries. From this database, Dimos Arhodidis and I first selected all alliances in computer hardware for the twenty-four firms and then coded the information on 198 of these alliances. Because ITSA contains many small relationships, software alliances, and other news about alliances, we selected only those observations that seemed to match the earlier data in terms of substance and size. Simple statistics on the distribution of alliances across partners, type, and so on confirmed that the profile of the alliances selected in this second phase corresponded closely to that of those selected in the first.

In total, the data used here contain 647 domestic and international alliances, formed mostly between 1975 and 1994, each of which involves at least one of the twenty-four firms listed above. About one-quarter of these alliances are among two or more of these twenty-four firms. These "duplicates" are counted only once when the data are aggregated across the firms.

Data on RISC alliances. The analysis of RISC groups draws on a separate database of 171 alliances of the leading RISC firms—Mips, Sun, HP, IBM, and Motorola. These data were gathered in similar fashion to that already described, using a combination of press reports and ITSA data. These observations have not been merged with the general database on computers, because the RISC data include software alliances.

Additional Case Studies

This appendix contains three case studies on U.S.-Japanese alliances that were used in the analysis in the text.

Amdahl Helps Fujitsu Catch Up with IBM

In 1970, IBM had annual revenues five times greater than its nearest competitor, R&D spending of over $1 billion, and a sales and marketing network embracing the globe. IBM was so dominant that most of its competitors believed they could do little more than struggle for Big Blue's scraps.

Gene Amdahl did not share this view. That year he left his position as IBM's chief engineer to launch his own company, the Amdahl Corporation. Underfunded and without the slightest prospect of generating revenue for five years, Amdahl aimed to take on IBM. He planned to build so-called plug-compatible machines (PCMs), that is, computer hardware that could run IBM software and could readily substitute for IBM equipment. Today, Amdahl's sales of IBM-compatible computers represent 15 percent of the world market for mainframes; and IBM, though still dominating the mainframe segment, no longer looks invincible. Amdahl's success was due partly to its founder's technical genius. Yet this was not enough. In taking on his Goliath, Gene Amdahl needed a weapon. He found one in his partnership with Japan's Fujitsu.

In the late 1960s, Fujitsu too had been planning an assault on IBM's mainframe business. With sales over $500 million, Fujitsu was already Japan's biggest computer maker, but its global business was dwarfed by that of IBM. At first, Fujitsu attempted to take on IBM alone. In 1968 it established Fujitsu California to serve as a window on American technology and a "boot camp" for its engineers. The same year, it proudly brought its new mainframes to the World Computer Show in New York. Yet for all its effort, it left the show—and the decade—without a single mainframe sale in the United States. Fujitsu realized that it could not compete on its own against IBM.

In 1971 Fujitsu learned that Gene Amdahl's start-up company had exhausted its early venture capital and needed funding to survive. Fujitsu offered $5 million for a small ownership share in Amdahl and, more important, for the chance to participate in Amdahl's research and development. The companies signed a royalty-free cross-licensing agreement giving Fujitsu exclusive rights to Amdahl technology and products in Japan while maintaining Amdahl's exclusivity in the United States. This technical alliance revolved around the personal relationship between Gene Amdahl and Toshio Ikeda, Fujitsu's head computer engineer.

But Amdahl ran into new problems even before its first machine was completed. A slumping stock market thwarted its plans for the initial public offering that would have provided new funds. At the same time, the surprise introduction of IBM's 370 series rendered Amdahl's ongoing effort obsolete. Amdahl had to go back to the technical drawing board and to the deep pockets of its Japanese partner. Together with the original venture capital investors, Fujitsu contributed another $17 million to the venture and raised its ownership share. By 1975, after Amdahl's public offering, Fujitsu held about one-third of Amdahl's shares. As the original investors sold their holdings, Fujitsu's ownership rose to 43 percent and later to 49.5 percent.[1]

Amdahl finally hit pay dirt in 1975, when it became the first company to sell an IBM-compatible mainframe. The 470 V/6, designed by Amdahl and manufactured mostly by Fujitsu, offered price, power, and size advantages over the current IBM model. This initial victory led to others[2] and, over time, contributed to Fujitsu's rise to second place behind IBM.

When Amdahl and Fujitsu began working together, Amdahl needed help in making integrated circuits for its computers and Fujitsu needed help in developing a mainframe architecture like that of IBM.[3] Fujitsu's investment in Amdahl came in exchange for an agreement for patent licensing and joint development, as we saw. Under the terms of this agreement, Fujitsu was effectively blocked from competing in the U.S. market with its own mainframes.[4]

From the beginning, Fujitsu and Amdahl aimed to use common manufacturing processes in their computers. Fujitsu sent a cadre of engineers to California to develop a machine similar to the Amdahl product under development, but intended for the Japanese market. The proprietary machine that resulted (the M-190) ran the Fujitsu operating system, which was similar, but not identical, to the IBM operating system. The differences between the architecture of the M-series and that of IBM and Amdahl computers were small, but enough to make them incompatible. Still, the Fujitsu and Amdahl models used similar manufacturing processes and many common components. Of seventy printed-circuit boards (PCBs), only a few were different.

Amdahl was not successful in selling its first-generation machines, in part because IBM had leapfrogged Amdahl's technology with its 370 series. In the development of its second-generation machine, the highly successful 470, Amdahl contributed the key design concepts, but Fujitsu initially manufactured the computer itself. Later, Amdahl took over final assembly, and left Fujitsu to manufacture subassemblies and components (mostly PCBs and packaging). The special semiconductors for the machines came from Motorola. After about three years, when the companies needed a more specialized chip, Fujitsu became the sole chip supplier to Amdahl.

With every new product after these initial ones, Fujitsu and Amdahl would coordinate early to ensure that they would use the same semiconductor technology and packaging, but the circuitry would be different and independently designed. Amdahl would design the circuitry for its own machines, Fujitsu would manufacture it and do simple tests, and Amdahl would do logic tests and final assembly. In this way, they developed a third-generation Amdahl series in 1982–83, and a fourth in 1988–89. In the process, Amdahl's design changed and diverged from that of Fujitsu. Still, the two companies used the same process technologies—semiconductors, packaging, testing, PCB technologies, and so on.

With each generation of computers, the decision regarding who would manufacture what part of the machines sold by Amdahl was based on cost/benefit analyses. Fujitsu typically made about 60 percent of the components, and Amdahl 40 percent. This proportion remained fairly stable, with some variation from one project to the next.[5] Amdahl

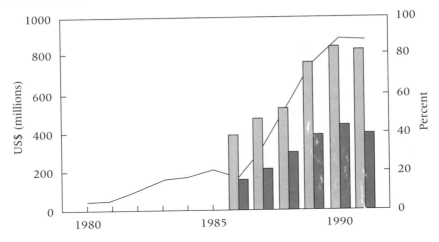

— Fujitsu sales to Amdahl (left axis)
▨ As % of Fujitsu's U.S. sales (right axis)
▨ As % of Fujitsu's total computer manufacturing costs (right axis)

Figure 25 Fujitsu sales of computer components to Amdahl, 1980–1991.
"Fujitsu's total computer manufacturing costs" represent an estimate of the
manufacturing cost of all Fujitsu mainframe computers, whether or not they
were sold in the United States.
(Sources: Based on Amdahl annual reports and data from the Gartner Group.)

did all final assembly, design, and sales and service, usually at its
California location.

This arrangement had substantial advantages for Amdahl. The PCBs
used in the computers were among the most complex in the world and
included over sixty layers; only Fujitsu and IBM reportedly had the
sophistication to make them.[6] Fujitsu shipped the PCBs and semiconductor wafers to Amdahl, which assembled them and put the wafers
on the boards. Other firms that bought Fujitsu PCBs and chips did not
gain access to the new technology as early as did Amdahl. At the same
time, Amdahl dependence on Fujitsu was substantial—it had no second source for these components.[7]

From its side, Fujitsu benefited from the supply relationship by
gaining substantial sales and experience in a demanding market. First,
feedback from Amdahl pushed the development of Fujitsu capabilities.
The changes in Amdahl design over the years were driven by fierce
competition in the United States with IBM. Because Amdahl sold

plug-compatible equipment that did not have IBM's brand image, its computers had to be more cost effective than IBM's. Fujitsu did not experience such direct pressure from IBM in Japan, because the proprietary design of the M-series insulated it from short-run competition in terms of price and performance, at least with existing customers.[8] As a result, Amdahl design engineers continually pressured Fujitsu to improve its manufacturing process so as to enable production of higher-performance chips and PCBs. This in turn benefited the Fujitsu line of products, which used the same manufacturing processes.

Second, business with Amdahl helped increase the scale of Fujitsu's production of key components. By 1990 Amdahl purchases of sub-assemblies from Fujitsu amounted to almost $890 million.[9] These purchases represented over 80 percent of Fujitsu sales of data processing equipment in the United States, over 20 percent of Fujitsu worldwide sales of mainframe equipment, and an estimated 40 percent of the production cost of these mainframe sales (see Figure 25).

IBM and Toshiba Share Innovation

A full decade after IBM's dominance had driven Amdahl and Fujitsu to work together, new competitive pressures impelled IBM itself to seek a Japanese partner. With sales of $52 billion in 1986, IBM was still the world's largest computer maker, but it was not dominant in the micro-computer segment. In particular, it lagged in several technologies that were becoming central to success in this market.

The color flat-panel display was one of these technologies. In the late 1980s, Sharp, Mitsubishi, Hitachi, and NEC were advancing rapidly in the development and production of color active-matrix liquid-crystal displays (AMLCDs) driven by thin-film transistors (TFTs). IBM recognized that it lacked the resources to develop this technology in time to meet the competition. As it happened, Toshiba found itself in the same predicament. With sales of $37 billion, Toshiba was one of Japan's electronics giants, and it had substantial business in laptop microcomputers using monochrome displays. The two companies first collaborated to develop new display technologies and later invested jointly in manufacturing facilities.

The origins of this alliance date to 1985, when IBM's corporate research group identified color flat-panel displays as a critical technology. IBM Japan proposed that a joint R&D project with Toshiba would shorten development time and save resources. By May 1988, a joint R&D team had developed an excellent 14-inch, 16-color display, the most advanced in the industry at the time. Having reached its goal, this joint R&D program was soon terminated.

A few months later, IBM developed a second generation of the screen at its new lab in the United States. To manufacture this screen, IBM and Toshiba formed Display Technologies Incorporated (DTI), a 50/50 joint venture headquartered in Japan. With an initial investment of $100 million in a plant located on Toshiba's site, the partners expected to make one million screens per year by about 1994.[10] The parent firms agreed to transfer the necessary technology to the joint venture. Toshiba would make a new production line available, and each parent agreed to purchase 50 percent of the output. The venture would not market the product independently of the parents, and it did no R&D by itself. Both parents continued in-house R&D, and they collaborated in a new joint R&D project separate from DTI.

IBM expected several benefits from this arrangement. First, the companies would share the investment and the risk inherent in this rapidly changing technology and market. The novelty of AMLCD and TFT technologies heightened the risk of capital overruns. Projected demand for DTI's displays was also highly uncertain; it depended on the success of competitors, on the demand for new-style computers, and on untested assumptions about process improvements and future prices.

Second, IBM expected to benefit from Toshiba's manufacturing experience in TFT production and the related design strengths of the Japanese company. These contributions from Toshiba were critical to IBM, not because IBM could never match them,[11] but because it could not hope to do so quickly. IBM Japan's executives estimated that collaboration with Toshiba might shorten the time to product introduction by about eighteen months, putting them twelve months ahead of the competition. In other words, without the alliance, IBM's products might have come out six months behind equivalent products of competitors—a long, and perhaps fatal, lag time in the fast-paced computer market.[12]

Joint Decision Making at Yokogawa-Hewlett-Packard

The birthplace of the Silicon Valley can be traced to David Packard's garage in Palo Alto, California. In 1938 Packard and his Stanford classmate William Hewlett joined forces to build their own electronic test equipment business. World War II transformed Hewlett-Packard into a major supplier to the U.S. government and to customers in the electronics, telecommunications, aviation, and automotive industries.

In the late 1950s, HP began looking abroad for expansion.[13] In 1959 it opened a wholly owned factory in West Germany, and in 1961 it opened one in Britain. After that, HP set its sights on Japan; here too Hewlett and Packard favored a wholly owned subsidiary that would afford them full control over quality, technology, and strategy.

But the Japanese government did not allow wholly owned foreign subsidiaries at the time.[14] IBM Japan had been an exception to this rule, but only because IBM agreed to license its technology to Japanese computer firms and to limit its domestic market share.[15] Most other companies had to settle for joint ventures with local firms. With sales of only $120 million in 1963, HP could not expect much leniency from MITI.

Like other firms trying to gain a toehold in Japan, Hewlett-Packard set out to find a local partner. With the help of a business research firm, the company generated a list of fifty potential partners in the electronics industry; using criteria of size and expertise, it narrowed the list down to fourteen. Among these, HP was quickly drawn to Yokogawa Electric Works, because this company had earlier approached HP for a license and because it was the leading electronic instrument maker in Japan.

Yokogawa, which was one-quarter the size of HP in 1963, had been trying to enter the test and measurement business on its own, but with limited success. In its view, joining hands with HP was a way to gain access to technology and expertise. The companies quickly agreed to form Yokogawa-Hewlett-Packard (YHP), a joint venture owned 49 percent by HP and 51 percent by Yokogawa. Yokogawa agreed to transfer its measurement business to the venture, and HP agreed to transfer technology and products.

The only stumbling block in the negotiations concerned YHP's sales and marketing strategy. Yokogawa wanted to use its existing distribution channels for YHP products, an approach typical of U.S.-Japanese joint ventures at the time. Yokogawa believed that it would be difficult and costly to launch an independent sales force. But Hewlett-Packard, bolstered by the success of direct selling in its European ventures, wanted an independent campaign led by the joint venture's own sales force. The debate was resolved in HP's favor.[16] In the decades that followed, HP continued to push for greater control over its joint venture in Japan.

Alliance development stages. All alliances have a beginning, and eventually all have an ending. Other authors working on alliance evolution have focused almost exclusively on the ending, that is, on when and why alliances break up. Much attention has also been paid to why firms enter into alliances, but little to the process of starting up a collaborative venture. Finally, the process of change in the "middle" years has been seriously neglected. Through their lives, alliances go through four stages of development, which appear inherent in the progress of collaboration: (1) start-up; (2) early adjustments; (3) operation; and (4) review and renegotiation.

Among the alliances examined in this book, Yokogawa-Hewlett-Packard best illustrates these stages of development, perhaps because other drivers of change intervened the least. Neither partner in this alliance acquired dramatically new skills, the division of labor between partners varied little, and changes in the environment were gradual. Until 1983, the formal structure of the alliance remained unchanged. Still, this alliance went through distinct stages that we also observe, though less clearly, in the other alliances studied.

The start-up stage. Although the negotiations between Yokogawa and Hewlett-Packard proceeded smoothly, the early years of their joint venture were rocky. In its first three years, YHP lost money at the rate of 10 percent of sales each year. By the end of 1965, the accumulated loss was $1 million,[17] and the partners had to resort to a bank loan to keep the venture afloat. Stunned by this turn of events, HP dispatched a team of managers to investigate.

These envoys found inefficiency and mismanagement in every aspect of YHP's operations. In manufacturing, "there seemed to be too many people to get the job done," and the "idle machines told their own story."[18] All hiring, staffing, and financial plans had been based on the "sales forecast done by a young, relatively inexperienced sales engineer."[19] Furthermore, there was "no recognizable system for tracking the backlog, . . . [with] very long wait times for customers [and] inventory . . . spread all over the floor."[20] The HP team report summed up the difference in management style of the partners: "We thought we knew what we were doing. So did they. They got the sound but not the music. They got the products but not the culture. Some of the answers lie in the different expectations of the two parents. YEW's view: it would work out well, long-term; HP's view: if it's broke, fix it, don't wait until tomorrow to make a profit."[21]

The partners, in other words, began to find out what they really had to offer each other, and what it would take to make collaboration work. This is typical of start-up phases in other alliances.

The early adjustment stage. As a response to these problems, HP decided to get directly involved. This time it dispatched five "co-managers" to Japan; they had expertise in accounting, manufacturing, marketing, R&D, and service. Originally, only Yokogawa Electric had taken a direct role in YHP management. But the American envoys now worked with the Japanese in making joint decisions in each area of the business.

The co-management pairs made several key decisions. Sales targets were reduced; production targets were scaled back; one-fifth of the fixed assets were sold off; and one-third of the workers were sent back to Yokogawa Electric. These moves led to immediate cost savings.

The new managers also reconfigured YHP's product line. Fifty products were retired, and four mid-volume HP products were transferred from the United States; YHP was given responsibility for manufacturing these four products for HP customers worldwide. The sales strategy was redirected even more aggressively toward direct contact with the end-user. To build further personal exchanges between Japan and California, training programs at HP sites were expanded.

The strategy worked. In 1966 YHP made its first profit—200 million yen on sales of 2.2 billion yen. From then on, annual profits grew steadily with sales. By 1970 its yearly profits averaged about 8 percent of sales,[22] and the American co-managers could be reduced from five to three; in 1979 they left for good.

Early adjustments served to modify the division of labor and redirect the alliance based on the new information from the start-up stage. The first two stages, therefore, are closely related: a concept is developed, tested, and adjusted. As a group, these steps can be thought of broadly as the design and debugging phase of the alliance.[23] During these stages the strategy and structure of the alliance, including major elements such as equity shares, division of labor, and control, may be altered.

The operation stage. The early changes in YHP's strategy and management led to a long period of profitable growth. During the late 1960s and early 1970s, YHP also received an injection of new high-margin products from Hewlett-Packard—computers and medical products. By the 1980s, YHP's main function in the HP world was as a channel for selling U.S.-made computers in Japan. Between 1973 and 1993, the share of computers in YHP revenues rose from 25 percent to 60 percent, while the share of the company's traditional test-and-measurement products dropped.

The test-and-measurement business, however, was still the pride of YHP management. This business relied on products developed and manufactured at YHP, not on imports from HP. These products were exported worldwide, because YHP had two global "charters" in this field.[24]

YHP also became more autonomous in management during the 1970s; by the end of that decade, HP recalled its resident director from Japan. In the same period, YHP found a niche for itself in the area of quality management. Under the leadership of CEO Kenzo Sasaoka, YHP began a quality campaign that led to dramatic results.[25] Now it was YHP which influenced HP to improve its quality when it repeatedly complained about HP products that were "dead on arrival," that is, that were defective or somehow incomplete. When YHP won the Deming Prize in 1982, the committee congratulated the company for influencing its U.S. parent.[26]

It is during the period of operation that alliances begin to generate economic results. At the same time, learning through experience takes place. Feedback loops, too, occur in this period, leading to changes in objectives and roles. In addition, the partners begin to accumulate experience with collaboration, which influences the next stage of the process.

The review and renegotiation stage. Growth in YHP was also accompanied by shifts in the roles, capabilities, and interests of the partners. These shifts led to renegotiation and restructuring of the relationship.

In 1983 Hewlett-Packard increased its ownership in YHP from 49 percent to 75 percent. This decision had deep historical roots. The American partner had originally wanted a wholly owned subsidiary, but had to settle for a joint venture. HP tried several times in the years that followed to gain full ownership of YHP. When the agreement came up for renewal in 1973, the government still had not liberalized its foreign investment laws; but when the agreement came up for renewal again in 1983, government policy had changed, and foreign companies were allowed to establish wholly owned subsidiaries in Japan.

In its petition to gain full ownership of YHP, Hewlett-Packard detailed the ways in which the alliance had changed since its inception, arguing that Yokogawa Electric's role had diminished and that its own involvement had increased dramatically: "The first ten years of YHP's operation was truly a period of both partners providing equal contributions to the success of the joint venture. . . . During the second ten-year period, HP has been the dominant supporter of YHP both in the areas of technology as well as in sales and management. . . . HP has extended its technology . . . into many new areas which have been a substantial source of new transferred product, growth, and profits for YHP."[27]

Giving HP full ownership, the petition argued, would reflect the realities of the business and provide a fairer return to HP. Yokogawa Electric, however, was not willing to accede to HP's desires. Kenzo Sasaoka proposed that the partners split the difference, that is, that HP's share increase to 75 percent, not 100 percent. The partners agreed, and the transaction was swiftly completed. Shu Asai, YHP vice president for finance, described the changes that followed: "The restructuring released all the yokes that had been established at the start of the joint venture. Literally overnight, YHP had a freer relationship with HP. The relationship between the parents also changed in other ways. HP became more willing to receive Yokogawa people in its R&D labs."[28]

From HP's point of view, too, the restructuring achieved its chief aims. YHP was more closely integrated into the HP world, and HP derived greater financial benefits. Dividend policies were changed to yield higher returns to the partners. In 1983, $1 million was paid out to partners; in 1984, this figure jumped to $23 million.[29]

The results of reviews and renegotiations in an alliance are idiosyncratic—they depend on the circumstances of each alliance. All alliances, however, go through this stage. That these adjustments will take place, therefore, is predictable; they are an inherent part of the progress of collaboration.

Data on Selected
U.S.-Japanese Alliances

The following data concern the principal U.S.-Japanese alliances examined in this book. Each entry provides information on both the original partners and their alliances. Data on alliance formation and recent performance are included.

	Partners		Alliance
Fuji Xerox			
Company name	Xerox Corp.	Fuji Photo Film	Fuji Xerox Co.
Founded	1906	1934	1962
Home country	U.S.	Japan	Japan
Main businesses	Document processing	Film and photo equip.	Document processing
Recent Performance			
Total revenues	$15 billion	$9.0 billion	$5.1 billion
Total assets	$17 billion	$14 billion	$4.3 billion
Return on assets	3.3%	4.5%	4.3%
Number of employees	99,000	25,000	15,000
At Alliance Formation			
Total revenues	$105 million	$90 million	
Structure of alliance			50% Fuji Photo 50% Rank Xerox (a Xerox joint venture in Europe)
Yamatake-Honeywell			
Company name	Honeywell Inc.	Yamatake Trading Co.	Yamatake-Honeywell
Founded	1885	1906	1953
Home country	U.S.	Japan	Japan
Main businesses	Home, building, and industrial controls; aerospace	Industrial controls	Home, building, and industrial controls

Yokogawa-Hewlett-Packard

	Hewlett-Packard Co.	Yokogawa Elec. Works	Yokogawa-Hewlett-Packard
Company name	Hewlett-Packard Co.	Yokogawa Elec. Works	Yokogawa-Hewlett-Packard
Founded	1938	1915	1963
Home country	U.S.	Japan	Japan
Main businesses	Test and measurement equip.; computers	Industrial controls; test and measurement equip.	Test and measurement equip.; computers

Recent Performance			
Total revenues	$6.2 billion	(see under Alliance)	$1.5 billion
Total assets	$4.9 billion	"	$1.3 billion
Return on assets	6.4%	"	4.4%
Number of employees	55,000	"	4,600

At Alliance Formation			
Total revenues	$210 million	$1 million	
Structure of alliance			Honeywell bought 50% of Yamatake; share later decreased

	Partners		Alliance
Recent Performance			
Total revenues	$16 billion	$2.0 billion	$1.2 billion
Total assets	$14 billion	$3.2 billion	$640 million
Return on assets	6.9%	0.4%	3.8%
Number of employees	93,000	7,000	4,000
At Alliance Formation			
Total revenues	$120 million	$25 million	
Structure of alliance			51% Yokogawa and 49% Hewlett-Packard; HP share later increased
Amdahl and Fujitsu			
Company name	Amdahl Corp.	Fujitsu	Amdahl Corp.
Founded	1970	1935	1971
Home country	U.S.	Japan	U.S.
Main businesses	Mainframe computers	Computers and related equip.	Mainframe computers
Recent Performance			
Total revenues	(see under Alliance)	$28 billion	$2.5 billion
Total assets	"	$33 billion	$2.7 billion

Return on assets	"	−0.8%	−0.3%
Number of employees	"	162,000	8,800
At Alliance Formation			
Total revenues	None (start-up phase)	$520 million	
Structure of alliance			Fujitsu bought 25% of Amdahl; share later increased

IBM and Toshiba (DTI)

	IBM	Toshiba	DTI
Company name	IBM	Toshiba	Display Technologies Inc.
Founded	1910	1896	1989
Home country	U.S.	Japan	Japan
Main businesses	Computers	Computers; consumer electronics; other electronics	Flat-panel displays
Recent Performance			
Total revenues	$65 billion	$37 billion	$480 million
Total assets	$87 billion	$49 billion	$292 million
Return on assets	−7.7%	0.4%	N/A
Number of employees	300,000	173,000	600
At Alliance Formation			
Total revenues	$63 billion	$31 billion	None (start-up)
Structure of alliance			50% IBM; 50% Toshiba

Sources: Annual reports and company documents.

Note: All recent data are for 1992, except for data on Fuji Xerox, which are for 1993. Xerox financial data are for document-processing part of the business (excludes financial services). Data for DTI are estimates based on press releases and press reports. N/A = not available.

Data on RISC Alliance Groups

The following data concern the principal RISC alliance groups examined in this book. Each entry provides information about the lead firm as well as about one or two of the main partners in each group. The performance data refer to the year in which each firm joined the group.

Group	Lead firm	Two main partners	
Mips (RX000)			
Company name	Mips Computer Systems	Digital Equipment Corp.	NEC
Founded	1984	1957	1899
Home country	U.S.	U.S.	Japan
Main businesses	RISC microprocessors	Minicomputers	Computers; electronic equip.
Performance at Joining			
Joined alliance group	1987	1988	1989
Role in alliance group	Chip and O/S design	Systems sales	Chip production
Total revenues	$14 million	$12 billion	$25 billion
Revenues in fields related to alliance	$14 million	$6 billion	$5 billion
Total assets	$45 million	$10 billion	$25 billion
Return on assets	−23%	13%	1.6%
Number of employees	700	122,000	104,000
Sun (SPARC)			
Company name	Sun Microsystems	Fujitsu	Texas Instruments
Founded	1982	1935	1930
Home country	U.S.	Japan	U.S.
Main businesses	Workstations	Computers	Semiconductors
Performance at Joining			
Joined alliance group	1987	1987	1988
Role in alliance group	Architecture and O/S design; systems sales	Chip design/production; systems sales in Japan	Chip design/production

Total revenues	$760 million	$17 billion	$6.3 billion
Revenues in fields related to alliance	$760 million	$5 billion	$4 billion
Total assets	$524 million	$19 billion	$4.4 billion
Return on assets	7.0%	1.9%	8.3%
Number of employees	4,200	94,800	76,000

Hewlett-Packard (PA-RISC)

Company name	Hewlett-Packard Co.	Hitachi	Samsung
Founded	1938	1910	1952
Home country	U.S.	Japan	So. Korea
Main businesses	Test and measurement equip.; computers	Computers; electronic and other machinery; other	Electronics; chemicals; other

Performance at Joining

Joined alliance group	1989	1989	1989
Role in alliance group	Chip design/production; systems sales; O/S design	Chip design/production	Systems production, sales, esp. in So. Korea
Total revenues	$13 billion	$52 billion	$13 billion
Revenues in fields related to alliance	$5 billion	$1 billion	N/A
Total assets	$16 billion	$49 billion	$8 billion
Return on assets	8.2%	2.7%	2.7%
Number of employees	94,900	291,000	N/A

IBM (PowerPC)

Group	Lead firm	Two main partners	
Company name	IBM	Apple	Motorola
Founded	1910	1976	1928
Home country	U.S.	U.S.	U.S.
Main businesses	Computers	Microcomputers	Semiconductors; telecomm. and computer equip.
Performance at Joining			
Joined alliance group	1991	1991	1991
Role in alliance group	Chip design/production systems; sales; O/S	Systems sales; O/S	Chip design/production
Total revenues	$65 billion	$6.3 billion	$11 billion
Revenues in fields related to alliance	$16 billion	$5 billion	$4 billion
Total assets	$92 billion	$3.5 billion	$9.4 billion
Return on assets	−0.6%	8.9%	4.8%
Number of employees	345,000	14,000	102,000

Motorola (88000)

Company name	Motorola[a]	Data General
Founded	1928	1968
Home country	U.S.	U.S.
Main businesses	Semiconductors; telecomm. and computer equip.	Minicomputers
Performance at Joining		
Joined alliance group	1988	1988
Role in alliance group	Chip design/production; systems sales	Systems sales
Total revenues	$8.3 billion	$1.4 billion
Revenues in fields related to alliance	$3 billion	$1.4 billion
Total assets	$6.7 billion	$1.1 billion
Return on assets	6.6%	−1.4%
Number of employees	102,000	15,000

Sources: Annual reports and company documents.

Note: The name of each group's RISC architecture is given in parentheses (RX000, SPARC, etc.). The partners shown are two of the largest and most influential in each group. Revenues related to the alliance group are revenues from mini- and microcomputers and semiconductors. O/S = operating system software; N/A = not available.

a. Motorola stopped promoting its own 88000 design when it joined with IBM in 1991.

Notes

Introduction: Competition despite Cooperation

1. Adam Smith, *An Inquiry into the Nature and Causes of the Wealth of Nations,* edited with an introduction, notes, marginal summary, and an enlarged text by Edwin Cannan; with an introduction by Max Lerner (New York: Modern Library, Random House, 1937), p. 128. Originally published in 1776.
2. The view has a long literature behind it; see Chapter 5. The view also finds popular expression in business periodicals. See, for example, Michael E. Porter, "Don't Collaborate, Compete," *Economist,* June 9, 1990, p. 17.
3. My notion of collective competition, described further below, is related to the "collective capitalism" described by William Lazonick. He uses that term to differentiate capitalism in Japan from that in the United States and Britain. In Japan, enterprise groups *(keiretsu)* are common, business and government together guide economic development, and relationships between workers and managers are more cooperative than confrontational. These and other features define a distinctive type of capitalism, according to Lazonick. See also Michael H. Best's discussion of how cooperation among small firms in industrial districts—for example in Italy—help create a "New Competition." See William Lazonick, *Business Organization and the Myth of the Market Economy* (New York: Cambridge University Press, 1991); and Michael H. Best, *The New Competition: Institutions of Industrial Restructuring* (Cambridge, Mass.: Harvard University Press, 1990).

   My definition of collective competition is in some ways narrower and in other ways broader than the concepts of Lazonick and Best. I do not use the term to define a whole national economy—rather, it refers to a pattern of competition in a specific business. Furthermore, I do not include business-government and worker-management cooperation in my definition. In these ways, my concept is more narrowly defined. In my view, patterns of collective competition arise in Japan, United States, Europe, and in global industries. I apply the term to competition that involves groups of small firms, or just pairs and triads of large firms. A simple joint venture, in my view, can be engaged in collective competition, even if it is not embedded in the social and political-economic fabric that characterizes Lazonick's and Best's collective capitalism. In this sense, my concept can be applied more broadly.

4. Adam Smith, *The Wealth of Nations,* book 1, chaps. 1–3.

5. The term "constellation" is used in the generic sense of "any brilliant group of persons or things," *Funk and Wagnalls Standard College Dictionary* (New York: Funk and Wagnalls, 1963). My usage is similar to that of Richard Normann and Rafael Ramírez in "From Value Chain to Value Constellation: Designing Interactive Strategy," *Harvard Business Review* (July–August 1993): 65–77.

6. After saying that firms are defined by "the direction of resources," R. H. Coase admitted in a footnote that "it is impossible to draw a hard and fast line which determines whether there is a firm or not. There may be more or less direction." See "The Nature of the Firm," *Economica* (November 1937): 386–405. The treatment of alliances in the modern theory of the firm is not much different. Oliver E. Williamson, in *Markets and Hierarchies: Analysis and Antitrust Implications* (New York: Free Press, 1975), drew a sharp distinction between markets and hierarchies, and only later did he admit to the existence of governance forms in between these two extremes; see his "Transaction-Cost Economics: The Governance of Contractual Relations," *Journal of Law and Economics* 22 (October 1979): 233–261.

7. For example, Edith T. Penrose recognized the importance of the alliance groups I discuss in this book, but she was at a loss in dealing with their growth: "For an analysis of economic power there is no doubt that the industrial firm is *not* the most relevant unit; indeed individual men as well as corporations may extend their economic power by extending their ownership interests, and an attempt to define the firm according to power groupings would produce too amorphous a concept to handle." See her *Theory of the Growth of the Firm* (White Plains, N.Y.: M. E. Sharpe, 1980), p. 22. First published in 1959. In a new foreword to the third edition of her book, Penrose reviews the major theoretical and empirical developments since her original work. Among these is the "metamorphosis" of firms into groups that compete with one another. See *The Theory of the Growth of the Firm,* 3rd ed. (New York: Oxford University Press, 1995).

8. Quoted in "The Virtual Corporation," *Business Week,* February 8, 1993, p. 100.

9. Good collections of recent work on this topic are Farok J. Contractor and Peter Lorange, eds., *Cooperative Strategies in International Business* (Lexington, Mass.: D. C. Heath, 1988); David C. Mowery, *International Collaborative Ventures in U.S. Manufacturing* (Washington, D.C.: American Enterprise Institute, 1988); Lynn Krieger Mytelka, ed., *Strategic Partnerships: States, Firms, and International Competition* (Rutherford, N.J.: Farleigh Dickinson Univer-

sity Press, 1991); Joel Bleeke and David Ernst, eds., *Collaborating to Compete* (New York: John Wiley and Sons, 1993). The following articles report on cross-industry patterns of alliance formation: P. Mariti and R. H. Smiley, "Co-Operative Agreements and the Organization of Industry," *Journal of Industrial Economics* 31 (June 1983): 437–451; Deigan Morris and Michael Hergert, "Trends in International Collaborative Agreements," *Columbia Journal of World Business* (Summer 1987): 15–21; Pankaj Ghemawat, Michael E. Porter, and Richard A. Rawlinson, "Patterns of International Coalition Activity," in *Competition in Global Industries,* ed. Porter (Boston: Harvard Business School Press, 1986), pp. 345–365; Vern Terpstra and Bernard L. Simonin, "Strategic Alliances in the Triad: An Exploratory Study," *Journal of International Marketing* 1, no. 1 (1993): 4–25; and John Hagedoorn, "Understanding the Rationale of Strategic Technology Partnering: Interorganizational Modes of Cooperation and Sectoral Differences," *Strategic Management Journal* 14 (July 1993): 371–385.

10. D. H. Robertson and S. Dennison, *The Control of Industry* (Cambridge: Cambridge University Press, 1960), p. 73. First published in 1923.

11. "Mips" is often spelled with capital letters ("MIPS"), because it originally stood for Multiple Interlocking Pipeline Stages, a technical term related to the type of microprocessor sold by the company. But the company itself never used this full term as its name. In addition, the company name represents a play on words, as MIPS also stands for Millions of Instructions Per Second, a common measure of microprocessor speed. To avoid confusion with these other acronyms and following the practice of others in the business press, I will use the "Mips" to signify the company.

12. In other words, when I compare constellations with single firms in this book, I do not mean to imply that the single firms operate in complete isolation from other firms. Rather, the relationships between "single firms" and other firms are arm's length agreements, which are not alliances by my definition. See further discussion in Chapter 1.

13. This is, of course, an oversimplified view of the world. But it is employed as a basic framework by leading economists; see F. M. Scherer, *Industrial Market Structure and Economic Performance* (Boston: Houghton Mifflin Company, 1980), p. 10. In practice, the number of players is not the only characteristic that matters. There may be many players, but only a few "top tier" competitors that compete with one another as if the market only contained a few players.

14. The leading graduate-level textbook on industrial organization spends one chapter on the theory of the firm and then all but ignores that theory in the remaining eleven chapters. It does so because the author believes that, for most purposes, it does not matter how the firm is organized. Even so, the author apologetically inserts (Jean Tirole, *The Theory of Industrial Organization,* Cambridge, Mass.: MIT Press, 1988, pp. 50–51): "It is not meant to convey the impression that 'separability' between internal organizations and product-market or input-market decisions is the rule. Indeed, one of the most exciting research agendas in industrial organization for years to

come is the determination of the scope and importance of such interactions." Leading textbooks on the theory of the firm reflect the other side
of this coin: they explain in great detail why firms exist and how they are
structured, but seldom connect these ideas to how the firms behave in the
market. See, for example, Paul Milgrom and John Roberts, *Economics,
Organization, and Management* (Englewood Cliffs, N.J.: Prentice Hall, 1992).

At the root of this disconnect between the theory of the firm and theories
of industrial organization lies the distinction that Oliver Williamson and
others have made between the "economizing" and the "strategizing" approaches to economic behavior. The former focuses on the role of firms as
efficient ways of organizing production; the latter focuses on how firms
gain advantage through strategic behavior. See especially the cognitive
map of contracts and the surrounding discussion in Oliver E. Williamson,
*The Economic Institutions of Capitalism: Firms, Markets, and Relational Contract-
ing* (New York: Free Press, 1985), p. 24. Fortunately, new work in economics is beginning to bridge this gap. See, for example, Julio J.
Rotemberg, "Benefits of Narrow Business Strategies," *American Economic
Review* 84 (December 1994): 1330–1349; Joseph Farrell, Hunter K. Monroe, and Garth Saloner, "The Vertical Organization of Industry Systems
Competition versus Component Competition," mimeograph, 1994; and
Pankaj Ghemawat, "Competitive Advantage and Internal Organization:
Nucor Revisited," *Journal of Economics and Management Strategy* 3 (Winter
1995): 685–717. Furthermore, students of the multinational enterprise
have sometimes been implicitly concerned with the relationship between
firm structure and market competition. Richard Caves reviews the relationships between the degree of foreign investment and patterns of market
competition in his *Multinational Enterprise and Economic Analysis* (Cambridge: Cambridge University Press, 1982), chap. 4.

15. George J. Stigler gave this as one explanation for why firms seeking to
monopolize their industry in late nineteenth-century America formed
mergers rather than cartels. See p. 30 of his "Monopoly and Oligopoly by
Merger," *American Economic Review* (May 1950): 23–34.

16. Oliver E. Williamson, *Markets and Hierarchies: Analysis and Antitrust Implications* (New York: Free Press, 1975), chap. 12. He critiques the claim that a
small group of firms could exercise monopoly power much like a single
firm could (p. 234): "I take exception to this position here. It fails to make
allowance for the advantages of internal organization as compared to
interfirm contracting in adaptational respects, and it gives insufficient
standing to the differential incentives and the related propensity to cheat
that distinguish internal from interfirm organization." The remainder of
this short chapter reviews the approaches of others to oligopoly, and then
elaborates on the contracting perspective. He concludes that the various
costs of contracting under uncertainty will prohibit oligopolists from acting
like a single firm.

17. The structure of a competitor also matters in other ways not studied here.
If we admit that the number of firms per player affects the pattern of

competition, then why not consider also the effects of *internal firm organization* on competition between traditional single firms? In other words, the vertical axis in Figure 3 might show multinational firms versus domestic firms, or firms with divisionalized structures versus firms with functional organizations. Do these firms with different internal organizations behave differently from each other?

There are isolated arguments consistent with such an approach. There is a long-standing debate about whether conglomerates behave differently from focused firms—not only performing more poorly, but also colluding more with other conglomerates. There is also the notion that firms shift to divisionalized structures to improve their efficiency in implementing strategy. If so, we should expect different behaviors from different structures. Finally, there are arguments about how large, integrated firms might have deeper pockets or use cross-subsidies to compete more fiercely than other types of firms. But research that addresses the impact of internal firm organization on competitive behavior is still the exception, not the rule, in economics (see note 14 above).

18. This is discussed further in Chapter 5. For a review of the results of empirical studies on these and other variables, see Richard Schmalensee, "Inter-Industry Studies of Structure and Performance," in *Handbook of Industrial Organization,* vol. 2, ed. Schmalensee and Robert D. Willig (New York: North-Holland, 1989), chap. 16.

19. Joseph A. Schumpeter, *Capitalism, Socialism, and Democracy,* 3rd ed. (New York: Harper, 1950).

20. Benjamin Gomes-Casseres, "Computers: Alliances and Industry Evolution," in *Beyond Free Trade: Firms, Governments, and Global Competition,* ed. David B. Yoffie (Boston: Harvard Business School Press, 1993), chap. 3.

21. Key features of the RISC industry are described in the case study preceding Chapter 3.

Case Study: How Fuji Xerox Saved Xerox

1. The rise of new competitors was in part enabled by the Federal Trade Commission's (FTC) antitrust actions against Xerox. In 1973 the FTC charged that Xerox's pricing, leasing, and patent-licensing practices violated the Sherman Antitrust Act. It demanded that Xerox offer royalty-free licenses on all its copier patents, that it divest itself of Rank Xerox and Fuji Xerox, and that it allow third parties to service copiers leased from Xerox. Xerox signed a consent decree in 1975, in which it agreed, among other things, to license more than 1,700 past and future patents for a period of ten years. Competitors were permitted to license up to three patents free from royalties, to pay 0.5 percent of revenues on the next three, and to license additional patents royalty-free. Kodak, IBM, Canon, Ricoh, and other Japanese firms were among the firms to secure Xerox licenses under this arrangement.

2. Personal interview, January 1991.
3. It was IBM's introduction of its Copier series in 1970 that signaled the end of the Xerox monopoly in its home market. This line of products, however, was dogged by performance problems. A more serious threat came from Kodak's popular and high-performance Ektaprint series, introduced in 1972.
4. The joint venture with Rank was formed in 1956, with Xerox holding 50 percent of the equity. In 1969 the Xerox share was increased to 51 percent, and Xerox took over management control of Rank Xerox. In 1995 Xerox purchased additional shares from Rank to bring its ownership up to 71 percent.
5. As part of its technology licensing agreements with Rank Xerox, Fuji Xerox had exclusive rights to sell the machines in Japan, Indonesia, South Korea, the Philippines, Taiwan, Thailand, and Indochina. In return, Fuji Xerox would pay Rank Xerox a royalty of 5 percent on revenues from the sale of xerographic products. Rank Xerox would, of course, also be entitled to 50 percent of Fuji Xerox's profits. By agreement, 66 percent of Rank Xerox profits (that is, 33 percent of Fuji Xerox profits) flowed to Xerox between 1969 and 1995. After Xerox increased its share of Rank Xerox to 71 percent in 1995, 80 percent of Rank Xerox profits flowed to Xerox (that is, 40 percent of Fuji Xerox profits).

   Originally, Fuji Xerox was designed to be purely a marketing joint venture to sell copiers made by Xerox or by Fuji Photo. When the Japanese government refused to approve a joint venture intended solely as a sales company, however, the agreement was revised to give Fuji Xerox manufacturing rights. In the early years, Fuji Xerox subcontracted Fuji Photo Film to manufacture the products.
6. Personal interview, February 1991.
7. Rank Xerox became a passive partner because Xerox acquired control of Rank Xerox in 1969, when it increased its shareholding from 50 percent to 51 percent; from then on, Rank Xerox decisions were controlled by Xerox. The reasons behind Fuji Photo's passive stance are more complex. In 1971 Fuji Photo transferred its copier plants to Fuji Xerox. In a personal interview in September 1990, Yoichi Ogawa, one of the executives transferred from Fuji Photo to launch Fuji Xerox, explained how the contract with Xerox raised barriers to technology flow between Fuji Xerox and Fuji Photo: "According to Fuji Photo's agreement with Xerox, the company, as a shareholder, could collect information from Fuji Xerox, but it could not use it in its own operations. In addition, a technology agreement between Fuji Xerox and Xerox provided that any technology acquired by Fuji Xerox from outside sources (including from Fuji Photo) could be passed on freely to Xerox."
8. Personal interview, October 1990.
9. Gary Jacobson and John Hillkirk, *Xerox: American Samurai* (New York: Macmillan, 1986), p. 299.
10. Personal interview with Kennard, December 1990.

11. Jacobson and Hillkirk, *Xerox: American Samurai.*

12. Personal interview, February 1991.

13. Although Xerox had acquired control of Rank Xerox in 1969 by raising its share of equity to 51 percent, the line operations of the two firms were not integrated until 1978. Rank Xerox could thus make this decision in relative autonomy.

14. In the 1990s, Xerox too increased its number of patents as part of an overall corporate strategy to strengthen the patent portfolio.

15. Royalties were again renegotiated in 1993. Xerox then expected the royalties to increase over time, in recognition of the rising value of Xerox technologies supplied to Fuji Xerox.

16. Many of these models were manufactured by Fuji Xerox and transferred to Rank Xerox and Xerox for sale in Europe and the United States. This trend started with the FX2200 and the FX3500.

17. Allaire was referring to the three ultimate parents of Fuji Xerox—Xerox Corporation, Fuji Photo Film, and Rank Organization. Personal interview, February 1991.

18. Personal interview, October 1990.

19. By 1989, an estimated 1,000 young Fuji Xerox employees had spent three years each as residents at Xerox, and about 150 Xerox people had done the same at Fuji Xerox. These residents were directly involved in the work of their host companies. Every year there were also some 1,000 shorter visits by engineers and managers.

20. Most of this section is based on interviews at Xerox and Fuji Xerox in October and November 1993.

21. Personal interview, October 1993.

22. Personal interview, December 1990.

23. Personal interview, October 1993.

24. Personal interview, November 1993.

25. Ibid.

26. Personal interview, October 1993.

1. Firms, Alliances, and Constellations

1. I interpret capabilities quite broadly here; see G. B. Richardson, "The Organisation of Industry," *Economic Journal* (September 1972): 883–896; and Paul H. Rubin, "The Expansion of Firms," *Journal of Political Economy* 81 (July/August 1973): 936–949; and Edith T. Penrose, *The Theory of the Growth of the Firm* (White Plains, N.Y.: M. E. Sharpe, 1980), p. 22 (first published in 1959).

2. This idea is common in the literature on organizational behavior and business strategy. One of the first statements of it is in James D. Thompson, *Organizations in Action: Social Science Bases of Administrative Theory* (New York: McGraw-Hill, 1967). For a review of the relevant literature, see Nitin Nohria and Ranjay Gulati, "Firms and Their Environments," in *Handbook*

of Economic Sociology, ed. Neil J. Smelser and Richard Swedberg (Princeton, N.J.: Princeton University Press, 1994), chap. 21.

3. An arm's length contract is a transaction between separate parties that involves little or no mutual dependence and no joint decision making. The transaction is made on terms common in the market, without special considerations. In the economics and legal literature, arm's length contracts are also referred to as "complete contracts." For an excellent discussion of the role of this and other types of contracts in economics, see Oliver Hart and Bengt Holmström, "The Theory of Contracts," in *Advances in Economic Theory: Fifth World Congress,* ed. Truman F. Bewley (Cambridge: Cambridge University Press, 1987), pp. 71–155.

4. The need for heavy investments in relationship-specific assets, for example, may lead to bilateral monopolies that create incentives for opportunistic recontracting. It is often impossible or costly to write contracts that avoid this problem. Knowing this, firms will likely decline to conduct such transactions through contracts, choosing arm's length arrangements instead. See Benjamin Klein, Robert G. Crawford, and Armen A. Alchian, "Vertical Integration, Appropriable Rents, and the Competitive Contracting Process," *Journal of Law and Economics* 21 (1978): 297–326; and Oliver E. Williamson, *Markets and Hierarchies: Analysis and Antitrust Implications* (New York: Free Press, 1975).

Another set of conditions may lead to the embeddedness of certain capabilities, because they are costly to transfer across firm boundaries, or because they create economies of scope that make it beneficial to keep them tied to other firm capabilities. Alliances may be the only way to gain access to inputs not available on the market or to capabilities that are embedded in firms. See David J. Teece, "The Multinational Enterprise: Market Failure and Market Power Considerations," *Sloan Management Review* (Spring 1981): 3–17; and Joseph L. Badaracco, Jr., *The Knowledge Link: How Firms Compete through Strategic Alliances* (Boston: Harvard Business School Press, 1991).

Difficulties with monitoring the output of an alliance or of the partners' contributions can also make contracting costly. See Armen Alchian and Harold Demsetz, "Production, Information Costs, and Economic Organization," *American Economic Review* (December 1972): 777–795. For a good review of the principals-and-agents literature, which stresses monitoring costs, see John W. Pratt and Richard J. Zeckhauser, eds., *Principals and Agents: The Structure of Business* (Boston: Harvard Business School Press, 1985).

5. The mere existence of interdependence among partners is not enough for a relationship to be classified as collaborative. Scholars in the field of noncooperative game theory study how interdependent parties make decisions *in the absence of collaboration.* My definition is akin to Arthur Stein's definition of collaboration between nations: "behavior [that] results from joint rather than independent decisionmaking." See his "Coordination and

Collaboration: Regimes in an Anarchic World," *International Organization* (Spring 1982): 310.

6. The circumstances that typically give rise to alliances are usually such that complete contracts are either impossible or too costly to write. For example, they may involve small-numbers bargaining or investment in specific assets in the presence of uncertainty and bounded rationality; see Williamson, *Markets and Hierarchies;* and Hart and Holmström, "The Theory of Contracts."

7. Hart and Holmström ("The Theory of Contracts") write: "[I]ncompleteness raises new and difficult questions about how the behavior of contracting parties is determined. To the extent that incomplete contracts do not specify the parties' actions fully (i.e., they contain 'gaps'), additional theories are required to tell us how these gaps are filled in. Among other things, outside influences such as custom or reputation may become important under these conditions. In addition, outsiders such as the courts (or arbitrators) may have a role to play in filling in missing provisions of the contract and resolving ambiguities, rather than in simply enforcing an existing agreement. Incompleteness can also throw light on the importance of the allocation of decision rights or rights of control. If it is too costly to state precisely how a particular asset is to be used in every state of the world, it may be efficient simply to give one party 'control' of the asset, in the sense that he is entitled to do what he likes with it, subject perhaps to some explicit (contractible) limitations." Without saying so, the authors have listed several features commonly found in alliances and that typically help partners manage the incomplete contract between them—reputation, arbitration, allocation of decision rights, limitations on control. It is striking, however, that in most of the models in the property rights school of thought, jointly owned ventures are explicitly ruled out. See Oliver Hart and John Moore, "Property Rights and the Nature of the Firm," *Journal of Political Economy* 98 (1990): 1119–1158, esp. p. 1132. For a less technical treatment of these and related issues in the theories of the firm and of contracts, see Hart's "An Economist's Perspective on the Theory of the Firm," *Columbia Law Review* 89 (November 1989): 1757–1774. A classic study of how common incomplete contracts are in business is Stewart Macaulay, "Non-Contractual Relations in Business: A Preliminary Study," *American Sociological Review* 28 (February 1963): 55–70.

8. Arthur L. Stinchcombe describes how long-term contracts often contain features of organizations, and the reverse; see his "Organizing Information Outside the Firm: Contracts as Hierarchical Documents," in *Information and Organizations,* ed. Stinchcombe (Berkeley: University of California Press, 1990), pp. 194–239.

9. For a discussion of mutual forbearance in alliances, see Peter J. Buckley and Mark Casson, "A Theory of Cooperation in International Business," in *Cooperative Strategies in International Business,* ed. Farok J. Contractor and Peter Lorange (Lexington, Mass.: D. C. Heath, 1988), pp. 31–54.

10. In practice, my definition of an alliance does not differ much from those of other scholars. The requirement of separate firms is almost universal. And most authors exclude arm's length contracts from alliances. See, for example, the various studies in Contractor and Lorange, eds., *Cooperative Strategies*. Neverthless, my emphasis on incomplete contracts and incomplete control—while consistent with earlier definitions—focuses attention on the unique characteristics of alliances as a governance mechanism.

11. For a discussion of major supplier-buyer relationships that are clearly deeper than arm's length, see K. J. Blois, "Vertical Quasi-Integration," *Journal of Industrial Economics* 20 (July 1972): 253–272. A pioneering analysis of alliances, defined broadly as I do here, is in Richardson, "The Organisation of Industry."

12. For the role of equity in alliances, see Jean-Francois Hennart, "A Transaction Costs Theory of Equity Joint Ventures," *Strategic Management Journal* (July–August 1988): 361–374; and Gary P. Pisano, "Using Equity Participation to Support Exchange: Evidence from the Biotechnology Industry," *Journal of Law, Economics, and Organization* (Spring 1989): 109–126. For differences in the activities carried out in the alliance, see Pankaj Ghemawat, Michael E. Porter, and Richard A. Rawlinson, "Patterns of International Coalition Activity," in *Competition in Global Industries*, ed. Porter (Boston: Harvard Business School Press, 1986), pp. 345–365. For the different strategic aims of alliances, see Bruce Kogut, "Joint Ventures: Theoretical and Empirical Perspectives," *Strategic Management Journal* (July–August 1988): 319–332. For alliances specifically in R&D, see Michael L. Katz, "An Analysis of Cooperative Research and Development," *Rand Journal of Economics* (Winter 1986): 527–543.

13. Because of these considerations, a constellation of firms linked by alliances will often be more efficient than a single firm that is linked to other firms through arm's length relationships.

14. This classic trade-off between loss of control and access to resources was first analyzed in John M. Stopford and Louis T. Wells, Jr., *Managing the Multinational Enterprise* (New York: Basic Books, 1972), part 2.

15. "Investment" should be interpreted broadly to mean sunk expenditures of capital or effort; see Hart and Moore, "Property Rights."

16. This argument is common to several schools of thought in the theory of the firm, including the agency, transaction-cost, and property-rights approaches. For representative treatments in each school, see Pratt and Zeckhauser, eds., *Principals and Agents;* Williamson, *Markets and Hierarchies;* and Hart and Moore, "Property Rights."

17. It is important to hold all else equal in this analysis of organizational advantage. Clearly, a competitor might have an advantage over another because it has greater capabilities; here we hold this variable constant and inquire into differences in the structure of control of a given set of capabilities.

18. Richardson, "The Organisation of Industry."

19. There is a growing empirical literature on the failure of firms to manage

disparate businesses acquired through "unrelated diversification." Among the earliest studies is Richard P. Rumelt, *Strategy, Structure, and Economic Performance* (Cambridge, Mass.: Harvard University Press, 1974). A recent study is Michael E. Porter, "From Competitive Advantage to Corporate Strategy," *Harvard Business Review* (May–June 1987): 43–59. A recent survey is Cynthia A. Montgomery, "Corporate Diversification," *Journal of Economic Perspectives* 8 (Summer 1994): 163–178. See also an explanation for these patterns in David J. Teece, "Toward an Economic Theory of the Multiproduct Firm," *Journal of Economic Behavior and Organization* 3 (1982): 39–63.

Although there is little doubt about the practical limits to firm size, economic theorists have not yet found a convincing reason for it. Oliver Williamson attributed the inefficiency of a large firm to the failure of "selective intervention"; see *The Economic Institutions of Capitalism: Firms, Markets, and Relational Contracting* (New York: Free Press, 1985), chap. 6. In an earlier piece, he argued that "control loss" and distortions arose as information and decisions were transmitted along layers of a hierarchical organization; see his "Hierarchical Control and Optimum Firm Size," *Journal of Political Economy* 75 (April 1967): 123–138. Paul Milgrom and John Roberts explain the inefficiency of large firms by arguing that internal political influences on the central authority bias its decision in favor of one organizational unit or another. These "influence costs" can distort centralized decision making and lead to suboptimal outcomes when compared with decentralized decision making; see their *Economics, Organization, and Management* (Englewood Cliffs, N.J.: Prentice Hall, 1992), pp. 192–194. A related argument is that bureaucracies create opportunities for formation of coalitions of co-workers that collude to distort information in their favor; see Jean Tirole, "Hierarchies and Bureaucracies: On the Role of Collusion in Organizations," *Journal of Law, Economics, and Organization* 2 (Fall 1986): 181–214.

20. A capability that is used in several businesses may be the "core competence" of a firm; see C. K. Prahalad and Gary Hamel, "The Core Competence of the Corporation," *Harvard Business Review* (May–June 1990): 79–91. More broadly, these capabilities represent the "embedded knowledge" discussed by Badaracco, *The Knowledge Link.*

21. Scholars examining the choice between acquisitions and joint ventures have come to similar conclusions. One study found that Japanese firms are more likely to use a joint venture—rather than an acquisition—when the U.S. target is part of a diversified company. See Jean-François Hennart and Savine Reddy, "The Choice between Mergers/Acquisitions and Joint Ventures: The Case of Japanese Investors in the United States," University of Illinois at Urbana-Champaign, CIBER Working Paper no. 93-011 (October 1993).

22. Ronald Coase described this dilemma, but did not have a solution for it (p. 395): "Suppose *A* is buying a product from *B* and that both *A* and *B* could organise this marketing transaction at less than its present cost. *B*,

we can assume, is not organising one process or stage of production, but several. If *A* therefore wishes to avoid a market transaction, he will have to take over all the processes of production controlled by *B.*" The problem with the merger solution, Coase concluded, was that *A* was not likely to be able to organize all of *B*'s processes more efficiently than *B* already did, because, he argued, of the much larger size of the merged firm. As a result, *A* would only acquire all of *B* if the loss of reorganizing *B*'s business were less than the gain of internalizing the original market transaction between *A* and *B*. He did not consider the possibility of an alliance between *A* and *B*, although he admitted elsewhere that "it is not possible to draw a hard and fast line which determines whether there is a firm or not. There may be more or less direction" (p. 392). An alliance enables joint decision making between *A* and *B*, and thus for some "direction" from both firms. An alliance in this situation might thus yield a lower governance cost than either the market or merger. See Coase, "The Nature of the Firm."

23. In addition, a complete contract would be costly or impossible to write and enforce, given the specific and uncertain nature of the investments in capability. Thus IBM and Toshiba had to conclude an incomplete contract and govern it through an alliance.

24. Management Review Committee minutes of July 15, 1971, quoted in Leo A. Morehouse and John W. Rosenblum, "IBM World Trade Corporation," Harvard Business School Case no. 9–374–303 (1974), p. 7.

25. Such cross-subsidies are the essence of a global strategy; see Gary Hamel and C. K. Prahalad, "Do You Really Have a Global Strategy?" *Harvard Business Review* (July–August 1985): 139–148.

26. See Lawrence G. Franko, *Joint Venture Survival in Multinational Corporations* (New York: Praeger, 1971).

27. In this example, Intel was using alliances because there were as yet no dominant players in the emerging industry. Rivals in such environments often use alliance groups to establish dominance. See Jonathan McLeod, "PC Videoconferencing Debuts at ComNet '94," *Electronics,* January 24, 1994, p. 1; and his "Building a Bandwagon for PC-Based Videoconferencing," ibid., p. 2.

28. I am not assuming that the constellations have a different set of capabilities than firms, merely that they have more freedom in creating the set and in changing it over time. For related arguments, see Walter W. Powell, "Neither Market Nor Hierarchy: Network Forms of Organization," *Research in Organizational Behavior* 12 (1990): 295–336; and Raymond E. Miles and Charles C. Snow, "Organizations: New Concepts for New Forms," *California Management Review* (Spring 1986): 62–73.

29. Adam Smith, *An Inquiry into the Nature and Causes of The Wealth of Nations,* edited with an introduction, notes, marginal summary, and an enlarged text by Edwin Cannan; with an introduction by Max Lerner (New York: Modern Library, Random House, 1937), book 1, chaps. 1–3. Originally published in 1776.

30. At a conference at Harvard Business School (October 7, 1994) Walter S. Mossberg, a columnist who reviews computer products for the *Wall Street Journal,* attributed the failure of the early PDAs partly to the lack of integration among the technologies of alliance partners.

31. According to the evolutionary theory of the firm, the intangible resources and capabilities of firms guide their patterns of expansion and diversification. Put differently, the patterns of expansion of firms are constrained by their history and are "path dependent." See Richard R. Nelson and Sidney G. Winter, *An Evolutionary Theory of Economic Change* (Cambridge, Mass.: Harvard University Press, 1982); Penrose, *Theory of the Growth of the Firm;* Cynthia A. Montgomery and S. Hariharan, "Diversified Expansion by Large Established Firms," *Journal of Economic Behavior and Organization* 15, no. 1 (1991): 71–89; Montgomery, ed., *Resources in an Evolutionary Perspective* (Norwell, Mass.: Kluwer Academic Publishers, 1995); and Giovanni Dosi, David J. Teece, and Sidney Winter, "Toward a Theory of Corporate Coherence: Preliminary Remarks," in *Technology and Enterprise in a Historical Perspective,* ed. Dosi, Renato Giannetti, and Pier Angelo Toninelli (Oxford: Clarendon Press, 1992), chap. 6.

32. There is a long literature on technology transfer; see a review in Benjamin Gomes-Casseres, "Technology Flows and Global Competition: A Framework for Research and Management," *Advances in International Comparative Management* 7 (1992): 3–22. For a discussion of how alliances help transfer technology, see Badaracco, *The Knowledge Link.*

33. Claudio U. Ciborra, "Alliances as Learning Experiments: Cooperation, Competition, and Change in High-Tech Industries," in *Strategic Partnerships: States, Firms, and International Competition,* ed. Lynn K. Mytelka (Rutherford, N.J.: Farleigh Dickinson University Press, 1991), p. 51.

34. Richard N. Langlois calls these "dynamic transaction costs" in "Transaction-Cost Economics in Real Time," *Industrial and Corporate Change* 1, no. 1 (1992): 99–127. He also defines these costs as "the costs of persuading, negotiating and coordinating with, and teaching others" in the process of changing a firm's capabilities.

35. Penrose, *Theory of the Growth of the Firm.*

36. Dorothy Leonard-Barton, "Core Capabilities and Core Rigidities: A Paradox in Managing New Product Development," *Strategic Management Journal* 13 (Summer 1992): 111–125; and Richard P. Rumelt, "Inertia and Transformation," in Montgomery, ed., *Resources in an Evolutionary Perspective.*

37. Personal interviews at IBM Japan, October 1990.

38. The changing antitrust climate in the United States, and to a lesser extent in Europe, may also have had an effect on IBM's attitude toward alliances. As an example, the alliance with Apple—IBM's chief competitor in PCs—would have been unlikely to be approved by the U.S. Justice Department if it had occurred in the early 1980s.

39. See Figure 1.

40. See further discussion in Benjamin Gomes-Casseres, "Computers: Alliances and Industry Evolution," in *Beyond Free Trade: Firms, Governments, and*

Global Competition, ed. David B. Yoffie (Boston: Harvard Business School Press, 1993), chap. 3.

41. Although these data span a large number of years, during which the industry underwent dramatic change, the bulk of the alliances occurred in the second half of the 1980s and the early 1990s. The patterns in the table thus represent that period better than earlier periods. Even so, aggregate patterns in the late 1970s were not very different from those shown here.

42. Nancy Foy, *The Sun Never Sets on IBM* (New York: Morrow, 1974), p. 158.

43. Some refused to do so and either left or were deterred from entering these countries. See Joseph M. Grieco, "Between Dependence and Autonomy: India's Experience with the International Computer Industry," *International Organization* (Summer 1982): 609–632; Dennis J. Encarnation, *Rivals beyond Trade* (Ithaca, N.Y.: Cornell University Press, 1992); and Benjamin Gomes-Casseres, "Firm Ownership Preferences and Host Government Restrictions: An Integrated Approach," *Journal of International Business Studies* (First Quarter, 1990): 1–22.

44. Gomes-Casseres, "Computers: Alliances and Industry Evolution."

45. Alfred D. Chandler, Jr., *Scale and Scope: The Dynamics of Industrial Capitalism* (Cambridge, Mass.: Harvard University Press, 1990), pp. 21–25.

46. This is termed "modularity" in Richard N. Langlois and Paul L. Robertson, "Networks and Innovation in a Modular System: Lessons from the Microcomputer and Stereo Component Industries," *Research Policy* 21 (August 1992): 297–313; a related distinction between assembled and nonassembled systems is made in Michael L. Tushman and Lori Rosenkopf, "Organizational Determinants of Technological Change: Toward a Sociology of Technological Evolution," *Research in Organizational Behavior* 15 (1992): 311–347. For an analysis of the benefits of modularity using options theory, see Carliss Y. Baldwin and Kim B. Clark, "The Benefits and Costs of Modularity in Design," December 1992, Harvard Business School, mimeograph.

47. A related question is addressed in an economic model in Joseph Farrell, Hunter K. Monroe, and Garth Saloner, "The Vertical Organization of Industry Systems Competition versus Component Competition," 1994, mimeograph. This paper treats a constellation as if it were full integration; the organizational choice examined is between operational integration and arm's length transactions. The paper then finds that a "closed organization" is often preferred by firms; but it does not analyze whether that organization is a single firm or a constellation.

48. None of the studies collected data systematically enough for us to be definite about these industry differences. Still, the weight of the evidence is consistent with this conclusion. See Ghemawat, Porter, and Rawlinson, "Patterns of International Coalition Activity"; John Hagedoorn, "Understanding the Rationale of Strategic Technology Partnering: Interorganizational Modes of Cooperation and Sectoral Differences," *Strategic Management Journal* 14 (July 1993): 371–385; and Vern Terpstra and Ber-

nard L. Simonin, "Strategic Alliances in the Triad: An Exploratory Study," *Journal of International Marketing* 1, no. 1 (1993): 4–25.

49. The use of alliances as options is discussed in Bruce Kogut, "Joint Ventures and the Option to Expand and Acquire," *Management Science* (January 1991): 19–33.

50. The static rationale for alliances does not completely ignore the effects of change and uncertainty. In fact, the likelihood of unforeseen change is one of the chief reasons why contracts may be costly to negotiate. Uncertainty in the environment thus tends to favor integration. For example, when the price for an intermediate good is subject to variation that cannot be predicted or hedged, the governance costs of internalizing the transaction will be lower than those of using contracts. Still, the type of uncertainty included there typically surrounds *features* of the external transaction, such as prices, quantities, and qualities, not the very need for the transaction.

51. See Kogut, "Joint Ventures and the Option to Expand and Acquire."

52. This distinction between single firms, pairs, triads, small groups, and large groups emerged from the data in this book. But it also has a distinguished history in sociology. See Georg Simmel, "On the Significance of Numbers for Social Life," in *The Sociology of Georg Simmel*, trans. and ed. Kurt H. Wolff (New York: Free Press, 1950). See also further discussion in Chapter 2.

53. This definition of an alliance network differs from other meanings often attached to the term "network." First, electronic networks linking computers and communications equipment may be part of the fabric of collaboration in a group, but this is not required by my definition. Second, the term "network organization" is often used to describe organizational and social arrangements that are geared to just-in-time production and rapid responses to market demands. (See William H. Davidow and Michael S. Malone, *The Virtual Corporation*, New York: HarperBusiness, 1992.) The alliance networks examined here may well be capable of such feats, but these are not their defining characteristics. Third, the idea of the "networked firm" sometimes is meant to describe a lack of hierarchy inside a firm, and it is often applied to formerly hierarchical firms that have been decentralized. For an overview of this and related parts of the network literature, see Nitin Nohria and Robert G. Eccles, *Networks and Organizations* (Boston: Harvard Business School Press, 1993). For conceptual discussions of networks inside and among firms, see Hans B. Thorelli, "Networks: Between Markets and Hierarchies," *Strategic Management Journal* (January–February 1986): 37–51; J. Carlos Jarillo, "On Strategic Networks," *Strategic Management Journal* (January–February 1988): 31–41; and Miles and Snow, "Organizations: New Concepts for New Forms."

54. For examples of such industrywide networks in various information technology sectors, see John Hagedoorn and Jos Schakenraad, "Leading Companies and Networks of Strategic Alliances in Information Technologies," *Research Policy* 21 (April 1992): 163–190.

55. Using tools of statistical network analysis it is possible to identify "blocks" of firms inside an industrywide network based on the density of relation-

ships among firms. The firms inside such a block have more connections with each other than with firms outside the block. But the definition of such a block depends on arbitrary assumptions about where to draw boundaries between blocks, that is, what density levels are used to differentiate internal block from interblock linkages. See John Scott, *Social Network Analysis: A Handbook* (New York: Sage, 1991). For an application of this technique to the automobile industry, see Nitin Nohria and Carlos Garcia-Pont, "Global Strategic Linkages and Industry Structure," *Strategic Management Review* 12 (Summer 1991): 105–124; for application to the computer industry, see Hagedoorn and Schakenraad, "Leading Companies and Networks of Strategic Alliances." The alliance groups analyzed in this book have been identified without these statistical techniques, because they stand out clearly from the fabric of the industry.

56. David J. Teece explains why economies of scale—and transactions costs—lie beneath every economy of scope; see his "Economies of Scope and the Scope of the Enterprise," *Journal of Economic Behavior and Organization* (September 1980): 223–247.

57. See "Swissair's Alliances," in David B. Yoffie and Benjamin Gomes-Casseres, *International Trade and Competition: Cases and Notes in Strategy and Management,* 2nd ed. (New York: McGraw-Hill, 1994), chap. 14.

58. Nathan Rosenberg describes a similar pattern in mechanical technologies in the United States in the nineteenth century; the petroleum and chemical industries experienced technological convergence from the 1940s to the 1960s. See his *Inside the Black Box: Technology and Economics* (Cambridge: Cambridge University Press, 1982).

59. The evolution of firm capabilities is path-dependent, as noted above.

60. For discussion of how a dominant architecture can provide a competitive advantage, see Charles R. Morris and Charles H. Ferguson, "How Architecture Wins Technology Wars," *Harvard Business Review* (March–April 1993): 86–96.

61. For a discussion of the role of "sponsors" in technology adoption, see Michael L. Katz and Carl Shapiro, "Technology Adoption in the Presence of Network Externalities," *Journal of Political Economy* (August 1986): 822–841.

62. For the history of the VCR standards battle, see Michael A. Cusumano, Yiorgos Mylonadis, and Richard S. Rosenbloom, "Strategic Maneuvering and Mass-Market Dynamics: The Triumph of VHS over Beta," *Business History Review* (Spring 1992): 51–94. For the quadraphonics story, see Steven R. Postrel, "Competing Networks and Proprietary Standards: The Case of Quadraphonic Sound," *Journal of Industrial Economics* (December 1990): 169–185.

63. Walter W. Powell sees networks as a form of economic organization that is distinct from markets and firms. I find it more useful to decompose networks into alliances, and then treat the alliances as the distinct form that lies "between" markets and firms. The component alliances are thus the mechanisms for governing incomplete contracts; the networks can

then be seen as an aggregation of these alliances. Compare with Powell's "Neither Market Nor Hierarchy."

64. Notwithstanding these arguments, alliance networks are sometimes substitutes for individual partnerships, at least if the latter are given broad scopes. When Xerox recognized in the mid-1950s that it needed additional resources to go abroad, it chose one major partner, the Rank Organization. It then gave Rank Xerox the exclusive rights to xerography in all markets outside the Americas. In principle, Xerox might have used a series of alliances to achieve the same ends, perhaps forming relationships with leading firms in different countries or regions. This option might not have occurred to Xerox at the time, or perhaps it preferred not to get involved in managing so many different relationships. Today, with alliances becoming ever more popular and Xerox having developed deep expertise in managing them, it may be expected to choose a different course. Indeed, when Xerox announced in 1993 a new high-resolution, dry-processing film not based on silver halide technology, it said that it would market the product in collaboration with nine graphic arts firms, including 3M and Agfa.

65. Simmel described how larger groups depersonalize relationships and lower the commitment of members to the joint effort. See his "On the Significance of Numbers for Social Life."

66. For definitions of "centrality" in networks, see Scott, *Social Network Analysis*. In most of the cases discussed here, the identity of the central firm is easy to discern; in other cases, statistical analysis can be used to find them. For an attempt to measure centrality in automobile networks, see Nohria and Garcia-Pont, "Global Strategic Linkages."

67. These structural choices are discussed further in Chapter 3.

68. See Michael L. Gerlach, *Alliance Capitalism: The Social Organization of Japanese Business* (Berkeley: University of California Press, 1992); Akira Goto, "Business Groups in a Market Economy," *European Economic Review* (September 1982): 53–70; and Marie Anchordoguy, *Computers, Inc.: Japan's Challenge to IBM*, Harvard East Asian Monographs, 144 (Cambridge, Mass.: Council on East Asian Studies, Harvard University, 1989).

69. See Nathaniel H. Leff, "Industrial Organization and Entrepreneurship in the Developing Countries: The Economic Groups," *Economic Development and Cultural Change* 26, no. 4 (1978): 661–675; and Mark Granovetter, "Business Groups," in *Handbook of Economic Sociology*, ed. Neil J. Smelser and Richard Swedberg (Princeton, N.J.: Princeton University Press, 1994), chap. 18. The "federated enterprises" are mentioned in Michael J. Piore and Charles F. Sabel, *The Second Industrial Divide: Possibilities for Prosperity* (New York: Basic Books, 1984), p. 267.

70. See George W. Stocking and Myron W. Watkins, *Cartels in Action: Case Studies in International Business Diplomacy* (New York: Kraus Reprint Co., 1975). Originally published in 1946. Stocking and Watkins define a cartel as "an arrangement among, or on behalf of, producers engaged in the same line of business, with the design or effect of limiting competition among

them" (p. 3). In this sense, cartels are constellations. Furthermore, because constellations suppress internal competition, as we shall see, they may fall under this definition of a cartel. The difference, however, is that in a true cartel, the sole purpose is to suppress competition; in the constellations I study, the suppression of internal rivalry is a means to an end—more effective competition with external parties.

Case Study: Did Honeywell Create a Competitor?

1. Telephone interview, October 1993. In the 1990s this was Yamatake-Honeywell's most successful business, one in which it had a dominant market share in Japan.
2. Telephone interview, November 1993.
3. This reluctance is partly explained by the fact that the Micro Switch division, too, grew out of a Honeywell acquisition, and headquarters gave this division a great deal of autonomy.
4. "[W]e rushed ahead of other firms into the then non-existent Japanese market for automation control equipment," wrote Kazuma Takeisi, Omron's founder. "As a result, for several years Omron was the only company serving the market, and that laid the foundation for the company's current prosperity." See his *Eternal Venture Spirit: An Executive's Practical Philosophy* (Cambridge, Mass.: Productivity Press, 1989), p. 58.
5. Telephone interview, October 1993.
6. Like General Motors, Chrysler, Levi Strauss, and other American firms, Honeywell saw its Japanese assets as a way to improve its balance sheet. In 1989 General Motors, Chrysler, and Levi Strauss all sold a portion of their Japanese assets. GM sold part of its interest in Isuzu, Chrysler sold part of its ownership in Mitsubishi Motors, and Levi Strauss had an initial public offering for Levi Strauss Japan KK, its Japanese affiliate (*Japan Economic Journal*, December 23, 1989, pp. 1, 6). Renier reasoned that Honeywell's share in Yamatake-Honeywell was worth over $1 billion, thanks in large part to high real estate prices in Tokyo, where Yamatake-Honeywell had five factories. Furthermore, the current price of Yamatake-Honeywell stock, which had risen with the Japanese stock market boom, was never reflected on Honeywell's books. The value of Yamatake-Honeywell had never been adequately reflected in Honeywell's financial statements. Income was accounted for on an equity basis. Honeywell did not treat Yamatake-Honeywell as a source of funds; it kept royalties and dividend payouts low; and Yamatake-Honeywell profits were reinvested in Japan. Like other embattled corporate leaders during this period, Renier set out to unlock this value.
7. *Industry Week*, March 5, 1990.
8. "Operating within the Framework of the Honeywell/Yamatake-Honeywell Strategic Alliance Agreement: Management Summary," Honeywell internal document, December 1991, p. 3.

9. The SAA states: "Future license grants for products and/or technology are to be worldwide in territorial scope for purposes of development and low-cost manufacturing, but territorially limited for purposes of marketing, support and usage" ("SAA: Management Summary," p. 11).

10. "SAA: Management Summary," p. 9.

11. Ibid., p. 10.

12. Telephone interview, November 1993; and personal interview, August 1991.

13. Telephone interview, October 1993.

14. Ibid.

15. *Industry Week,* March 5, 1990, p. 24.

16. Telephone interview, October 1993.

17. Ibid.

18. Telephone interview, December 1993.

19. The SAA agreement divided the world into three domains: one the exclusive responsibility of Honeywell, one the responsibility of Yamatake-Honeywell, and one in which responsibility was shared. Honeywell would be responsible for the Americas, Europe (including Eastern Europe, the Middle East, and Africa), Australia, and New Zealand. Yamatake-Honeywell would remain responsible for Japan. Within each area, the responsible partner would "coordinate and manage the marketing, selling and distribution of *all* products within the scope" of the SAA. ("SAA: Management Summary," p. 6.) By early 1993, responsibilities in "Other Asia" had, according to Yamatake-Honeywell chairman Haruo Okinobu, been defined as follows: Honeywell would be responsible for Hong Kong, Malaysia, Taiwan, and Singapore; Thailand and Indonesia were the "mutual" responsibility of Yamatake-Honeywell and Honeywell; South Korea was to be served by the Honeywell-Goldstar joint venture; and China was to be served "independently" by Yamatake-Honeywell and Honeywell. (Personal interview, November 1993.)

20. Mike Meyers, "Honeywell Engaged in High Stakes 'Bridge Building,'" *Minneapolis Star Tribune,* December 13, 1993, p. A1.

21. This was in recognition of the fear of abandonment felt by Yamatake-Honeywell after the sale of equity (see Chapter 2).

22. Quoted in Meyers, "Honeywell."

23. Telephone interview, December 1993.

24. Telephone interview, October 1993.

2. Allies or Rivals?

1. See, for example, Louis Kraar, "Your Rivals Can Be Your Allies," *Fortune,* March 27, 1989, pp. 66–70.

2. The term "coopetition" was coined by Ray Noorda, president and CEO of Novell Inc., to describe his company's relationship to licensees that are also its competitors. It has since been used by others in the computer hardware

and software industry. See, for example, Samuel Weber, "Anatomy of 'Coopetition,' " *Electronics*, August 1991, pp. 37–38, which applies the term to an alliance between Hewlett-Packard Company and Lotus Corporation. More recently, business economists have defined and used this term more precisely to describe the way in which every business relationship contains elements of both competition and cooperation. See Adam M. Brandenberger and Barry J. Nalebuff, "The Right Game: Use Game Theory to Shape Strategy," *Harvard Business Review* (July–August 1995): 57–71.

3. Smith's statement has to be read in context. It comes in a chapter devoted to the ways in which continental European countries used corporations to restrain competition in certain trades. His classic analysis of the division of labor illustrates a different kind of cooperation—one that improves efficiency and lowers prices. Compare p. 128 and book 1, chaps. 1–3 in Adam Smith, *An Inquiry into the Nature and Causes of The Wealth of Nations*, edited with an introduction, notes, marginal summary, and an enlarged text by Edwin Cannan; with an introduction by Max Lerner (New York: Modern Library, Random House, 1937). Originally published in 1776.

4. For a model of how the incentives for collusion in one market increase when two firms already collude in another, see Douglas Bernheim and Michael D. Whinston, "Multimarket Contact and Collusive Behavior," *Rand Journal of Economics* 21 (Spring 1990): 1–26. Two collaborative projects may also reinforce each other because the contribution of one party can be withheld in the first project if the other party does not fulfill obligations on the second project. See Oliver E. Williamson, "Credible Commitments: Using Hostages to Support Exchange," *American Economic Review* 73 (September 1983): 519–540. For an empirical test of the hostages hypothesis and for evidence that continued rivalry between partners hurts cooperation, see Bruce Kogut, "The Stability of Joint Ventures: Reciprocity and Competitive Rivalry," *Journal of Industrial Economics* 38 (December 1989): 183–198.

5. The classic statement of this argument, with experimental tests, is Robert Axelrod, *The Evolution of Cooperation* (New York: Basic Books, 1984). Future expectations—the "shadow of the future"—have been found to affect the stability of alliances; see Arvind Parkhe, "Strategic Alliance Structuring: A Game-Theoretic and Transaction-Cost Examination of Interfirm Cooperation," *Academy of Management Journal* 36 (August 1993): 794–829; and Jan B. Heide and Anne S. Miner, "The Shadow of the Future: Effects of Anticipated Interaction and Frequency of Contact on Buyer-Seller Cooperation," *Academy of Management Journal* 35 (June 1992): 265–291.

6. As discussed below, this is the problem with precompetitive collaborative R&D in MCC, Sematech, Esprit, and other such ventures.

7. I have employed the following criteria to evaluate constellation performance. First, performance is judged relative to an estimate of how partners would have fared had they not formed the alliance. Second, the focus is not on the alliance per se, but on the effects of collaboration on the partners. Third, the performance of a constellation is measured separately

for different tasks and over time. For a good discussion of the difficulties in judging the performance of constellations, see Erin Anderson, "Two Firms, One Frontier: On Assessing Joint Venture Performance," *Sloan Management Review* (Winter 1990): 19–30.

8. In social network analysis, the first case is referred to as a "balanced" triad, the second as an "unbalanced" triad; see John Scott, *Social Network Analysis: A Handbook* (New York: Sage, 1991), pp. 13–14; and further discussion below.

9. Personal interview with Jeff Kennard, October 1993.

10. The term "precompetitive" was first used by Europeans designing the Esprit program but is now more generally applied to cases such as Sematech, the Microelectronics and Computer Technology Corporation (MCC), and others in the United States. For a good discussion of the European experience with precompetitive collaborative research, see Wayne Sandholtz, *High-Tech Europe* (Berkeley: University of California Press, 1992).

11. The literature in sociology and political science has explored why external conflict generates internal cohesion. For a review, see Arthur A. Stein, "Conflict and Cohesion: A Review of the Literature," *Journal of Conflict Resolution* 20 (March 1976): 143–172.

12. This is similar to the "technology cartel" described by William J. Baumol, "Horizontal Collusion and Innovation," *Economic Journal* 102 (January 1992): 129–137.

13. For an account of collaboration among potential competitors in the aerospace industry, see Thomas W. Roehl and J. Frederick Truitt, "Stormy Open Marriages Are Better: Evidence from U.S., Japanese, and French Cooperative Ventures in Commercial Aircraft," *Columbia Journal of World Business* (Summer 1987): 87–95.

14. The best discussion of Esprit and Eureka, another European cooperative R&D program, is Sandholtz, *High-Tech Europe*.

15. See Peter Grindley, David C. Mowery, and Brian Silverman, "Sematech and Collaborative Research: Lessons in the Design of High-Technology Consortia," Consortium on Competitiveness and Cooperation Working Paper no. 39–21, January 1994. On the Japanese consortia, see Kiyonori Sakakibara, "R&D Cooperation among Competitors: A Case Study of the VLSI Semiconductor Research Project in Japan," *Journal of Engineering and Technology Management* 10 (1993): 393–407; and Gerald Hane, "R&D Consortia: Contrasting U.S. and Japanese Strategies," MIT Japan Program Working Paper no. 94–02, 1994.

16. This may be one reason why there was reportedly substantial technical collaboration in the interwar chemical cartels: Du Pont, Imperial Chemical Industries (ICI), and IG Farben had the world market divided among themselves, and so had little to fear from sharing research in the "precompetitive" phase. This conclusion is also consistent with a number of economic models of R&D collaboration that show that downstream competition tends to discourage cooperation in upstream R&D. See Mi-

chael L. Katz and Janusz A. Ordover, "R&D Cooperation and Competition," *Brooking Papers on Economic Activity,* 1990, pp. 137–203; and Michael L. Katz, "An Analysis of Cooperative Research and Development," *RAND Journal of Economics* (Winter 1986): 527–543.

17. For further analysis of how firms can lose competitiveness through these vicious circles, see Gary Hamel, "Competition for Competence and Inter-Partner Learning within International Strategic Alliances," *Strategic Management Journal* (Summer 1991): 83–104; and Robert B. Reich and Eric D. Mankin, "Joint Ventures with Japan Give Away Our Future," *Harvard Business Review* (March–April 1986): 78–86.

18. For a discussion of how "core rigidities" keep the firm from changing and adopting new technologies, see Dorothy Leonard-Barton, "Core Capabilities and Core Rigidities: A Paradox in Managing New Product Development," *Strategic Management Journal* (1992): 111–125.

19. This argument is consistent with the view in game theory that the shadow of the future and reputation enhance cooperation even without a change in the formal payoff structure of a game. See Axelrod, *Evolution of Cooperation,* and Kenneth A. Oye, ed., *Cooperation under Anarchy* (Princeton, N.J.: Princeton University Press, 1986), especially the introductory chapter (by Oye) and concluding chapter (by Axelrod and Robert O. Keohane).

20. This concept borrows from the idea of "social capital" introduced by James S. Coleman and elaborated by Robert D. Putnam. See Coleman's "The Rational Reconstruction of Society: 1992 Presidential Address," *American Sociological Review* 58 (February 1993): 1–15. Putnam defines social capital as "features of social organization, such as trust, norms, and networks, that can improve the efficiency of society by facilitating coordinated actions" (p. 167); see his *Making Democracy Work: Civic Traditions in Modern Italy* (Princeton, N.J.: Princeton University Press, 1993), esp. chap. 6.

21. Rosabeth Moss Kanter, "Collaborative Advantage," *Harvard Business Review* (July–August 1994): 96–108.

22. Yves L. Doz, "From Intent to Outcome: Managing the Dynamic of Strategic Alliances between Firms," September 1993, INSEAD, mimeograph.

23. For a model in which alliances survive or dissolve based on partner learning through a series of experiments in collaboration, see Ashoka Mody, "Learning through Alliances," *Journal of Economic Behavior and Organization* (February 1993): 1–20. For a discussion of how firms learn about collaboration itself, see M. A. Lyles, "Learning among Joint Venture Sophisticated Firms," *Management International Review* 28 (special issue, 1988): 85–98.

24. In game theory, players are said to develop reputations that give other players a better sense of how they will behave in the future. This, combined with infinitely repeated games, leads to collaboration even in prisoner's dilemma–type games. See Axelrod, *Evolution of Cooperation.*

25. Matthew Rabin, "Incorporating Fairness into Game Theory and Economics," *American Economic Review* (December 1993): 1281–1302.

26. The role of trust in business is discussed in Mark Casson, *The Economics of*

Business Culture (New York: Oxford University Press, 1991); Mark Casson and Howard Cox, "Reinterpreting the 'Wheel': International Networks in Business History," 1993, University of Reading, mimeograph; Diego Gambetta, *Trust: Making and Breaking Cooperative Relations* (New York: Basil Blackwell, 1988); and Jeffrey L. Bradach and Robert G. Eccles, "Price, Authority, and Trust: From Ideal Types to Plural Forms," *Annual Review of Sociology* 15 (1989): 97–118. For an application to alliances, and evidence that repeated transactions generate trust, see Ranjay Gulati, "Does Familiarity Breed Trust? The Implications of Repeated Ties for Contractual Choice in Alliances," *Academy of Management Journal* 38 (February 1995): 85–112.

27. Peter J. Buckley and Mark Casson, "A Theory of Cooperation in International Business," in *Cooperative Strategies in International Business,* ed. Farok J. Contractor and Peter Lorange (Lexington, Mass.: D. C. Heath, 1988), pp. 31–54.

28. In game theoretic terms, these factors affect the shadow of the future. An excellent treatment of the various subjective and objective influences on collaboration is Avinash K. Dixit and Barry J. Nalebuff, *Thinking Strategically* (New York: W. W. Norton, 1991). A striking example of how the shadow of the future affected willingness to cooperate even in the absence of common goals and culturally based "trust" can be found in the "live and let live" practices that arose among rival armies in World War I trench warfare. See Axelrod, *Evolution of Cooperation,* chap. 4.

29. See Chapter 1, note 52.

30. John Scott, *Social Network Analysis: A Handbook* (New York: Sage, 1991), pp. 13–14.

31. There is a long literature on triad effects in social networks. See Leslie Lane Salzinger, "The Ties That Bind: The Effect of Clustering in Dyadic Relationships," *Social Networks* 4, no. 2 (1982): 117–145.

32. It covered five deals: two joint ventures (called Taligent and Kaleida), an agreement to create interoperability in systems, a cross-license for operating-system software, and a commitment by Apple to adopt IBM's RISC chip. Taligent and Kaleida were dissolved in 1995.

33. Simmel described these roles using examples from a wide variety of fields, including personal relations, marriage, alliances between nations, and political parties. See "On the Significance of Numbers for Social Life." See also a modern exposition of the role of the third player in Ronald S. Burt, *Structural Holes: The Social Structure of Competition* (Cambridge, Mass.: Harvard University Press, 1992), esp. chaps. 1 and 7. Burt argues that the third player can exploit "structural holes" in the network by spanning parts of the network that are otherwise unconnected or competing; this strategy generates benefits and profits to the player.

34. Fujitsu bought the Ross division of Cypress in Spring 1993, when Cypress decided to leave the microprocessor business. Fujitsu had been a customer of Cypress before, and both were licensees of Sun.

35. Dorwin Cartwright and Frank Harary defined the "degree of balance" in a

group of more than three actors as the ratio between the number of balanced triads to the total number of triads; see their "Structural Balance: A Generalization of Heider's Theory," *Psychological Review* (September 1956): 277–293. This measure is not used here, because it assumes that the power of an actor depends solely on its position in a network. Here, the identities and strategies of the actors also matter.

36. Patent counts, too, are not always reliable measures of innovation. Counts weighted by number of subsequent citations are more so. The data for the mid-1980s suggest that the average number of subsequent citations per office equipment patent was similar for Canon and Xerox (compiled from data from Chi Research).

Case Study: Tiny Mips Takes On the Giants

1. The CISC microprocessor was designed to execute directly many complex mathematical and logical instructions—instructions "embedded" in the hardware of the chip. CISC designers saw this as the best way to optimize computer performance. RISC designers challenged this premise, claiming that, in practice, only 20 percent of the embedded instructions were called upon to perform 80 percent of a computer's functions. They set out to increase processing speeds by reducing and simplifying the instruction set built into the microprocessor. To do that, many of the more complex commands and functions included in conventional designs were transferred to the compiler software. Compilers translated language commands into machine-readable instructions. In RISC designs, the speed and efficiency of program execution was substantially determined by the quality of the compiler.

2. Ridge Computer Systems and Pyramid Computer had both introduced early RISC designs, but had been unsuccessful in converting many customers to their technologies. These early RISC products were not considered "pure" RISC. That is, although their design incorporated some RISC principles, some complex instructions were left in the design to avoid redesigning system and compiler software.

3. IBM reentered the RISC field in 1986, as discussed later.

4. An operating system is the software code that controls the computer and provides interface between application software, the user, and the microprocessor. DOS and UNIX are both operating systems common in desktop computers. Traditionally, computer companies had attempted to protect their markets by developing proprietary operating systems and software to match. The IBM 370 operating system had long dominated the market for mainframes, for example, while DEC VMS held the majority of the minicomputer market. "Open" systems, in contrast, allowed hardware and software made by different companies to be used, and promised greater competition between vendors.

5. In 1989, revenues from sales for commercial applications represented just

over 7 percent of total workstation revenues, and industry analysts expected this to rise to one third by 1994.

6. In 1989 HP acquired Apollo, one of the pioneers in the workstation segment.

7. The 386,000 workstations sold in 1990, nevertheless, were dwarfed by the 24 million PCs sold that same year.

8. Intel's Pentium chip, for example, which came out in 1992, combined RISC principles for improved performance with the original Intel design, and so was compatible with existing software designed for the X86 family.

9. Computer "architecture" generally refers to the technical design of components, such as the microprocessors, as well as to the way in which components are linked to make the whole system. "Standard" architectures are those with substantial, or dominant, shares of the relevant market.

10. Telephone interview, July 1991.

11. Ibid.

12. The balance between global and local strategies in the computer industry is discussed in Benjamin Gomes-Casseres, "Computers: Alliances and Industry Evolution," in *Beyond Free Trade*, ed. David B. Yoffie (Boston: Harvard Business School Press, 1993).

13. Board products are subassemblies of computers—chips and other electrical parts mounted on prewired plastic boards.

14. Personal interview, October 1990.

15. This list does not reflect alliances created under the Advanced Computing Environment (ACE) initiative, which is discussed in the case study preceding Chapter 4.

16. Soon after this cancellation, however, a small group of DEC designers began work on what was later to become Alpha, the RISC chip that DEC introduced in 1992. See Richard Comerford, "How DEC Developed Alpha," *IEEE Spectrum* (July 1992): 26–31; and Ralph Katz, "How a Band of Technical Renegades Designed the Alpha Chip," *Research and Technology Management* (November–December 1993): 13–20.

17. More partners could be added to make embedded processors, as discussed below.

18. Telephone interview, July 1991.

19. DEC, which signed a license agreement with Mips shortly after this episode, never stopped work on RISC, as noted above.

20. In 1991 Sun licensed SPARC for $15,000, with no royalties.

21. Telephone interview, July 1991.

22. Level I semiconductor licensees had access to the Mips instruction set for internal use only—for example, for research purposes to build systems around the Mips chip—but could not sell chips. Level II semiconductor licensees were allowed access to the Mips instruction set without the actual hardware design of the chip; they then built their own version of the Mips chip. These chips could be used for special "embedded control" applications, which were estimated to account for half the total market for RISC

chips. For embedded control applications, the microprocessor was slightly redesigned and built into a system other than a general purpose computer. In 1990, for example, Sony became a Level II licensee from Mips to use modified versions of Mips chips in an array of consumer products.

23. Telephone interview, July 1991.

3. Competing in Constellations

1. Timothy F. Bresnahan and Shane Greenstein came to a similar conclusion in "Technological Competition and the Structure of the Computer Industry," Center for Economic Policy Research Working Paper no. 315, Stanford University, June 1992. After a review of the recent history of the computer industry, they wrote: "The 'thing which competes' is not a firm or a product but a cluster of firms and products, including buyers and sellers of several complementary technologies. Rents accrue to the effective coordination of technical progress more than to technical progress itself" (p. 45).

2. Encouraging other firms to make clones will pay only if the lead firm maintains a higher quality and price than the clone makers, that is, if it maintains a firm-specific advantage within the group; see Kathleen Conner, "Obtaining Strategic Advantage from Being Imitated: When Can Encouraging 'Clones' Pay?" *Management Science* 41 (February 1995): 209–225. J. Kenneth Benson also found that network structure and extra-network linkages determine the degree of power of specific governmental agencies inside their bureaucratic networks; see his "Interorganizational Network as a Political Economy," *Administrative Science Quarterly* (June 1975): 229–249.

3. Jeffrey Church and Neil Gandal, "Network Effects, Software Provision, and Standardization," *Journal of Industrial Economics* (March 1992): 85–103.

4. It is possible for a group to form voluntarily on the basis of only the expectation of a group surplus. But the firms will not stay together if the positive network effects do not materialize. We will see in Chapter 4 that a group may temporarily expand beyond a point of diminishing returns.

5. The analysis of group-based advantages draws on two aspects of network theory and departs from the theory in one important way. First, the idea that total network effects depend on the structure of the group relies on analysis of the overall structure of networks. Second, the idea that a firm's power depends on its position in a group relies on analysis of actors within a network. But my emphasis on the capabilities of firms as determinants of bargaining power departs from "pure" network theory, because the latter ascribes all power and behavior to an actor's structural position, not its attributes. For an empirical study that discusses how bargaining power depends on the position of an actor in a network, see J. Kenneth Benson,

"The Interorganizational Network as Political Economy," *Administrative Science Quarterly* 20 (June 1975): 229–249.

6. Intel, of course, was more important than any of the others in CISC microprocessors for personal computers. Some of the RISC groups targeted this market. Furthermore, Intel's RISC chip became popular in "embedded" applications, particularly after HP chose it for the Laserjet 4 series of printers. The analysis here focuses on general-purpose microprocessors, not on embedded uses.

7. An alternative way of referring to these groups, used sometimes here and often in the press, is by the name of the RISC architectures: the Mips chips are referred to as the Rx000 family; the Sun chips as SPARC; the HP chips as PA-RISC; and the IBM chips as the PowerPC.

8. Motorola was a lead firm in its own group before it joined IBM. Its chip was called the 88K.

9. Almarin Phillips developed a parallel list of variables for effective coordination in an oligopoly. He says that number of firms, symmetry among firms, value systems of companies, and buyer and supplier power all affect how formally the groups have to be organized in order to collude effectively. See Phillips, "A Theory of Interfirm Organization," *Quarterly Journal of Economics* (November 1960): 602–613. The aim of the RISC groups, as noted, is not collusion to suppress overall competition in an industry, but coordination to improve competitive advantage for the group. Still, the difference between this type of coordination and the collusion analyzed in Phillips's work lies more in the goals of the groups and in the interaction between groups than in their internal structures.

10. For a normative approach to these questions, see Benjamin Gomes-Casseres, "Managing International Alliances: Conceptual Framework," Harvard Business School Case no. 9-793-133 (1993).

11. This was critical in the standards battle between JVC and Sony. See Michael A. Cusumano, Yiorgos Mylonadis, and Richard S. Rosenbloom, "Strategic Maneuvering and Mass-Market Dynamics: The Triumph of VHS over Beta," *Business History Review* (Spring 1992): 51–94.

12. The shares of the lead firm shown in this table are also a measure of internal competition, which is discussed later in this chapter.

13. This is, of course, a rough measure of relevant capabilities. Much semiconductor capacity and some of the underlying skills are not applicable to the RISC field. Even so, Mips designed its chip so that it could be produced on semiconductor lines intended for S-RAM chips, a common type of memory device. In this way it hoped to benefit directly from its partners' capacity in S-RAMs.

14. *Electronics*, November 22, 1993, p. 4.

15. For discussion of this matching pattern in the automobile industry, see Nitin Nohria and Carlos Garcia-Pont, "Global Strategic Linkages and Industry Structure," *Strategic Management Review* 12 (Summer 1991): 105–124.

The authors show that each of the alliance groups in that industry contained representatives from several strategic groups. As a result, the pooled capabilities of each group matched those of rival groups.

16. Michael L. Gerlach, *Alliance Capitalism: The Social Organization of Japanese Business* (Berkeley: University of California Press, 1992), pp. 197–198.

17. Church and Gandal call these effects the "network" and the "competitive" effects; see their "Network Effects, Software Provision, and Standardization."

18. In the computer industry, a clone is a machine using the same hardware design as the original. As a result, clones can run the same software as the original.

19. By comparison, this pricing strategy had worked well for clones of the IBM-PC, because IBM operated with much higher margins than did Sun.

20. Gary Andrew Poole, "Sun in Their Eyes," *Unix World,* October 1991, p. 79.

21. Personal interviews at Sun, August 1993.

22. The Sun allies tended to sell mostly to other members of their own *keiretsu;* Toshiba and Fujitsu, for example, belonged to different *keiretsus* and so did not compete head to head; see Gerlach, *Alliance Capitalism.* Furthermore, their customers were often loyal to them because of historical relationships and business ties in other fields. Toshiba, for example, was a major and traditional supplier to Tokyo Electric for a range of products; providing SPARC workstations was part of this relationship. In part because of this relationship and the fact that Toshiba had supplied Tokyo Electric with many SPARC-based machines, Toshiba's system group did not switch to Mips when Toshiba's semiconductor group did so in 1992.

23. For an economic analysis of how firms might use various contractual terms as commitments to multiple partners, see R. Preston McAfee and Marius Schwartz, "Opportunism in Multilateral Vertical Contracting: Nondiscrimination, Exclusivity, and Uniformity," *American Economic Review* 84 (March 1994): 210–230.

24. In Joseph Farrell and Garth Saloner's standard-setting model, explicit coordination and communication through "committees" can improve upon use of a market "bandwagon." See their "Coordination through Committees and Markets," *RAND Journal of Economics* (Summer 1988): 235–252.

25. Based on personal interviews with Thomas E. Mace, president of 88Open, August 1993. See also Andrew Updegrove, "Forming, Funding, and Operating Standard-Setting Consortia," *IEEE Micro* (December 1993): 52–61.

26. Technically, they sought to create and adhere to an application binary interface (ABI) standard.

27. The adoption of the 88000 was further stalled by Motorola's difficulties with the 68040, the latest in its CISC line. Delays and problems with this chip gave some the impression that Motorola was no longer a reliable supplier. In fact, the 88110 chip—the next generation in the so-called 88K line—did come out a year late.

28. Furthermore, Motorola put the 88000 under the same management as its

68K line, even though the two were incompatible. There was no separate sales force for the 88000. To many observers, the effort to push the 88000 seemed half-hearted.

29. Data General remained as the only major firm still tied to the 88K; it did not have much of a choice, having built up a $500 million business with the chip. Motorola's computer division had a business of similar size with this chip.

30. This initiative was never a formal consortium with the status of a separate legal entity, as the other governance mechanisms in this discussion.

31. As if to emphasize the debt to 88Open, in 1993 the PowerOpen Association hired Thomas E. Mace, formerly president of 88Open, to be its president.

32. Updegrove, "Standard-Setting Consortia."

33. The analogy is from Joseph Farrell and Garth Saloner, "Competition, Compatibility, and Standards: The Economics of Horses, Penguins, and Lemmings," in *Product Standardization and Competitive Strategy,* ed. H. Landis Gabel (New York: Elsevier Science Publishers, 1987), pp. 1–21. A related effect has been hypothesized in a model of arms races. Because of the uncertainties of elections, democratic regimes in this model have less constant a commitment to defense spending, and so will appear less aggressive to other countries. The result is reduction in the severity of conflict. See Michelle R. Garfinkel, "Domestic Politics and International Conflict," *American Economic Review* 84 (December 1994): 1294–1309.

34. For an excellent discussion of these problems in the context of firm organization, see Paul Milgrom and John Roberts, *Economics, Organization, and Management* (Englewood Cliffs, N.J.: Prentice Hall, 1992), chap. 4. The classic statement of the value of decentralization—applied to the problem of central planning in the whole economy—is F. A. Hayek, "The Use of Knowledge in Society," *American Economic Review* 35 (1945): 519–530. Economists have argued that decentralization promotes learning by doing (Masahiro Aoki, "Horizontal vs. Vertical Information Structure of the Firm," *American Economic Review* 76, December 1986, 971–983); but at the cost of duplication and delays in decision making (Patrick Bolton and Joseph Farrell, "Decentralization, Duplication, and Delay," *Journal of Political Economy* 4, no. 98 (1990): 803–826. One empirical study of decision making in high-technology businesses, however, concluded that centralized decision making is not necessarily faster than a well-managed process with multiple layers of advisors; see Kathleen M. Eisenhardt, "Making Fast Strategic Decisions in High-Velocity Environments," *Academy of Management Journal* 32 (September 1989): 543–576.

35. For another discussion of the balance between integration and specialization in computers, see Carliss Y. Baldwin and Kim B. Clark, "Sun Wars: Competition within a Modular Cluster," paper presented at the Colliding Worlds Colloquium, Harvard Business School, October 1994, mimeograph. For a general discussion of the role of integration and interdependence in design, see Christopher Alexander, *Notes on the Synthesis of Form* (Cambridge, Mass.: Harvard University Press, 1964).

36. Charles R. Morris and Charles H. Ferguson, "How Architecture Wins Technology Wars," *Harvard Business Review* (March–April 1993): 86–96.

37. Susumu Kohyama of Toshiba explained in a personal interview (November 1993) that the R4000 was late for two reasons. First, Mips management kept changing the feature set; they did not freeze the design early enough. Second, the design rules were not standard across semiconductor partners, because very advanced process technology was involved. As a result, many critical technical issues had to be addressed, and there were no generic rules that would apply to all semiconductor partners. Instead, Mips designers worked from their own generic rules, and then customized the design for each partner. By comparison, when the R2000 was designed, Mips used rules that were almost industry standard by then, and certainly very mature.

38. This measure is different from the RISC systems revenues reported in Table 9, because the number in the table only included RISC-based workstations. In Figure 16 the sales of all kinds of systems, including larger and more expensive machines, such as minicomputers and servers, are plotted. HP and IBM had more sales of these larger machines than did Sun and Mips, which specialized in workstations. HP therefore has a higher market share in Figure 16 than is implied by the numbers in Table 9.

39. Telephone interview, July 1991.

40. For a discussion of the role of sponsors in promoting new technology, see Michael L. Katz and Carl Shapiro, "Technology Adoption in the Presence of Network Externalities," *Journal of Political Economy* 94 (1986): 822–841.

41. John Clyman wrote in *PC Magazine* ("Battle for the Desktop," May 31, 1994, p. 114): "The newest kid on the RISC block, the PowerPC has the potential to make the deepest inroads on the desktop. With its high performance and unprecedented industry backing, the PowerPC family could give the [Intel] Pentium a good fight."

42. The processes of creating and claiming value in negotiations are discussed in David A. Lax and James K. Sebenius, *The Manager as Negotiator: Bargaining for Cooperation and Competitive Gain* (New York: Free Press, 1986).

43. Toshiba's system business, however, continued to supply Sun-based machines, because existing customers required compatibility with earlier models.

Case Study: The ACE Bandwagon Runs Out of Steam

1. Telephone interview, July 1991.

2. The requirements for joining ACE were minimal. The membership fee was $1,000, payable to Mips Computer Systems; ACE was not a separate legal entity.

3. Toshiba's systems division remained in the Sun camp.

4. *Business Week,* October 1991.

5. First quarter 1992 revenues, at $47.3 million, were down 46 percent from

the first quarter of 1991 and down 50 percent from the previous quarter. Mips had a net loss of $12.7 million in the period. A year earlier it had had a profit of $624,000, and in the fourth quarter of 1991 it had a profit of $2.6 million. "Both product and technology revenue did not achieve anticipated levels," said Mips CFO David Ludvigson. "The revenue decline is principally due to deferrals in customer orders and licensing activities as a result of the announcement of our proposed merger with Silicon Graphics." Mips press release.

6. Mips press release.

7. Note that, by the time of the merger, DEC—an original licensee—had dropped out of the Mips group, and Toshiba had joined.

8. The R4200, developed by NEC and MTI, was to be a low-power chip optimized for notebook computers. Toshiba and SGI worked on the Total Floating Point (TFP) chip intended for high-end workstations and super-computers. Toshiba and NEC worked on the R4400, targeted at mid-range workstations. Separately, Toshiba, IDT, and QED worked on the R4600, another low-power chip. Finally, Toshiba, NEC, and IDT worked on the T5 chip for multiprocessor machines. IDT, LSI, and Performance Semiconductor focused on embedded applications.

9. By comparison, the R2000 was developed in a relative vacuum, as there were no adopters yet. The R3000, too, was completed before all the semi-conductor partners were signed on. Thus the first two Mips chips were developed almost in isolation, even though they were commercialized through an alliance group. The third-generation chip, however, was developed in a group. Personal interview with David Corbin, MTI, August 1993.

4. The Spread of Collective Competition

1. These assertions are based on casual observation. But see Figure 1 for alliance waves in several industries. Data and analysis of waves in the use of joint ventures by U.S. multinational firms are in Gomes-Casseres, "Joint Venture Cycles: The Evolution of Ownership Strategies of U.S. MNEs: 1945–1975," in *Cooperative Strategies in International Business,* ed. Farok J. Contractor and Peter Lorange (Lexington, Mass.: D. C. Heath, 1988).

2. See, for example, "The Latest Business Game," *The Economist,* May 5, 1990, p. 18, which argued: "[C]ross-border alliances are reaching fad proportions . . . this fad comes adorned with elaborate theories designed to make it seem inevitable."

3. Pressures such as these may also drive firms to merge or to integrate vertically, particularly when they fear that such a move by a rival will foreclose them from future markets. For a discussion of this phenomenon, with some examples of where it might have occurred, see F. M. Scherer, *Industrial Market Structure and Economic Performance* (Boston: Houghton Mifflin Company, 1980), p. 90. More recently, Richard Caves argued: "Races to make acquisitions are frequently set off by the perception that

potential targets are few in number and may soon all be acquired (major motion-picture studios, small-volume luxury automobile producers). Acquirers pay high prices in order to complete deals quickly and avoid being left out." See his "Corporate Mergers in International Economic Integration," in *European Financial Integration,* ed. Alberto Giovannini and Colin P. Mayer (Cambridge: Cambridge University Press, 1991), pp. 137–171; quotation at 152.

4. HP's acquisition of Apollo may appear to be an example of collaboration between two leaders. In fact, Apollo was no longer a leader—it was in serious financial trouble at the time. Even so, the acquisition combined two companies with substantial market shares. As discussed in Chapter 5, such combinations are more likely to take place through mergers and acquisitions than through alliances.

5. See Carliss Y. Baldwin and Kim B. Clark, "Sun Wars: Competition within a Modular Cluster," paper presented at the Colliding Worlds Colloquium, Harvard Business School, October 1994, mimeograph.

6. The idea of oligopolistic imitation is common in the economics literature. For an application to foreign investment, see F. T. Knickerbocker, *Oligopolistic Reaction and Multinational Enterprise* (Boston: Division of Research, Graduate School of Business Administration, Harvard University, 1973); and for application to mergers, see Caves, "Corporate Mergers in International Economic Integration."

7. Based on interview with Randall Livingston, Taligent, August 1993.

8. Based on personal interview with Susumu Kohyama of Toshiba, November 1993.

9. Based on personal interviews at IBM Europe, November 1991.

10. Furthermore, the French government favored IBM, in part because it thought IBM would be a stronger counterweight to NEC, which also owned a share in Bull. See "France Chooses IBM to Bolster Groupe Bull," *Wall Street Journal,* January 29, 1992, pp. A3, A6.

11. Adam Smith, *An Inquiry into the Nature and Causes of The Wealth of Nations,* edited with an introduction, notes, marginal summary, and an enlarged text by Edwin Cannan; with an introduction by Max Lerner (New York: Modern Library, Random House, 1937), pp. 3–21; quotation at 17. Originally published in 1776. See also the essay about Charles Babbage's concept of the division of labor in Nathan Rosenberg, *Exploring the Black Box: Technology, Economics, and History* (Cambridge: Cambridge University Press, 1994), chap. 2. The argument about the extent of the market was developed further in George J. Stigler, "The Division of Labor Is Limited by the Extent of the Market," *Journal of Political Economy* (June 1951): 185–193.

12. Quoted in "HP Shares Its RISC," *Electronic Engineering Times,* August 14, 1989, p. 86. The HP-Samsung alliance has not worked wholly as planned. Samsung did not have all the capabilities needed to develop the systems, and HP had to transfer more technology and devote more efforts to get the job done. In the process, the alliance was renegotiated several times. Samsung continues to be a major chip supplier to HP (memories and other

chips), resells HP systems in Korea, and competes aggressively with HP in world markets.

13. Chip class is defined by the implementation, which determines power usage, performance, price, and so on.

14. This limit has a parallel in Penrose's analysis of limits on the growth of the firm. Aside from the constraints owing to internal management capabilities, Penrose recognizes that growth can be limited by the finite "productive opportunities" available externally. See Edith T. Penrose, *The Theory of the Growth of the Firm* (White Plains, N.Y.: M. E. Sharpe, 1980), chap. 3. But, in Penrose's view, these opportunities were not finite, but limited only by the ability of the firm's managers to recognize the commercial applications for their capabilities. In my framework, the external limits are finite, because they depend on the number of partners available. The possibility of a "saturation" effect that would slow the formation of alliances in biotechnology is examined in Bruce Kogut, Weijan Shan, and Gordon Walker, "The Structure of an Industry: Cooperative Agreements in the Biotechnology Industry," Working Paper, Reginald H. Jones Center, Wharton School, September 1989. Tests of the effect of alliance crowding on the rate of new entry in semiconductors appear in Bruce Kogut, Gordon Walker, and Dong-Jae Kim, "Cooperation and Entry Induction as an Extension of Technological Rivalry," 1992, mimeograph.

15. See Oliver E. Williamson in *Markets and Hierarchies: Analysis and Antitrust Implications* (New York: Free Press, 1975). See also my discussion in the Introduction of the lack of alliances in the purely competitive markets shown in Figure 3.

16. See Nitin Nohria and Carlos Garcia-Pont, "Global Strategic Linkages and Industry Structure," *Strategic Management Review* 12 (Summer 1991): 105–124.

17. Of course, IBM may not have needed the Japanese semiconductor partners as urgently as Mips and Sun, because IBM had its own strong capabilities and a major alliance with Motorola.

18. Telephone interview, July 1991.

19. Penrose, *Theory of the Growth of the Firm*.

20. The limits to growth predicted by Penrose have been addressed by managers in precisely this fashion.

21. The original semiconductor suppliers in the group were Fujitsu, Texas Instruments, LSI Logic, and Ross/Cypress; later ICL, Solbourne, Amdahl, and Sun were added.

22. Personal interview with Phillip Huelson, SI, August 1993.

23. Jeffrey L. Bradach found a similar pattern in franchising systems. Subgroups of outlets owned by individual franchisees were common in many groups. One explanation for these "chains within chains" is that they save on the costs of management and of transactions with the franchisor. See his "Chains within Chains: The Role of Multi-unit Franchisees," 1993, mimeograph.

24. Louis Wells, Lawrence Franko, and others pointed out in the early 1970s that having local joint venture partners limits the ability of a multinational

firm to rationalize its operations globally. See John M. Stopford and Louis T. Wells, Jr., *Managing the Multinational Enterprise* (New York: Basic Books, 1972), part 2; and Lawrence G. Franko, *Joint Venture Survival in Multinational Corporations* (New York: Praeger, 1971).

25. Conflicts may also arise when one of the partners has another alliance—that is, with a third firm—that influences the goals of the first alliance.

26. See Chapter 2.

27. Using evidence from international cooperation between governments, Kenneth A. Oye argues that a large number of players makes cooperation more difficult: (1) transactions and information costs rise; (2) the likelihood of defection increases as recognition and control of defection become more difficult; and (3) the feasibility of sanctioning defectors decreases. See his introductory chapter in his edited volume *Cooperation under Anarchy* (Princeton, N.J.: Princeton University Press, 1986).

28. A similar mechanism leads to limits to growth in James M. Buchanan's model of cooperatives where owners also consume the output of their joint production. In that model, the marginal benefit of adding a new member declines, but every member still will consume the average production. See his "Economic Theory of Clubs," *Economica* 34 (February 1965): 1–14.

29. To some extent, the loss of control and limited appropriability that firms experience when they use alliances extensively is inherent in their environment. As discussed in Chapter 1, rapid environmental change and the rising complexity of business have meant that few firms can compete on their own. The environment, in other words, forces these firms to share control and rents with alliance partners. Still, firms usually have a choice over how extensively they use alliances and over how many partners they have; the discussion in this section explores the control and appropriability issues involved in this choice.

30. This trade-off is the underlying theme in part 2 of Stopford and Wells, *Managing the Multinational.*

31. One empirical study found that, owing to a variety of imperfections in the market for technology, licensors only extract between one-third and one-half the rent due to their technology. See Richard E. Caves, Harold Crookell, and J. Peter Killing, "The Imperfect Market for Technology Licenses," *Oxford Bulletin of Economics and Statistics* 45, no. 3 (1983): 249–267. When there are network externalities, licensors may receive higher earnings than those that refuse to license. For example, JVC gained from licensing its VCR technology, while Sony lost by not doing so. Given the importance of network externalities in this business, none of these firms was in a position to exploit its technology by itself. See Michael A. Cusumano, Yiorgos Mylonadis, and Richard S. Rosenbloom, "Strategic Maneuvering and Mass-Market Dynamics: The Triumph of VHS over Beta," *Business History Review* (Spring 1992): 51–94.

32. Without product leadership, a technology firm can even lose sales to its

own partners, as IBM learned in the PC business. For a theoretical treatment of how a technology-diffusion strategy can either help or hurt a firm, see Kathleen Conner, "Obtaining Strategic Advantage from Being Imitated: When Can Encouraging 'Clones' Pay?" September 1992, mimeograph.

Case Study: The Thickening Web of Multimedia Alliances

1. This case study is based on research conducted jointly with Dorothy Leonard-Barton. See our paper "Alliance Clusters in Multimedia: Safety Net or Entanglement?" presented at the Colliding Worlds Colloquium, Harvard Business School, October 1994, mimeograph.
2. This three-part typology is developed and applied in Benjamin Gomes-Casseres, "Computers: Alliances and Industry Evolution," in *Beyond Free Trade,* ed. David B. Yoffie (Boston: Harvard Business School Press, 1993). See also the three theoretical approaches to joint ventures identified in Bruce Kogut, "Joint Ventures: Theoretical and Empirical Perspectives," *Strategic Management Journal* (July–August 1988): 319–332.
3. Microsoft could be expected to do the same, but its WinPad system was delayed.

5. Alliances and the Organization of Industry

1. Alfred Chandler provides evidence of the long-run stability of the competitive positions of leading firms across many industries; see Alfred D. Chandler, Jr., *Scale and Scope: The Dynamics of Industrial Capitalism* (Cambridge, Mass.: Harvard University Press, 1990).
2. See Joseph L. Bower and Eric A. Rhenman, "Benevolent Cartels," *Harvard Business Review* (July–August 1985): 124–132.
3. This list is a synthesis of lists in Richard E. Caves, "Industrial Organization, Corporate Strategy, and Structure," *Journal of Economic Literature* 18 (March 1980): 64–92; F. M. Scherer, *Industrial Market Structure and Economic Performance* (Boston: Houghton Mifflin Company, 1980), p. 4; Michael E. Porter, *Competitive Strategy* (New York: Free Press, 1985), pp. 17–21; and Sharon M. Oster, *Modern Competitive Analysis* (New York: Oxford University Press, 1990), p. 218. Some conditions cited by these authors are not included here because they are not affected by collective competition among vendors, such as demand conditions.
4. IBM refused to commercialize the invention for fear of cannibalizing its successful System 370 architecture, which was based on CISC technology. See Charles H. Ferguson and Charles R. Morris, *Computer Wars: How the West Can Win in a Post-IBM World* (New York: Random House, 1993), pp. 41–48.
5. The Intergraph technology was purchased from Fairchild.
6. Economists and antitrust authorities often use the Herfindahl Index to

summarize the number and size distribution of firms in an industry; the index is defined as the sum of the squared market shares of the firms. By this measure, too, the degree of competition increases in these businesses when we include alliances. The Herfindahl Indices for the four panels are:

	Semiconductors	Systems
Lead firms alone	.33	.43
Group totals	.24	.32

7. Porter, *Competitive Strategy*, pp. 20–21.
8. Barriers to entry were first defined in Joe S. Bain, *Industrial Organization* (New York: John Wiley and Sons, 1959); Porter's *Competitive Strategy* is the current classic. Barriers to mobility are defined in Richard E. Caves and Michael E. Porter, "From Entry Barriers to Mobility Barriers: Conjectural Decisions and Contrived Deterrence to New Competition," *Quarterly Journal of Economics* 91 (May 1977): 241–261. In this text, the term *barriers to entry* will be used to refer to both types of barriers.
9. For a succinct review, see Jean Tirole, *The Theory of Industrial Organization* (Cambridge, Mass.: MIT Press, 1988), chap. 10.
10. Rajan R. Kamath and Jeffrey K. Liker, "Supplier Dependence and Innovation: A Contingency Model of Suppliers' Innovative Activities," *Journal of Engineering and Technology Management* 7 (September 1990): 111–127.
11. Michael L. Gerlach, *Alliance Capitalism: The Social Organization of Japanese Business* (Berkeley, Calif.: University of California Press, 1992), chap. 6.
12. William J. Baumol, "Horizontal Collusion and Innovation," *Economic Journal* 102 (January 1992): 129–137; Michael L. Katz and Janusz A. Ordover, "R&D Cooperation and Competition," *Brooking Papers on Economic Activity*, 1990, pp. 137–203; and Michael L. Katz, "An Analysis of Cooperative Research and Development," *RAND Journal of Economics* (Winter 1986): 527–543.
13. John A. Stuckey wrote in his exhaustive *Vertical Integration and Joint Ventures in the Aluminum Industry* (Cambridge, Mass.: Harvard University Press, 1983): "The evidence indicates that most of the successful new entrants into the industry over the last decade or two have relied heavily upon participation in joint ventures as part of their entry and growth strategies. Many of these firms would either have not entered or have failed if the opportunities for joint ventures had not been available. The significant decline in concentration of firms that has resulted should have improved the industry's allocative performance" (p. 211).
    Bruce Kogut, Weijian Shan, and Gordon Walker found that in the semiconductor industry "entry into industries increases when a firm forms a dominant coalition with other firms through technology-based agreements. Rivalry among incumbent firms, such as Intel and Motorola, leads

to cooperative behavior towards new entrants" (p. 73); see their "Knowledge in the Network and the Network as Knowledge," in *The Embedded Firm: On the Socioeconomics of Industrial Networks,* ed. Gernot Grabher (New York: Routledge, 1993), chap. 4.

David Encaoua and Alexis Jacquemin studied the rationale and impact of large business groups in France. They concluded that "administrative and organizational efficiency is an adequate explanation for the existence of these groups and that rivalry between groups differently integrated and diversified is more likely to be the case than collusion" (p. 25); see their "Organizational Efficiency and Monopoly Power: The Case of French Industrial Groups," *European Economic Review* 19 (September 1982): 25–51.

Finally, Sanford V. Berg and Philip Friedman, in a statistical analysis of data from a cross-section of industries, found that joint ventures were not necessarily anticompetitive. See their "Causes and Effects of Joint Venture Activity: Knowledge Acquisition vs. Parent Horizontality," *Antitrust Bulletin* (Spring 1980): 143–168.

14. This view goes back to Adam Smith, as noted earlier. But recent economic models that directly address the competitive effects of alliances also claim that joint venture or partial ownership tends to increase the incentives for firms to collude; see, for example, Robert J. Reynolds and Bruce R. Snapp, "The Competitive Effects of Partial Equity Interests and Joint Ventures," *International Journal of Industrial Organization* 4 (June 1986): 141–153; Timothy F. Bresnahan and Steven C. Salop, "Quantifying the Competitive Effects of Production Joint Ventures," *International Journal of Industrial Organization* 4 (June 1986): 155–175; and David Reitman, "Partial Ownership Arrangements and the Potential for Collusion," *Journal of Industrial Economics* 42 (September 1994): 313–322. Other recent models that have addressed the incentives for innovation claim that "R&D cartels" deter innovation; see John Vickers, "Pre-Emptive Patenting, Joint Ventures, and the Persistence of Oligopoly," *International Journal of Industrial Organization* 3 (September 1985): 261–273; and Morton I. Kamien, Eitan Muller, and Israel Zang, "Research Joint Ventures and R&D Cartels," *American Economic Review* 82 (December 1992): 1293–1306.

15. This is essentially the argument of Berg and Friedman in "Causes and Effects of Joint Venture Activity." See also the literature on R&D joint ventures and antitrust; for example, Thomas M. Jorde and David J. Teece, "Innovation and Cooperation: Implications for Competition and Antitrust," *Journal of Economic Perspectives* 4 (Summer 1990): 75–96; Janusz A. Ordover and Robert D. Willig, "Antitrust for High-Technology Industries: Assessing Research Joint Ventures and Mergers," *Journal of Law and Economics* 28 (May 1985): 311–333; and Gene M. Grossman and Carl Shapiro, "Research Joint Ventures: An Antitrust Analysis," *Journal of Law, Economics, and Organization* 2 (Fall 1986): 315–337.

16. The story of IBM's relationships to Microsoft and Intel is told in various books and articles. See, for example, Paul Carrol, *Big Blues: The Unmaking of IBM* (New York: Crown Publishers, 1993). The growing distance be-

tween IBM and Intel is more recent; in 1994 IBM decided to forgo licensing Intel's Pentium chip and began pushing its own PowerPC chip as an alternative to Intel.

17. See Michael A. Cusumano, Yiorgos Mylonadis, and Richard S. Rosenbloom, "Strategic Maneuvering and Mass-Market Dynamics: The Triumph of VHS over Beta," *Business History Review* (Spring 1992): 51–94.

18. The dilemma of promoting a standard through a constellation and yet maintaining a share of profits is analyzed in Kathleen Conner, "Obtaining Strategic Advantage from Being Imitated: When Can Encouraging 'Clones' Pay?" September 1992, mimeograph.

19. See Joseph Farrell and Carl Shapiro, "Horizontal Mergers: An Equilibrium Analysis," *American Economic Review* 80 (March 1990): 107–126. In their model, mergers raise prices if there is no rationalization of the firm after merger. But if there is learning or reallocation of resources after the merger, then the merger will have synergistic effects and might not raise prices.

20. Joel Bleeke and David Ernst, "The Way to Win in Cross-Border Alliances," *Harvard Business Review* (November–December 1991): 127–135; and Paul M. Healy, Krishna G. Palepu, and Richard S. Ruback, "Does Corporate Performance Improve after Mergers?" *Journal of Financial Economics* 31 (April 1992): 135–175.

21. Four different games are defined by William Poundstone, *Prisoner's Dilemma* (New York: Doubleday, 1992). Poundstone ranks the payoff structures for these games using C to denote cooperation and D to denote defection (noncooperation); CC then indicates mutual cooperation, DD is mutual defection, DC is unilateral defection, and CD stands for unrequited cooperation. These games are ranked in order of decreasing degree of conflict (p. 217):

DC > DD > CC > CD	Deadlock
DC > CC > DD > CD	Prisoner's Dilemma
DC > CC > CD > DD	Chicken
CC > DC > DD > CD	Stag Hunt
CC > CD > DC > DD	Harmony (not ranked by Poundstone)

For application of these ideas to international cooperation between governments, see the introductory chapter by Oye and the concluding chapter by Axelrod and Keohane in *Cooperation under Anarchy*, ed. Kenneth A. Oye (Princeton, N.J.: Princeton University Press, 1986). Oye cites the following reasoning from Harrison Wagner: "Stag Hunt, Chicken, and Prisoner's Dilemma are often inappropriate models of international situations. When you observe conflict, think Deadlock—the absence of mutual interest—before puzzling over why a mutual interest was not realized. When you observe cooperation, think Harmony—the absence from gains from defection—before puzzling over how states were able to transcend the temptations of defection" (p. 7). The same is no doubt true in business alliances—most of them are *not* Prisoner's Dilemmas. For a discussion of this point, see Ranjay Gulati, Tarun Khanna, and Nitin Nohria, "Unilateral Commitments and the Importance of Process in Alliances," *Sloan Management Review* 35 (Spring 1994): 61–69; and Arvind Parkhe, "Strategic Alliance Structuring: A Game-Theoretic and Transaction-Cost Examination of Interfirm Cooperation," *Academy of Management Journal* (August 1993): 794–829.

22. Axelrod and Keohane in *Cooperation under Anarchy,* ed. Oye.

23. For a discussion of how different payoff structures call for different governance mechanisms, see Gulati, Khanna, and Nohria, "Unilateral Commitments and the Importance of Process in Alliances."

24. For an analysis of the Prisoner's Dilemma in the OPEC game, see Avinash K. Dixit and Barry J. Nalebuff, *Thinking Strategically* (New York: W. W. Norton, 1991), chap. 4.

25. Alexis Jacquemin and Margaret E. Slade, "Cartels, Collusion, and Horizontal Merger," in *Handbook of Industrial Organization,* ed. Richard Schmalensee and Robert D. Willig, vol. 2 (New York: North-Holland, 1989), p. 421.

26. My argument here is consistent with Oliver E. Williamson's analysis of the inability of a group of oligopolists to act as a single monopolist. He writes (*Markets and Hierarchies: Analysis and Antitrust Implications,* New York: Free Press, 1975): "[C]heating is a predictable consequence of oligopolistic conspiracy; the record is replete with examples. The pairing of opportunism with information impactedness explains this condition. The monopolist, by contrast, does not face the same need to attenuate opportunism" (p. 246).

27. As noted in the Introduction, there is some discussion in the formal economics literature regarding whether cartels can act like single-firm monopolists. This literature is thin, however, and much remains to be done. In this same vein, Tirole poses the question of whether firms could duplicate the foreclosure effect of a merger through a contract. He suggests that if not, "the distinction is likely to stem from incomplete contracting and the allocation of residual rights of control" (p. 195); see his *Theory of Industrial Organization.*

Conclusion: Rethinking Alliances and Rivalry

1. Oliver E. Williamson, *The Economic Institutions of Capitalism: Firms, Markets, and Relational Contracting* (New York: Free Press, 1985), pp. 83–84.

2. Paul Milgrom and John Roberts have written an excellent textbook on this subject, but even they discuss business alliances in five pages, and then mostly in descriptive terms. See *Economics, Organization, and Management* (Englewood Cliffs, N.J.: Prentice Hall, 1992), pp. 575–580.

3. Benjamin Gomes-Casseres and Dorothy Leonard-Barton, "Alliance Clusters in Multimedia: Safety Net or Entanglement?" presented at the Colliding Worlds Colloquium, Harvard Business School, October 1994, mimeograph.

4. In physics, scientists have no problem with such multilevel analysis. Matter consists of protons, neutrons, electrons, and of even more basic particles, but it is often more useful to think in terms of atoms and molecules. And, to take the analogy further, molecules often disrupt one another's bonds; one can "preempt" another in bonding with free atoms; and certain contexts—for example, magnetic force fields—can strain them to the point of breakage. These events at the submolecular level can transform the matter we see and touch, just as alliances transform firms and markets.

5. The oversimplification, discussed in the earlier chapters, is that single firms can have varying degrees of unified control and rigidity in capabilities; constellations, too, vary in how flexible they are and how decentralized their control structure is.

6. Several scholars have argued that firms use franchising to expand when they have a shortage of internal resources. See Seth W. Norton, "Franchising, Brand Name Capital, and the Entrepreneurial Capacity Problem," *Strategic Management Journal* 9 (Summer 1988): 105–114; and Mick Carney and Eric Gedajlovic, "Vertical Integration in Franchise Systems: Agency Theory and Resource Explanations," *Strategic Management Journal* 12 (November 1991): 607–629.

7. Michael L. Katz and Carl Shapiro come to a similar conclusion in their review article "Systems Competition and Network Effects," *Journal of Economic Perspectives* 8 (Spring 1994): 93–115. They write, for example: "Because a firm with a small, initial advantage in a network market may be able to parlay its advantage into a larger, lasting one, competition in network industries can be especially intense—at least until a clear winner emerges" (p. 107).

8. The normative literature on antitrust policy is extensive and beyond the scope of this book. For opposing views on the antitrust implications of research alliances, see Thomas M. Jorde and David J. Teece, "Innovation and Cooperation: Implications for Competition and Antitrust," *Journal of Economic Perspectives* 4 (Summer 1990): 75–96; and Joseph F. Brodley, "Antitrust Law and Innovation," *Journal of Economic Perspectives* 4 (Summer 1990): 97–112. For attempts to tailor antitrust rules to alliances in high-technology industries, see Janusz A. Ordover and Robert D. Willig, "Antitrust for High-Technology Industries: Assessing Research Joint Ventures and Mergers," *Journal of Law and Economics* 28 (May 1985): 311–333; and Gene M. Grossman and Carl Shapiro, "Research Joint Ventures: An Antitrust Analysis," *Journal of Law, Economics, and Organization* 2 (Fall 1986): 315–337.

9. Sun Tzu considered that the first-best strategy was to attack an enemy's plans; next came the disruption of the enemy's alliances; only after that did he recommend engaging the army. Sun Tzu, *The Art of War,* translated

and with an introduction by Samuel B. Griffith, with a foreword by B. H. Liddell Hart (New York: Oxford University Press, 1963), p. 78.

10. Credible commitments are essential in other preemptive strategies too; see Jean Tirole, *The Theory of Industrial Organization* (Cambridge, Mass.: MIT Press, 1988), pp. 349–352. See also Mathias Dewatripont, "Commitment through Renegotiation-Proof Contracts with Third Parties," *Review of Economic Studies* 55 (July 1988): 377–390.

11. Michael E. Porter, *Competitive Strategy* (New York: Free Press, 1985), pp. 10–11; and P. Aghion and P. Bolton, "Contracts as a Barrier to Entry," *American Economic Review* 77 (June 1987): 388–401.

12. Steven C. Salop and David T. Scheffman, "Raising Rivals' Costs," *American Economic Review* 73 (May 1983): 267–271.

13. See a review in Stanley M. Besen and Joseph Farrell, "Choosing How to Compete: Strategies and Tactics in Standardization," *Journal of Economic Perspectives* 8 (Spring 1994): 117–131.

14. Sun Tzu, *The Art of War*, p. 83.

15. Not only is the quest for "strategic alliances" often a red herring for firms, but scholars too get bogged down in semantics when trying to define the term in their own unique ways. Michael Y. Yoshino and U. Srinivasa Rangan, for example, insist that the Fuji Xerox joint venture and Mips's partnerships are not strategic alliances. In contrast, a Caterpillar-Mitsubishi joint venture in Japan—which is in many ways similar to Fuji Xerox—and Nike's network of Asian suppliers—which is not unlike Mips's network—are strategic alliances in their analysis. See their *Strategic Alliances: An Entrepreneurial Approach to Globalization* (Boston: Harvard Business School Press, 1994), p. 6. This book does contain a useful discussion of the managerial aspects of alliances (chaps. 5–8).

16. In a related argument, Peter F. Drucker recently exhorted managers to "know and manage the *entire* cost of the economic chain" including those of their partners; see "The Information Executives Truly Need," *Harvard Business Review* (January–February 1995): 54–62; quotation at p. 58 (emphasis in the original).

17. For other work suggesting that a wholesale change in our view of competition is in order, see David J. Teece, "Competition, Cooperation, and Innovation: Organizational Arrangements for Regimes of Rapid Technological Progress," *Journal of Economic Behavior and Organization* (June 1992): 1–25. He considered whether the rise of alliances signals the end of the scale-intensive enterprises that Alfred D. Chandler, Jr., studied in his *Scale and Scope: The Dynamics of Industrial Capitalism* (Cambridge, Mass.: Harvard University Press, 1990). Teece's more thorough critique of Chandler's work is in his "Dynamics of Industrial Capitalism: Perspectives on Alfred Chandler's *Scale and Scope*," Journal of Economic Literature 31 (March 1993): 199–225. An early sketch of how networks might change the economic landscape—including some ideas about competing networks—is in Hans B. Thorelli, "Networks: Between Market and Hierarchies," *Strategic Management Journal* 7 (January–February 1986): 37–51. A popular, wide-

ranging opinion of the ultimate implications of "network economics" is in Kevin Kelley, *Out of Control: Rise of Artificial Evolution* (London: Fourth Estate, 1994), chap. 11.

18. Raymond Vernon, *Sovereignty at Bay* (New York: Basic Books, 1971), p. 3.

19. In fact, as Vernon described them, multinational corporations share important features with international alliances (*Sovereignty at Bay*, p. 6): "[A] multinational enterprise cannot be said to have a clear, unambiguous will. Such an enterprise represents a coalition of interests, sometimes collaborating over the achievement of a common objective, sometimes warring over conflicting priorities. In some multinational enterprises the sense of common objectives and common identity is strong; in others much less so. If the objectives of the constituent parts are sufficiently unrelated or antagonistic, can one say meaningfully that he is dealing with a single 'enterprise'?"

Appendix C: Additional Case Studies

1. Fujitsu had agreed early on to limit its ownership of Amdahl to 49.5 percent.

2. A 1984 study attributed a 1975 decline in computer hardware prices to Amdahl's introduction of the first IBM-compatible machine. A decade later it was possible to look back and assign a 19 percent savings *every year* for every customer in the industry—those who bought from Amdahl and those who did not—to Amdahl's challenge to IBM. See "Amdahl Predicts a Billion Dollar Year," *Information Week*, July 13, 1987, p. 23.

3. MITI had been encouraging, guiding, and funding joint efforts by Hitachi and Fujitsu to develop such machines. See Marie Anchordoguy, *Computers, Inc.: Japan's Challenge to IBM*, Harvard East Asian Monographs, 144 (Cambridge, Mass.: Council on East Asian Studies, Harvard University, 1989). In addition, Hitachi had an alliance with RCA, which produced IBM-compatible equipment, and Fujitsu had realized that, in the words of its chairman, "with computers that could not take advantage of software already widely used throughout the world, breaking the barrier into new markets would indeed be difficult." Taiyu Kobayashi, *Fortune Favors the Brave: Fujitsu—Thirty Years in Computers,* trans. Richard Cleary (Tokyo: Toyo, Keizai Shinposha, 1986), pp. 80–81.

4. By the early 1980s, the Amdahl patents ran out; therefore, technically, Fujitsu could have begun selling the M-series in the United States. But an intellectual property dispute that Fujitsu had with IBM at the time (from 1982 to 1988) kept it from selling its M-series software in the United States; doing so might have aggravated the dispute.

5. The proportion is defined as share of assembly hours at the component level; these components are in turn about 20 to 30 percent of the manufacturing cost of a finished system. The sale price is approximately double the manufacturing cost.

6. PCBs with six to forty layers are more common and available from more sources.

7. Amdahl's dependence on Fujitsu and its strategy of emulating IBM machines created a popular misperception that the company had minimal internal capabilities. Amdahl president Joseph Zemke felt compelled to set the record straight in 1987 when he said: "We've got a thousand engineers here. We've built four generations of machines that are one-third the weight, sixty-percent the size, and thirty to fifty percent faster than IBM's. We do not just copy." He was quoted in "Learning from Disaster," *Forbes*, October 19, 1987, p. 96.

8. On the role of standards in global competition in computers, see Benjamin Gomes-Casseres, "Computers: Alliances and Industry Evolution," in *Beyond Free Trade*, ed. David B. Yoffie (Boston: Harvard Business School Press, 1993).

9. The value of these purchases represented about 40 percent of Amdahl's sales. This includes the disk-drive business. Amdahl sold Fujitsu disk drives, which were also PCMs, although this business was smaller than the mainframe business. Here again, Amdahl designed the circuitry and software in the controller and Fujitsu did the physical, chemical, and mechanical work.

10. By the summer of 1992, the firms had invested an estimated $253 million and production had fallen short, as it proved difficult to raise yields. Other flat-panel display producers suffered similar problems, and, by all accounts, the DTI product was of comparable quality to those of its competitors. See Lori Valigra, "New Generation Screens Are a Tough Nut to Crack," *Computerworld*, May 25, 1992, p. 28.

11. In fact, in September 1993, IBM announced that it would begin making AMLCD products at its Yorktown Heights, N.Y., plant. Although Toshiba was not directly involved in this plant, the operation did plan to use "the process developed by IBM Japan." Andrew Jerks, *Washington Technology*, September 23, 1993.

12. As expected, timing proved to be critical for IBM. In mid-1993 there was a general shortage in the industry of color AMLCDs, owing to the slow improvement in yields everywhere and a boom in the sale of notebook computers, which used the screens. Without access to the output from DTI, this shortage might have cut into IBM's sales of its popular Thinkpad series of color notebook computers, introduced in early 1993. (Interview with industry expert David Mentley, July 1993.)

13. This section draws on "Hewlett-Packard's Experience in Negotiating and Operating a Joint Manufacturing and Marketing Venture in Japan," Hewlett-Packard company document, October 1970.

14. For a discussion of how Japan slowly opened its borders to foreign investment, see Dennis J. Encarnation, *Rivals beyond Trade: America versus Japan in Global Competition* (Ithaca, N.Y.: Cornell University Press, 1992).

15. For a discussion of how MITI constrained IBM Japan's growth, see Anchordoguy, *Computers, Inc.* IBM agreed to these restrictions because of the

importance of the Japanese market. In contrast, IBM chose to exit the Indian market in 1978 rather than give in to demands for local ownership; Joseph M. Grieco, "Between Dependence and Autonomy: India's Experience with the International Computer Industry," *International Organization* (Summer 1982): 609–632.

16. Two decades later, William Doolittle, HP Senior Vice President for International, saw this decision as a key to YHP's success. "US Trade with Japan can be both successful and profitable," presentation by William P. Doolittle, Japan Electric Measuring Instruments Manufacturers' Association, Los Angeles, March 16, 1982, p. 2.

17. By comparison, the partners had contributed $1.8 million in paid-in capital in 1963.

18. "Co-management: Case History of a Successful Experiment in Japan," HP internal company document, n.d., pp. 2–3.

19. Ibid., p. 7.

20. Ibid., p. 6.

21. Ibid., p. 7.

22. All financial data are from YHP internal documents.

23. These stages have much in common with the phases of introducing a new product or process into production. See Robert H. Hayes, Steven C. Wheelwright, and Kim B. Clark, *Dynamic Manufacturing: Creating the Learning Organization* (New York: Free Press, 1988).

24. Each HP division or foreign subsidiary typically had a charter that gave it the responsibility to design, develop, and manufacture certain products for sale by other HP units. During the 1960s, YHP was without such a niche. In the early 1970s, the company developed the 4260-A LCR meter, which became the forerunner of its component testing line. By the 1980s, YHP held the charter for component measurement instruments and for semiconductor testing equipment, and it was competing with other HP divisions for a new charter in communications testing products.

25. In one famous example, the failure rate of YHP's dip soldering process was reduced from 4 parts per thousand to 3 parts per million between 1978 and 1982. As a result of progress like this, one of YHP's product lines went from making a loss to being the most profitable in HP. Personal interview with Kenzo Sasaoka, November 1993.

26. Personal interview with Kenzo Sasaoka, November, 1993.

27. "Why Hewlett-Packard Desires to Acquire Full Ownership," internal company document, pp. 4–5.

28. Personal interview, August 1991.

29. Data from YHP.

Index

Advanced Computing Environment (ACE), 57; collaboration and competition within, 76, 189, 214; context of, 36, 37, 55; downfall of, 137–140, 283n5; origins of, 136–137, 282n2; as RISC competitor, 142, 149, 152, 154, 157–158, 161, 164–165; in RISC development, 116, 125, 126, 129, 131, 132, 133

Advanced Micro Devices (AMD), 104

Aerospace industry, alliances in, 273n13

Airline industry: alliances in, 4, 143, 204; globalization in, 41, 42, 53, 185

Allaire, Paul, 17, 19, 25, 26, 259n17

Alliance networks, definition of, 52–59, 267n53, 268n63, 269nn64,66, 278n2. *See also* Alliances; Constellations

Alliances: comparison with mergers, 198–199; competitive effects of, 10–14, 195–196, 225–227; competitive environment of, 7–10, 177–188; definition of, 34–35, 260n5, 262nn10–12, 267n53; dynamics of waves of, 142–147, 283–284nn1–3; as links between firms in constellations, 3–6, 35–38; managing barriers to formation of, 188–193, 209–215; motivations in computers, 49; pace of innovation in, 193–195; in reshaping industries, 175–201; types in PDAs, 171–174. *See also* Collective competition;

Constellations; Instability of alliances; Motivations for alliances; Risks of alliances; *names of specific alliance groups*

Alvarez, Raymond, 64, 66, 69

Amdahl Corporation, 12, 122, 160, 225, 285n21; alliance with Fujitsu, 36, 37, 73, 74, 76, 79, 80–81, 229–233, 244–245, 293nn1,2,4, 294nn7,9

American Airlines, 42, 43n, 53, 102

Amstrad, 168–172

Anticompetitive cooperation, 195, 197, 199–200, 201, 209, 288n13. *See also* Competition

Apollo Computer, 98, 148, 277n6, 284n4

Apple Computer, 28, 48, 57, 136, 225; alliance with IBM and Motorola, 74, 77–78, 90–91; in PDA development, 37, 168–174, 194; in RISC development, 36, 37, 113, 118, 125, 126–127, 131, 133–134, 152, 187, 197, 250, 275n32

Appropriability, limited, 165, 286nn29,31

Arm's length contracts, 33, 158, 255n12, 260nn3,4, 262n10

Asai, Shu, 239

AT&T, 204, 225; in PDA development, 44, 167–173, 195; in RISC development, 57, 98, 122, 148, 187

Automobile industry: alliances in, 4, 143, 204, 279–280n15; dominant firms in, 42

Axelrod, Robert, 272n5, 274n24, 275n28